BUDGET BIOMORPHS

THE MAKING OF THE GUYVER FILMS

To
Carolyn,
Enjoy my First Book!
Lots of love,
Dom. xx

To Cassy!

Enjoy my First Book!

Lots of love,

Dom. xx

BUDGET BIOMORPHS

THE MAKING OF THE GUYVER FILMS

DOM O'BRIEN

BearManor Media
2024

Published in the USA by
BearManor Media
1317 Edgewater Dr. #110
Orlando, FL 32804
www.BearManorMedia.com

ISBN: 979-8-88771-301-4
Printed in the United States of America

Table of Contents

For my wife, Sophie, who had confidence and faith in me even when I did not and put up with each of my overly animated ramblings after every interview I conducted. I couldn't have done this without you or your understanding.

Foreword

By David Hayter
(Sean Barker – *Guyver: Dark Hero*)

In the late winter of 1992, I was a broke actor/bartender, working at a seedy dance club on Ventura Boulevard in Studio City, California. I had moved to Los Angeles nearly two years prior, and my career was struggling at best.

I'd done a commercial or two, appeared in some crowd scenes as a film extra, and I occasionally got paid fifty dollars to go see private screenings of movies like *Green Card* and *Mr. Destiny*. Then, I'd put my arm around a girl I'd just met while we smiled like idiots in love, and I'd tell the camera, "It's the ultimate date movie!" Yes, nothing in Hollywood is real.

So, things weren't exactly going as planned. I'd come to Hollywood to be a movie star. An action hero, like Harrison Ford or Tom Cruise. And then one day, my manager sent me to an audition for a sci-fi action film called *Guyver: Dark Hero*, based on a Japanese anime series. I read the sides and realized I was reading for the *lead role*.

This was everything I'd come to Hollywood to do. I was determined to nail this audition.

I studied the scenes for days. On the day, I drove to a warehouse studio in Van Nuys, in the shadow of the Budweiser bottling plant, and parked my little red Nissan. I went over my lines, sucked up my courage, and went in. There were a few other guys there, young, handsome, and hungry. Some of them even looked like me. But I was young, and full of unearned confidence.

This was meant to be. The Guyver would be my ticket to stardom. My destiny. I read the scenes with the casting director, while the film's director, Steve Wang, sat watching me, stone-faced.

When I got to the part when the hero, who's been afflicted with the bio-boosting armor, Sean Barker, says his line to the unfeeling alien ship, "I want my <u>LIFE</u> BACK!" my voice echoed off the walls with power and frustration and loss. I grinned confidently, shook Steve Wang's hand, told him how much I would love to be a part of the film, and left.

And you know what? I got the part.

Confident or not, I walked back in for the first table read, *stunned*. I was so nervous in fact, that I met the woman who would be my wife of thirty years and the mother of my daughter that morning, and I have no recollection of it. (She reminds me of this annually.)

Early the next summer, we began shooting. My first film role. And I was the star.

I watched the first film, *The Guyver*, as part of my research. It's a fun, goofy action flick, with impressive creatures and some cool action. Mark Hamill gets turned into a giant insect, and Jimmy Walker plays a hilarious Zoanoid monster.

The script for the second film was different. Steve Wang, who had co-directed the first film with the subtly-but-aptly named Screaming Mad George, was determined to make the second film a dark, badass picture. A film adaptation that took the underlying anime *seriously*.

They built the cave, ship-hull and tunnel sets in the very same Van Nuys warehouse where I'd auditioned, and the dream began.

The alien creatures, including my superhero alter-ego, the Guyver, were sculpted by the director himself, Steve Wang, who I discovered had sculpted legendary creatures for huge movies, like the Mohawk Gremlin from *Gremlins 2: The New Batch* and the Predator from, well… *Predator*.

On top of that, Steve was a master of Hong Kong style action moviemaking. The stunts, the fight choreography, the shots, were all electric. We were punching far above our budget level.

Here's how good the fights were: In late 1999, I found myself in Toronto, writing the screenplay for the first *X-Men* film (I'd tell you how I went from being the Guyver to writing *X-Men*, but that's a whole other book). When Gary Jensen, *X-Men's* Stunt Coordinator, walked past my office carrying a VHS copy of *Guyver: Dark Hero*.

I ran out and grabbed him, "Gary, what are you doing with that?"

We were in the middle of choreographing the fight scenes between Wolverine and Sabretooth, and Gary said, "I was going to show it to Bryan (X-Men's director)."

"What for?" I asked, suspicious that he and the director meant to make fun of me or something.

Gary said, "Have you *seen* this movie? The fight scenes are incredible." I said, "Gary, turn over the box." He looked at the box photos and said, "Hey, that's you! Why is that you?"

I have never had so much fun as I did while shooting *Guyver: Dark Hero* with the cast and crew on location in the Angeles Crest Mountains that summer. It was like a summer camp where I got to be Batman. We shot our scenes, witnessed unbelievable stunt sequences; I slay monsters and ran full tilt towards a four-hundred-foot cliff.

And I met the love of my life, Marisa Cody. She plays Mary, the hot archeologist in the red tank top who first touches the side of the alien ship. Mary, "Feels like leather... soft." "Isn't she beautiful?". And a good many years later, we had Natasha, our amazing daughter, who was just one of at least three "Guyver Babies" to come out of that summer's production. The film was a literal labor of love.

Guyver: Dark Hero was a cult film in Hollywood terms: straight-to-video, shot on an eight hundred-thousand-dollar budget. But it has endured. I was in Manchester, England for a convention recently and I signed a good number of Guyver autographs for adoring fans.

If you are into anime adaptations, sci-fi action horror, or you're just a living human being, you will enjoy this movie. I know I did.

The Guyver gave me a family, lifelong friends and a sci-fi legacy that lasts to this day. In fact, it gave me a whole new life and I can't ever imagine asking for the old one back.

David Hayter
Los Angeles, California. December 2022

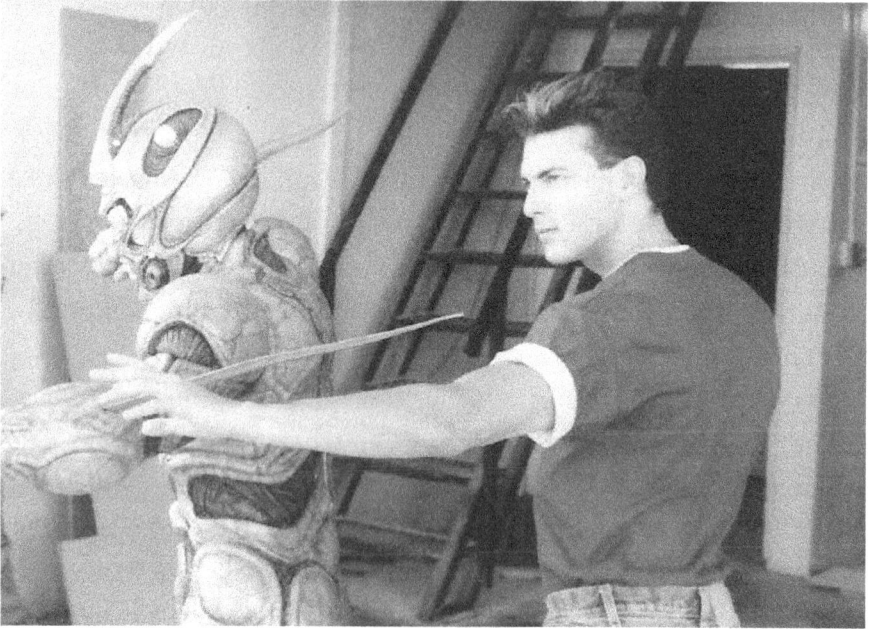

A young David Hayter poses with the *Guyver: Dark Hero* suit actor [Anthony Houk] for some behind-the-scenes photography. Still taken by Eric Lasher. Biomorph Incorporated/ LA Hero

Preface

It all started with a video shop poster!

That is what I tell people when they ask how my love affair with the Guyver films started; a single image that ignited my young imagination.

The poster in question, which was promoting *Guyver: Dark Hero* (1994), was a gift from my dad who had picked it up from the local video rental store in 1994. Coincidentally, this was also when *the Mighty Morphin Power Rangers* (1993-1996) were big business. My dad, possibly making a loose connection to the suited and masked martial artists, probably assumed this was the same thing.

Despite not knowing what a Guyver was, I proudly stuck it to my wall, above my bed, where I would stare at it in amazement every night for the next few years – often making up my own stories as to what this Guyver got up to (having yet to see the film).

A few years later, I was on a fortnightly trip to the video store where my eagle eye caught the image of something familiar. Walking past the cacophony of red plastic rental shelving, I saw a greener Guyver-like character similar to what had adorned my wall a few years prior. Bizarrely it was titled *Mutronics: The Movie* (1991). Was this a different take on the character or a sequel to *Guyver: Dark Hero* that I wasn't unaware of? Bear in mind, this was the mid-1990s and internet resources weren't readily available, so I wasn't able to do any fact-checking.

Although confused by the first film's title change (more on that later), my fascination and need to know what these two films were, was only fuelled further!

It wouldn't be until the summer of 1998 that I would finally see *Guyver: Dark Hero* for the first time. After some badgering from me, my dad had taken my sister and me (no doubt begrudgingly for her) to our first convention.

While touring the many seller stalls I spotted a very familiar image, that of a second-hand *Dark Hero* VHS. The Guyver himself was exactly as I remember him, drenched in black and blue clouds silhouetted by bolts of fierce lightning. I'm convinced I started drooling because, at a mere £3 (around $4), it was a bargain with the small amount of pocket money I had.

I excitedly gestured to my dad about the VHS case much to his bemusement. I relayed in detail what the film was. Due to its 15 rating in the U.K. from the BBFC (the equivalent of an R rating from the MPAA in the U.S.), my dad had to pre-screen it before I could view it.

This was the standard approach for my dad (and I have it on good authority, the same for parents of countless other Millennials who did the same), which led to me watching films like *Die Hard* (1988), *Terminator 2: Judgement Day* (1991), *Cliffhanger* (1993), and *Demolition Man* (1993) long before I should have (with dad fast-forwarding during certain overly violent moments).

I handed the change over to the seller, who was likely unaware of how much this humble VHS meant to me. I cradled the purchase to the car like it was the Holy Grail, studying every image on the front and back of the cover in fine detail. It would be a few weeks until I saw the VHS tape again. I am convinced I thought about it daily. When I saw my dad again, he had viewed it, remarking, *"It's a bit naff, Dom. But it is fine to watch."*

When I finally popped the VHS into the player, I sat slack-jawed throughout its 100-minute runtime (and yes, I mean 100-minutes as *MIA Video* cut the film when it was first released in the U.K.). Most British *Guyver: Dark Hero* fans would not get to see Steve Wang's full version (at least in physical form) until it was re-released on DVD in 2007.

During the initial viewing, my young mind could only see it as a more violent *Power Rangers* (which was no bad thing as I adored them). But as was my want during my pre-teens, I would re-watch certain films almost religiously, and *Dark Hero* found itself on frequent rotation. With each subsequent viewing, I fell in love with the martial arts wirework, adrenaline-fueled action set pieces, violent makeup effects and the detailed creature designs. It also felt edgy and almost taboo, like I shouldn't be watching it.

In the years following, *Dark Hero* (and to a lesser extent *The Guyver / Mutronics: The Movie*) would be one of the many films to shape my love of filmmaking, practical effects, animatronics, and fight choreography. I'd go on to university and study filmmaking, finding my creative happy place. Sadly, barring a handful of short films, it would not be an area I would ultimately have a career.

But my filmic love affair never wavered or left me, forever present, no matter what job I begrudgingly took to make ends meet. The passion for low-budget filmmaking never left me either; if I could not make films, I was damn well going to write about them.

Cut to several years later (and with a lot of writing under my belt), I set out to write an in-depth retrospective article on the making of one of my favourite low-budget films, *Guyver: Dark Hero*, which continued to live rent-free in my head in the decades since. As I researched and conducted interviews, a narrative started to form for something bigger than any feature article could contain. Seeing that a proper making-of-book for the Guyver films did not exist (outside of a 1991 Japanese-only photobook to tie-in with the first film's release) ultimately led to me embarking on this creative journey.

With *Budget Biomorphs,* I wanted to take a deep look at how Steve Wang, Screaming Mad George and the crew of both films created these cult gems from the VHS era. During the writing process, it also became a love letter to all the cast and crew who helped to create these slices of wonderfully schlocky entertainment on min-

xvi • Dom O'Brien

imal budgets, with ingenuity and creativity, despite being very different productions.

Passion, persistence, stubbornness, vision, and caffeinated mindsets are just a handful of the factors required to achieve these goals, and none more so was this the case than during both *The Guyver* and *Guyver: Dark Hero* productions. 30 years on, these low-budget creature features continue to inspire me and countless others in different mediums and creative ways.

Similar to the production of these films, there were many creative ups and downs throughout the writing of this book. Doing anything creative will always come with its unique challenges. Ultimately, it's about learning to adapt and power through to the finish line, despite the difficulties.

Dom O'Brien
Bath, England. January 2023

Part One

The Guyver
aka
Mutronics: The Movie
(1991)

Chapter One

Low-Budget Filmmaking Rascals

It is interesting to think how *The Guyver* aka *Mutronics: The Movie* (1991) and its sequel/reboot *Guyver: Dark Hero* aka *Guyver 2: Dark Hero* (1994) as it was titled in a few countries (or the alternative title of *Predator 3* as it's known in the Philippines), ultimately became a reality due to several individuals, all from different creative areas in filmmaking, indulged in their love of martial arts cinema and mixing it with Tokusatsu tinged undertones of shows they grew up with as kids. The film in question would be the micro-budget labour of love *Kung Fu Rascals* (1992), and it's here where the Guyver film's crew would hone their filmmaking skills.

These low-budget filmmaking rascals would include Steve Wang, Wyatt Weed, Ted Smith, Johnnie Saiko, Les Claypool, Eddie Yang, Michael Deak, Aaron Simms, Screaming Mad George, Asao Gato and (the late) Moto Hata.

The original *Kung Fu Rascals* short, titled *Kung Fu Rascals: Monster Beach Party* (filmed in 1985), was an early 8mm film that Steve Wang would direct prior to getting his start within the film industry, and while a copy doesn't exist (at least at the time of writing this) it would help form the basis of the *Kung Fu Rascals* feature film. This endeavour to expand and evolve on the short film, would once again be made over the course of several months (10 to be exact), mainly on weekends from the Fall of 1989 to Summer 1990.

It was also during this time that a number of the cast and crew had been breaking into various areas of the special effects industry.

Born in Taiwan and then moved to the United States at the age of nine, Wang was known to be a keen illustrator at an early age. "Ever since I was a kid, I was really artistic, and I think I started drawing when I was four years old," says Wang.

"My older brother started drawing and I was fascinated by it, so I started drawing. A couple of years later he stopped, and I just kind of kept going." As Wang continued to evolve his passion for drawing, he would find inspiration from a slew of Japanese Tokus-atsu shows, the most notable being Eiji Tsuburaya, Tohl Narita and Kazuho Mitsuta's long running *Ultraman* series and later Shotaro Ishinomori's equally long- running *Kamen Rider* (*Kamen Raidā Shirīzu*) series.

"I lived in Taiwan at the time – I was born there – and by the time I was nine years old I saw a poster for an Ultraman movie that was made in Thailand [*The 6 Ultra Brothers vs. the Monster Army* aka *Hanuman vs. 7 Ultra* (1974)], and it just blew my mind seeing all these guys in silver and red fighting these monsters," explains Wang.

"I went to the theatre to see it one day and ended up watching it three times. It just changed my life and at that point I didn't really know if I was going to be doing this kind of stuff, but I knew eventually this would somehow be a part of my life."

Whether he knew it or not, Wang would continue to develop his artistic skill set and it was *Ultraman* that would spur on this creative process. "They had a contest at the time where the winner would get a little three-dimensional plastic *Ultraman* mask," Wang describes.

"Up until that point I'd never seen anything like it before. All the masks in Taiwan were printed off cardboard where you pushed the eyeholes out and used a rubber band to put it round your ear – that was masks for us. So, seeing something three-dimensional was pretty mind-blowing to me."

This specific *Ultraman* mask would go on to percolate within Wang's creative brain and would spur him on to create his own masks once he and his family moved to the United States in 1975. Garnering an almost obsessive fascination with masks, it was in the U.S. where he would ultimately move past just collecting and teach himself the creative tricks of the trade.

"It was around Halloween time and in the local toy store there were hundreds of these latex rubber masks and that again blew my mind... it looked so life-like with hair, blood, and everything, so at that point I started collecting masks. About four years into it I realised that wasn't enough for me and I wanted to know how to make it."

It could be said that a knowledgeable and curious mind is often the bridging ground for ideas, and none more so was this the case with the young Steve Wang.

Inspired by a creative thirst and need to know more about how his hobby was created, he would devote his spare time research and eventually practice. "I started going to local libraries and looking up books on theatrical makeup and masks, and watching monster movies back then, and reading monster magazines like *Famous Monsters* and *Starlog*. Eventually I would see the photos of how guys like Stan Winston and Rick Baker did their work. From there I bought some clay and just started sculpting and teaching myself how to do this stuff."

After migrating from collecting masks to self-teaching how to sculpt in clay, Wang was devoted to practicing and perfecting this new craft, so much so that he says his mother was a bit concerned. "The summer before I started high school, I sat in my room the entire summer spending 18 hours a day sculpting," explains Wang.

"My mom thought something was wrong with me because I didn't want to do anything except come out to eat or to get the mail so I could see what kind of mask catalogues showed up." It was then that Wang's mother thought she had to intervene, by trying to coax him away from this new hobby and get some fresh air.

"I just made masks," continues Wang. "My mom got one of my older brother's friends to come and try to get me out of the house to go to parties and meet girls. Two weeks later, Mom found us in the garage, my brother's friend helping me create my first full body monster suit."

The friend in question would be Johnnie Saiko, who would go on to co-star and co-write *Kung Fu Rascals* with Wang and have his own special effects and stunt career post-*Guyver*.

"I had just moved to California from Virginia, because my father had retired out of the Navy," details Saiko. "So, I was one of those guys that people thought, just because I'm Asian, they assumed I knew martial arts. I was really into Bruce Lee at the time as well. I didn't make it a secret once people started to fuck with me, and they'd often say, *'what are you, like Bruce Lee'*, you know they'd actually call you out and you'd just end up fighting," recalls Saiko.

"So, I guess a few people had heard I was pretty good at fighting at the time, and it led to meeting other people in the area and one of the other martial artists that I ran into was Steve Wang's older brother. I let Steve's brother know I was interested in moving to Hollywood one day to do martial arts and he said he wanted to do that stuff too, but he was more into the business side. He said his younger brother [Steve] just kept playing with clay in his room and he wouldn't do anything else, he wouldn't even do martial arts because he's always playing with this clay. So, I said *'well, what do you mean he plays with clay?'*"

Saiko quickly found out that the younger Wang had a passion for creating and sculpting his own sci-fi creatures and monsters, an area that Saiko himself was also interested in, particularly with Rick Baker's work on the original *Star Wars: A New Hope* (1977).

Initially Saiko was introduced to the introverted Wang in the attempt to get him out of the house, but it quickly became clear that both Saiko and Wang (despite the age difference) were two peas in a nerdy pot. It wasn't long before both were up to makeup and sculpting shenanigans.

"I think Steve was only like 11 the first time I actually saw him, and he was already taller than me," reminisces Saiko.

"It took a few years before I finally actually got to talk to him and see all the things he had been doing, because his brother wanted me to knock on his door and take a look at the things he'd been working on. Bit by bit I found out that he was actually very talented and had a goal to one day meet Rick Baker."

Saiko and Wang would go on to learn and work with each other over the years, with Saiko teaching Wang martial arts. "Steve didn't want to learn it from his brother because he studied Korean Taekwondo. I said to Steve, '*you know what, I'll teach you some martial arts*', and Steve took to it like a fish to water," remembers Saiko.

It wasn't long before they both started making the short film which would later become the basis for *Kung Fu Rascals*, where Wang and Saiko would put their martial arts skills to comedic use.

"He was there choreographing along with me and the other guys for the original *Kung Fu Rascals* short we did in San Jose," says Saiko. "Even for that 30-minute extravaganza we shot on Super 8 film, we were doing our own stunts and our own kung fu."

"We just got all of our friends who knew martial arts and got them to participate in it," continues Saiko. "We shot this thing in like 85', just before everybody moved to Hollywood. And it was just a matter of meeting different people all along the way, such as meeting [the late] Matt Rose, who Steve would work with extensively after getting into feature films."

"Steve was interested in shooting it and we were literally editing it by using scotch tape, because we didn't have any money for editing tape to connect the pieces. The Super 8 camera we were using, we'd have to stick the film on a reel and turn it to capture the footage. Steve also taught himself how to edit during this process."

The final puzzle piece of this kung fu short would be the inclusion of one final rascal (who would sadly not return for the feature length film) in the form of Tokusatsu expert and author August Ragone.

Ultimately Ragone would stay in San Francisco and establish himself there as both a film critic and historian, while Wang, Saiko, and Rose would move to Los Angeles to kick-start their film careers.

Not only would the trio finally get to meet Rick Baker after moving to Los Angeles, but they'd also end up working for Baker as part of his Cinovation Studio (in a number of different capacities) with Joe Dante's satirical sequel masterpiece: *Gremlins 2: The New Batch (1990)*.

Prior to this feature, Wang would begin working on a number of local low budget Bay area productions, which he admits, "I don't know whatever happened to them." It appears they are now lost to the annals of time.

Following these two forgotten features, Wang and Rose would find themselves on their first Hollywood feature film – the late Tobe Hooper's *Invaders from Mars (1986),* a remake of William Cameron Menzies' schlock classic from 1953.

Hooper's version - filmed in 1985 and released the following year - would bring on Stan Winston's studio to create the various creature effects. Despite the film's poor critical and financial reception it received during its release in 1986, Wang would find himself heading to Rick Baker's Cinovation Studios to work as a sculptor on *Harry and the Hendersons* (1987).

In the same year, both Wang and Rose would be brought into several other productions, such as Sam Raimi's splatter masterpiece

Evil Dead 2 (1987) and cult gem *The Monster Squad* (1987) where Wang and Rose (who was his roommate at the time) were hired by Stan Winston to lead on one of the most iconic cinematic monsters.

This time round they got to reinterpret the classic design of The Creature from the Black Lagoon; effects pioneer and creature performer Tom Woodruff Jr. would bring the creature to physical life on-screen.

"We were only 20 years old at the time," remembers Wang, "but within a year we were given such a huge level of responsibility. We had to come up with a lot of techniques on how to create the suit for The Creature. It was just an amazing opportunity to give a couple of kids so young."

There was also a production which followed shortly after *The Monster Squad*; a film that would ultimately become even more of a calling card for both Wang and Rose, a little film by the name of *Predator* (1987).

It's well known among cinephiles that *Predator* was filled with a number of issues during production, ranging from problems of shooting in the sweltering Mexican heat while on location, the original alien suit actor (at the time a still unknown Jean Claude Van Damme) quitting the production. The original suit was created by Richard Edlund's Boss Film Studios – the same team responsible for the impressive ghost effects from *Ghostbusters* (1984), with it closer to resembling a space lobster and not the fearsome looking and otherworldly hunter it ultimately became, which would lead to its enduring legacy as one of the greatest and most recognisable cinematic creatures.

It was a film that almost became the stuff of production legend and could have potentially been lost to time or even shelved if Stan Winston Studios hadn't redesigned the Predator suit from the ground up. Thankfully a young, skilled crew came onboard, and the rest, as they say, is history. While the overall design was conceived by Winston, it would be Wang who'd help co-design and add the exquisite colouring and detail to the alien hunter's new look.

It would be on *Predator* where Wang and Rose would meet and work with a young and talented Eddie Yang, soon-to-be stunt man Brian Simpson, and a Japanese artist by the name of George (Joji) Tani aka Screaming Mad George.

At the time, Eddie Yang was also just starting out in the industry and found himself helping out a number of special effects protégés. Yang found himself first meeting Wang during the production of two seminal films - the first, the comedy-horror classic *Evil Dead 2* and the second being *Predator*. Yang would also work with both Wang, Rose, and Johnnie Saiko on effects work for Donald G. Jackson & R.J. Kizer's cult classic *Hell Comes to Frogtown* (1988).

For *Evil Dead 2,* Yang would run errands for the effects shop such as picking up supplies for fabrication, and in return, got to learn about how the effects work was created for Sam Raimi's splatter masterpiece.

Yang would also be an unpaid intern on *Predator,* often watching and learning how the creature work and airbrushing was done, which Wang was responsible for on that show. So, how did he end up being a runner for the would-be *KNB FX* guys prior to meeting Wang?

"It all started with a book called *Movie Monsters* by Alan Ormsby," says Yang. "I received a copy of it from a classmate while in second grade. I remember that the first half of the book explained classic movie monsters, like Frankenstein's monster, The Wolfman etc, but then at the end of the book it had these incredible drawings of kids applying makeup onto their faces and making themselves into those classic monsters," Yang enthuses.

"Then as I got older, I would read magazines like *Fangoria* and *Cinefex* which all continued to spur on my interest in effects work. I learned through these books and magazines of this fantastical chemical compound called latex, which was everywhere. So, I started looking at a phonebook and where it might be sold."

"My father was kind enough to pick up the supplies I would order because all the places that supplied the stuff were around the North Hollywood area, and I didn't drive at the time. But my parents allowed me to kind of make my own lab in our garage and I'd spend time doing experimental stuff in there or in our kitchen. My mom got super upset because it was like dental acrylic, and it smelt out the whole house," Yang chuckles.

Now that Yang's creative effects experimentation was in full swing, he continued to do more research and how one might earn a career in this particularly niche environment. He would be in luck; being born and raised in Los Angeles, Yang would find himself at the very epicentre of this constantly evolving creative field.

"I began reading about other artists that were these weird kids and would work in their parents' garage, like me, and were doing this crazy hobby that eventually became a career."

Despite his love and fascination in effects work and having a career in the industry, his parents would end up sending him to a private school in the hope of having a more prestigious career.

"In high school, during a summer vacation, my friend Simon and I just had a look in the phone book for makeup effects studios, and I'm like, '*you know what, I'm just gonna go and see if they'll let me do a tour visit*'. So, we found *Don Post Studios* which is a well-known mask company. My father dropped us off and me and my buddy Simon just went to talk with Don Post Jr., and he gave us a tour."

It was during this tour where Yang's heart sank a little bit. "He was being a very responsible adult," remembers Yang. "He basically said, '*go to medical school, be a doctor, don't get in this industry*', which I found a little depressing."

"So, after that tour we found another public phone and found that just 'round the corner was *Makeup Effects Lab, Inc.* which at the time was run by Allan Apone and Doug White. When we got there my friend literally pushed me through the door, because I was a little shy. Alan looked up and we just asked him, '*Hey, you know, even though we're kids, we're very interested in this stuff*, and he said, '*Oh, let me introduce you to Howard Berger, he can show you around*'."

It would be during this tour where Yang would ultimately lay the foundations of his friendship and mentorship, not just with Berger, but with Robert Kurtzman as well.

"So, Howard gave us a tour of the makeup effects lab," continues Yang. "He gave me his phone number and said he was leaving to shoot *Day of the Dead*. He said, '*There's another effects studio if you go 'round the corner, literally behind Makeup Effects Lab*', that was John Carl Buechler's MMI [Mechanical and Makeup Imageries]. We went over there and that's where I met Bob Kurtzman, and he gave me his phone number and said I could call him up anytime I needed some tips or whenever."

"I ended up hanging out with Bob Kurtzman over the summer, you know, and he showed me where to get supplies. Because I couldn't drive at the time he took me around Los Angeles, just showing me just everything related to effects work," recalls Yang.

"I would call on him when I was having problems while sculpting this or that, and he [Bob] would show me new techniques. Like, I had never seen a full head cast, because every time I tried to do a live cast mine always failed. I tried like six times and couldn't get it right, but that's all they're doing this one weekend, so he picked me up and took me to see how the other effects guys did it."

All of this would lead to a chain of events were Yang would get his first special effects gig. Firstly, the aforementioned errand runs for Kurtzman and the guys (prior to establishing KNB FX while still working for Mark Shostrom); getting to know other artists starting out on *Evil Dead 2* (Wang coincidently would do some minor work on the film); and from these relationships, it allowed Yang to work as lab technician on *Ghoulies II* (1987).

"The KNB guys (Robert Kurtzman, Greg Nicotero, Howard Berger) had heard John Carl Buechler was looking for extra people in the shop," says Yang. "MMI had just started production on *Ghoulies* and as I was currently on my summer vacation and they needed somebody, I interviewed and that ended up being my first job. I couldn't believe it," remembers Yang.

"I was just a lab tech, which is an entry level position for almost any studio, meaning I painted latex and molds, wrapped polyfoam, seamed up the Ghoulies and all that stuff. Nothing super artistic."

"Then I had to return to school as vacation was ending, but through that whole process I had met (the late) Matt Rose first, who was just an icon in our industry, and he was very much Rick Baker's sculpting right-hand man. He'd just come to L.A. a couple years prior along with Steve [Wang]."

"I'd not yet met Steve at the time, but their reputations preceded them, especially after winning a *Fangoria* contest where they made these grotesque copies of Siskel and Ebert, two movie critics who hated horror movies," chuckles Yang. "Their sculptures, paint jobs, and the artistic techniques were just amazing, even Howard [Berger] was excited they were coming to L.A.," remembers Yang.

The stars appeared to be aligning, particularly in regard to Yang cultivating further connections. It would be a brief meeting with the late Rose, which quickly led to a lifelong friendship with both him and Wang. "Howard was now working for Rick Baker at the time, I believe on *Harry and the Hendersons*," says Yang.

"At the time they had a shop baseball game for fun on a weekend and Howard said, 'Hey, once you finish mowing the lawn, if you head over to Brand Park, Rick Baker's crews gonna be there, he might show up'. I packed up the lawnmower and drove down to the park. The guy I met there was Matt Rose; he was like sitting off to the side. We struck up a conversation and that led to a 30-year friendship. He became, not just one of my mentors, but also one of my closest friends," reminisces Yang. "All of this eventually led to Matt introducing me to Steve Wang."

The final two additions to *Rascals* would also be instrumental components in Wang's future directorial filmography, both of whom were out-of-towners: Ted Smith and Wyatt Weed.

Both Smith and Weed came from different backgrounds compared to the rest of the *Rascal's* crew and have the distinction of working on all four of Wang's feature films.

"Ted and I are St. Louis boys," details Weed. "We're from the Midwest of the United States and had both moved out to Los Angeles. Well, prior to moving to L.A., we had been huge *Predator* fans. Like, we worship the Predator and thought it was the greatest science fiction action film we'd ever seen. At the time we were reading magazines such as *Cinefantastique* and *Fangoria*, so we knew who Steve Wang, Matt Rose, Eddie Yang, and Stan Winston were."

It wasn't until the late 1980s that Weed and Smith would move from St. Louis to L.A., with both men determined to make a change to their daily lives. At the time, both were in their own respective life ruts; it was time to make a change and seek out their passion for film and filmmaking.

"It was 1989, I believe, and I worked at a well-known store chain in the photography department at Sears. It was the era where you'd come in and get 35mm pictures taken of yourself and your kids, or family photographic portraits done," remembers Smith.

"So, I go for an interview where I'm in charge of quality control supervising because they love my pictures," says Smith. It wasn't long before he realised this wasn't the job progression he was after.

"They were like '*this guy has really got it down, like he knows how to do it. Let's just take his skill and dump them out of the studio*'. I initially jumped at it because it was a pay increase, but it was a miserable desk job, stuck in a cubicle."

Weed was, himself, stuck in a life rut and unsure of which direction to go in. Having been friends with Smith for a number of years; connecting over their love of filmmaking and a previously mentioned sci-fi creature, it was only a matter of time before they started pursuing their own creative endeavours to find solace outside of their day jobs.

A key short film they both worked on – titled *A Night in the Woods* (1987) – would allow both men to get a sense of each other's working process on different facets of film production, namely miniature effects work. "You could tell he [Wyatt] had a sense of my creative process," says Smith.

"The short was about a girl in a forest being harassed by this little fairy flying around her head," continues Smith. "It was all done inside a small studio with built miniature sets. It was a cute short and the sets were visually breath-taking. We didn't just want to create a story, we wanted to create the specific environment as well. We both kind of bonded over that."

Not only were both Smith and Weed on the same creative wavelength, but it also became quickly apparent how adept at problem solving (on a limited budget) they were.

"Wyatt had trouble with the fairy, so I had the idea of making a puppet and shooting it on a black background. We then put makeup on my (then) girlfriend and Wyatt would composite it all together. At the time, Wyatt was packing up his entire life and deciding to risk it all by moving to L.A. So, after the short film was all cut together and completed, that's when he left for L.A.," recalls Smith.

Despite returning to the reality of his cubicle of doom and drudgery, it wouldn't be long before Smith heard from Weed.

"I think it was a week later, I get a phone call from Wyatt saying, *'Hey, dude, I'm working on the zombie movie'* and I'm like, *'What! Dude, you haven't even been there for a week and you're already working on a zombie movie?'* I was so jealous and thought, *'That's it'*. I marched up to the main office, gave my 30-day notice and said I was leaving."

"They're like, '*What are you going to do, go to California? Oh, you'll be back'*. I decided to not just burn that bridge but set it on fire. I set out to pack my entire life into my old truck and head to L.A.," remembers Smith.

While Smith's young, impulsive, and determined (almost punk) attitude would pay off in the long run, this decision wasn't without its first incredibly bumpy start. Shortly before leaving to meet up with Weed, Smith was hit with some heartbreaking news that would ultimately be a big turning point for his vocational trajectory.

Prior to leaving for a clean break, Smith's father would die suddenly, upending his whole family. "My dad was athletic and played soccer, so it was a shock and very sad for us. My entire family suddenly had the carpet yanked out from underneath our feet, and at the time both my brothers had gone to college," recounts Smith.

"I'll never forget this – my mom was like, '*You have to go; you've always wanted to do something like this. This is an amazing opportunity, don't let me hold this up for you'*. I had some money saved up and when my father passed, he left us some money, so my mom gave me a bit of that, I packed up and drove to California. Prior to leaving, I had flown out to get an apartment, so when I arrived in the Valley, my apartment was literally next door to Wyatt's."

With Smith now settled in this new abode and in close proximity to Weed, it was the start of something new and exciting - far away from the miserable experience of a creatively stifling corporate environment. With no work available to him on his arrival, Smith went knocking for any opportunity he could find, or as he puts it "…I just started beating the pavement."

"It was really a trial by fire, because at the time in California you couldn't throw a rock without it hitting an effects shop somewhere. There were shops everywhere, but this also meant they were always starving for workers," remembers Smith.

"This was the birth of the straight-to-video-market, and then they learned how quickly films could be made and distributed, it was like '*Oh! You can make movies for theatrical release and good make movies straight for cable and VHS*'. I was in my early 20s' at the time and there was work everywhere because of this and I just started getting jobs."

Smith's first job in the industry would be for the CBS TV-Movie *Miracle Landing* (1990), where he'd help to make a replica airplane cockpit for a miniature effects sequence working within David B. Sharp's *Introvision Model Shop*. Sharp would go on to do miniature effects work as an uncredited model supervisor on *Tales from the Darkside: The Movie* (1990), a feature that Wang would also do uncredited work on.

It was here, while Smith was developing his creative skill set further within Ted Rae's special effects shop, that he crossed paths with Steve Wang, hot off Predator and currently working within Rick Baker's *Cinovation Studio* on *Gremlins 2: The New Batch*. Smith describes the meeting as, "I was just bouncing around effects shops and that's when I met Steve. The rest is history."

During this time, Weed was busy working on the low-budget zombie/creature feature *The Laughing Dead* (1989) as a production assistant. The makeup effects work for this feature would be handled by the late John Carl Buechler's MMI shop; the same company responsible for some of the gnarly effects work on *Bride of Re-Animator* (1990) and the Robert Englund starrer *The Phantom of the Opera* (1990).

Coincidently, *The Laughing Dead*, along with sci-fi tournament fight feature *Arena* (1989) and the aforementioned *Bride of Re-Animator*, would include a number of crew members from their respective creature effects teams, who Weed, Wang, and Co. would end up working with again during the *Kung Fu Rascals* production and beyond; most notably effects legend and occasional stunt man Michael Deak, who'd be credited for doing stunt work on *Tales From the Darkside: The Movie.*

Whether this was due to serendipity or just the insidious nature of the effects industry at the time, it seemed as though the stars were aligning for future collaborations.

Given their equidistant living locations, it was only a matter of time before Smith and Weed caught up on each other's projects and the latest from Smith was about to blow Weed's mind.

It was on *Tales from the Darkside: The Movie* where Wang spoke to Smith about his plan to direct a feature film based on his *Kung Fu Rascals* short. "When Ted told me he was working with Steve Wang I'm like, '*Oh, my God, the Predator guy!*,'" says Weed.

"I said to Ted, '*Tell you what, if Steve needs any help on this Kung Fu Rascals movie, I'll get involved*'. Steve was telling Ted about this movie and how it was a martial arts comedy. And Steve, like during lunch breaks, would enact the scenes from this martial arts comedy that he was going to do. And Ted is just cracking up. He's dying laughing," explains Weed.

It wasn't long after this discussion that *Kung Fu Rascals* would begin filming with all of the crew teaming up and dedicating a large portion of their free-time, in between paid work, to get Wang's vision onto the screen. The first of many future endeavours.

"One day Steve goes fully into production on *Kung Fu Rascals*," details Weed. "He has a production meeting and invites everybody over to his place and that was my first time showing up at Steve's house and being introduced, talking to him, and hanging out."

"So, our first experience together was basically making a $42,000 Super 8 feature film. It was just part of what, I think, endeared us to Steve and part of what brought us along for *Kung Fu Rascals*," Weed recalls fondly.

"We just put our hearts and souls into *Kung Fu Rascals*. I mean, we used our own resources, we used our own materials, we put in endless hours, and shot something like 60 days on it over the course of the Summer of 1990."

Like all good low-budget filmmakers, Wang and Co. were young and hungry, keen to make their mark on the L.A. film industry and establish themselves as a new breed of creatives who could make or craft anything from everything; all that was required was skill, imagination, and a few raw materials.

Wang could see potential in his crew, as Weed details. "Steve could see our dedication even though we weren't getting paid anything. All throughout *Kung Fu Rascals* we showed our dedication and devotion at just how insane and crazy we were. But Steve never said, '*If I get Guyver, I'll bring you on board*', but you got the sense that he was loyal and if he thought you did good work, he'll get you onboard projects," says Weed.

With principal photography on the *Kung Fu Rascals* feature underway, it would take just under a year to finish shooting the film, running from the Fall of 1989 through to the Summer of 1990.

The film, despite having a 30-page script written by Wang and Saiko, would be mostly improvised or ad-libbed by the cast, an interesting decision given how most low- budget features tend not to deviate too far from their own structure, due in large part to budget constraints.

This would work in *Rascals'* favour and help inject a raw, hyperactive energy onto the screen, due in large part to the crew's determination and young hedonistic mentality to get a film made. Wang and Saiko would wrangle the crew members to shoot mostly on weekends and any free time away from their day jobs on other projects.

Although it was a gruelling shoot for *Kung Fu Rascals*, it was clear just how much hard work each crew member put in, ultimately becominga valuable learning experience for all involved, especially with Wang able to see each crew member's individual skill set.

It inadvertently became a proving ground of sorts, with Wang able to entrust certain areas of the production to certain individuals. Yang remembers just how much Wang entrusted him with the suits for the monolithic Titans for the film's conclusion.

"I was young and didn't know what to expect when I volunteered to work with Steve," says Yang. "Luckily, I had a lot of energy and he [Steve] helped me along by getting me a lot of exposure as a creature creator. He had me make the final suits of the Titans at the climax of the film and kind of let me have full creative control, just like letting me do whatever I wanted. So that was the trade-off, and I was more than happy to showcase my skills at the time."

Kung Fu Rascals wouldn't see a release until 1992 and even then, it was still incredibly small. Over 30 years later and this micro-budget kung fu comedy gem has still (at the time of writing) yet to receive a proper home entertainment release.

Like any cult film worth its salt, it continued to grow in popularity with its small but devoted fan base, often whispered about on the film grapevine and convention circuits. Despite a limited VHS release (the film would finally release in 1992), bootlegs of the film would eventually start to circulate as the years rolled on.

What of the film itself? Well, at face value it's a highly silly, often juvenile homage to the Kung Fu classics churned out by studios such as Shaw Brothers from the 1970s, while at the same time combining elements of Japanese Tokusatsu features that Wang and Saiko had grown up with.

As his first full feature, there are occasional flaws, but it never hampers the overall entertainment on display. In fact, brushing film criticism aside, it feels very much like an Eastern infused live action *Looney Tunes*, with bags of creative talent on display, whether it's the impressively choreographed fight scenes, the final men-in-monster-suit showdown, or truly fantastic character and makeup designs for characters like Raspmutant the Mad Monk (Wyatt Weed) or the Bamboo Man from Ka Pow (Ted Smith).

It's a micro-budget film, made by friends with bags of creativity. Sometimes there is anoccasional a dash of subversive comedy. Whatever is thrown at the screen doesn't always stick, but it aims high, and remains a unique film among the low-budget pantheon, and for that it should be commended.

It wouldn't be long before Wang's directorial abilities would be called on again, and while the next project would be a co-directing gig with friend and collaborator Screaming Mad George, the end result would be seen as deeply flawed by a slew of critics and fans alike but would become instrumental in cultivating an enduring and inspiring low-budget creature feature legacy.

The film in question would be a live-action adaptation of Yoshiki Takaya's manga: *Kyōshoku Sōkō Gaibā* (*1985*), or what would be better known in the West as *Bio-Booster Armor Guyver.*

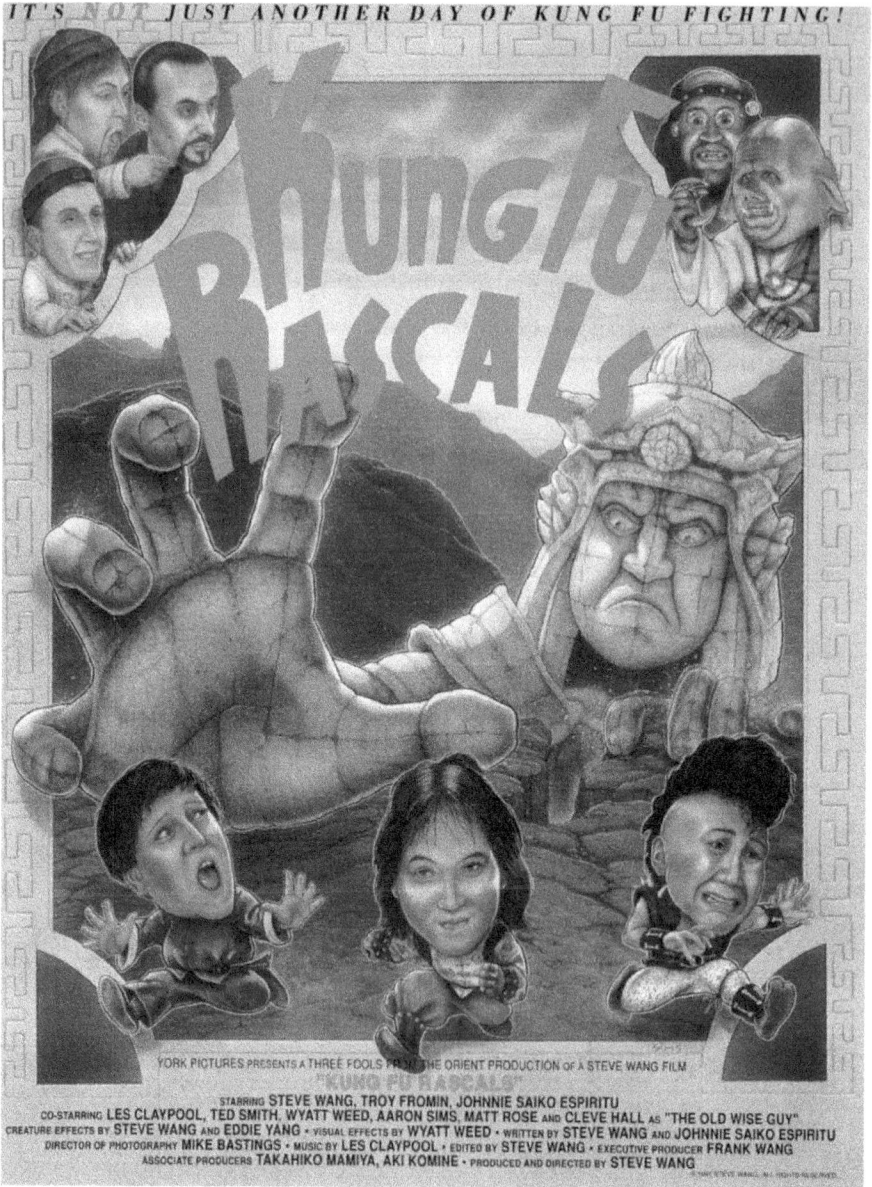

Poster for *Kung Fu Rascals* (1992) featuring Ted Smith, Aaron Simms, Les Claypool, Wyatt Weed, Steve Wang and Johnnie Saiko.

Japanese VHS Cover for *Kung Fu Rascals* invoking the classic Tokusatsu posters of yore. Hero Communications

Shot of Ted Smith as Bamboo Man from *Kung Fu Rascals (1992)*.
Photo courtesy of Steve Wang.

Ted Smith as Meta Spartan from the end of *Kung Fu Rascals'* giant monster/ Kaiju fight. Both this suit and the Neo Titan were created by Eddie Yang (who also suit-performed as the Neo Titan). Photo courtesy of Ted Smith.

Wyatt Weed in full Raspmutant makeup while on location shooting *Kung Fu Rascals*. Photo courtesy of Wyatt Weed.

Chapter Two

Crazy Bio-Organic Critters and Other Stories Part One

What exactly is *The Guyver* and why were two special effects guys selected as the directors for this particular film?

Created by manga artist Yoshiki Takaya in 1985, *Bio-Booster Armor Guyver* would be released in serialized form as part of *Monthly Shōnen Captain* (月刊少年キャプテン), published by *Tokuma Shoten*. Guyver would appear in the very first issue of *Monthly Shōnen Captain* in January 1985 for their February 1985 edition. In the nearly 40 years since its original publication, Guyver remains a unique manga rich in lore and Tokusatsu-inspired creature fights. As of 2023, *Bio-Booster Armor Guyver* hasn't been completed, with Takaya still to create an official ending for the long-running series.

Before the first manga appearance of *Bio-Booster Armor Guyver*, artist and creator Takaya was better known by his pseudonym Moriwo Chimi, having created a number of adult manga (more commonly known as Hentai) for the now-defunct magazine *Lemon People* (*Remon Pīpuru*). *Lemon People* became synonymous with having a less serious tone to other manga publications; often delving into parody despite the horror or cyberpunk genres it specialised in.

Takaya's most known manga under Moriwo Chimi would be *Hades Project Zeorymer* (*Purojekuto Zeoraimā*); published from 1983 to 1984. Looking back at this particular manga, filled with giant Mecha and Hentai within a sci-fi setting, it's easy to see just how *Guyver* would be a natural evolution from this prior work, albeit paired down in scale and with less explicit content, as *The Guyver* would evolve across various entertainment mediums.

After running for a year in *Monthly Shōnen Captain*, Guyver would make his transition to the small screen via a 60-minute OVA (Original Video Animation) in 1986, entitled *Guyver: Out of Control* (1986). Much like Takaya's previous OVA adaptation for *Hades Project Zeroymer*, the brief runtime for *Out of Control* would be filled with action, gore, and (unfortunately) moments of misogynistic violence towards one of the female characters, which errs into Hentai territory.

Viewing this as a historical document, it's evident why the live-action adaptation would stray from the original source material and this OVA.

How did the feature film come to fruition and why was Tani (Screaming Mad George) picked as the one to spearhead its gloopy birth onto the big screen?

Originating from Osaka, Japan, Tani would be influenced by the works of Salvador Dali at an early age. He would ultimately move to the United States, where he'd start doing a lot of paintings – mainly with oil paint – and sculpture, delving further into the surrealistic inspiration which Dali had on him during his younger years.

While in the U.S., Tani would begin to do music performances (at the height of the Punk Rock movement). It was here that he begun to experiment further with visual presentation during the shows. "I wanted to make it more of a performance piece, you know," remembers Tani.

"I want it to be more theatrical, that way I can fully express my artistic idea, not only just with the sound, but with the visual presentation as well. I start making a lot of physical appliances like fake guts and stuff like that. So, this way, you know, it was giving me a more three-dimensional piece of work, rather than just remain with the inside of the canvas framework."

At the time, Tani was enrolled at the School of Visual Arts in New York, and it would be a fateful viewing with a Joe Dante film that ultimately set him on his course to becoming a makeup effects pioneer. "I saw the movie *The Howling* (1981)," remembers Tani. "That and *An American Werewolf in London* (1981) really blew me away, because I was really seeing the transformation on-screen. You know, not the stop motion animation, but it's actually happening right in front of me. That was really amazing to me because I'd never seen things like that before."

"And then right after that I saw *Altered States* (1980), and that was like '*Whoa, this is really incredible*', you know, especially the images from the hallucinations. I found out it was the work of Dick Smith, and I knew this was something that I really wanted to go in to."

In just a short number of years, Tani would find himself working on some of the most iconic horror films of the 1980s, ranging from John Carpenter's martial arts schlock classic *Big Trouble in Little China* (1986); Renny Harlin's punk rock sequel *A Nightmare on Elm Street 4: The Dream Master* (1988); and Brian Yuzna's one-two punch of *Society* (1989) and *Bride of Re-Animator* (1990).

It would be with these latter two films that Tani would strike up a positive working relationship with Yuzna and would become the director's go-to effects artist for a slew of films post-*Guyver*. The two men became synonymous among gore-hounds as the ultimate purveyors of surreal body horror.

In the 1990s, if a horror fan saw a new Yuzna film hitting the VHS rental shelves, it was almost guaranteed that the viewer would be in for some fleshy, hellish delights from Tani's otherworldly imagination.

Outside of his work with Yuzna, Tani would also form a strong friendship with fellow sculptor and special effects prodigy, Steve Wang.

The two gentlemen would meet during the production of *Predator*, where Tani would be on the creature effects crew along with Wang. "We hit it off from day one," says Wang, "and became really good, close friends."

This close friendship also led to a mutual respect of each other's particular skill set; something that would lead to their joint co-directing collaboration in 1990. They would work together, prior to their directorial team up, on Peter Manoogian's sci-fi adventure schlock *Arena* (1989), with Tani heading up the effects shop for the alien and creature effects. It would be around this time that Tani was approached by one of the film's producers to do the effects work for the in-development live-action Guyver. "The Japanese producer for *The Guyver* wanted me to do effects for it," says Tani.

Having grown up with Japanese special effects films and programmes (called Tokusatsu) during his youth – from Toho to Toei, whether it was *Ultraman* or *Godzilla* – part of Tani must have seen an opportunity to live out a childhood dream of directing his very own creature film. "I said to him, '*Well, if this movie is all practical effects, why don't I direct it?*' and he agreed to it," said a surprised Tani.

"I read a lot of manga when I was in Japan, of course, but once I moved to the U.S. I wasn't reading as much, you know, and more getting into the artworks, music, and all that," remembers Tani. This didn't stop him from diving head-first into the original Japanese manga for Guyver once he got the directing gig. He would then inform Wang about this bizarre little creature feature.

"George called me up and says, '*Hey I'm directing this film, it's got a lot of action in it, do you want to direct second unit?*' remembers Wang. "At the time I was making *Kung Fu Rascals*, so I said to him, '*Well I'm in the middle of finishing my film and I don't really want to direct second unit'.* So, he says, '*Well, how about if you come on and co-direct it with me, and we do creature stuff together?*' At that point I thought okay, this is an opportunity to learn something new, so I agreed and that's kind of how it all began. I had just learned about *The Guyver* at that same time, and I was looking at it and thought it was really incredible and what a great opportunity it'd be."

With Wang now onboard to co-direct with Tani, all that was left was to secure some additional funding and distribution. This is where Tani turned to his friend, producer and director, Brian Yuzna.

During this time, *Society* had been released theatrically in the UK via Medusa Films and received a great response from critics and fans. Due to distribution issues, it wouldn't be released until 1992 in the States as Medusa didn't having a distribution arm within the U.S. at the time. Overseas Film Group would end up doing a very small theatrical release in the U.S. and despite its critical and financial success overseas, it was deemed a flop on its home turf.

While *Society* was awaiting release in the U.S., Yuzna begin pre-production on *Bride of Re-Animator* during early 1989 and would once again have Tani lending his wickedly surreal ideas to the body-horror sequel. It was clear Tani had found a frequent and understanding collaborator in Yuzna, which made approaching the writer/director with this bizarre and very Asian product the first port of call in its production process.

"*The Guyver* did not have a distributor in play," remembers Yuzna. "So, the way it came about was that Screaming Mad George had evidently had some backing directly, with it all being financed by Japanese investors. George and I had also been working with Japanese money up till then, with Japanese financing paying for both *Society* and *Bride of Re-Animator*," remembers Yuzna.

"There was a guy that was working on the Japanese side, representing the companies, called Aki Komine [credited as the executive producer] and he was working over here in the U.S. at the time. *Society* was where I met George and although it was produced by an American company called Wild Street, Paul White, who was the executive producer on it, was based in Japan doing business there and locating the funding."

"So, I did those two movies with him [*Society* and *Bride of Re-Animator*]. George came to me with Yutaka Wada, and they had pieced together some of the financing for *The Guyver*, with George suggesting that I produce it as I had production offices," says Yuzna.

"I think, actually, that there were two or three or more companies in Japan that put money into this. Actually, none of the Japanese executives were around for the production. It was really all done by fax machine, back when that was a thing. They came over to make the deal and then they basically sent the money over to put it in the production account, so we could start filming," recounts Yuzna.

1989 would see the release of a 12-part OVA (*The Guyver: Bio-Booster Armor*) which, outside of the feature films, became the interpretation the majority of Western audiences would associate with *The Guyver,* particularly in the U.K. where Manga Video would individually release each episode (known as Data 01, Data 02, etc.) during the mid-1990s. When the initial idea of a live-action American feature film was touted among the Japanese investors in the late 1980s, *The Guyver* was still relatively unknown.

At the time, the aforementioned 12-part OVA hadn't aired in the West (it would make its way to the States in 1992), and no English language translation of Takaya's manga existed yet.

With *The Guyver* being a relatively unknown and niche IP outside of Japan, Yuzna did what any good producer would do and delved headfirst into researching this unique project before the start of production. "I looked at the anime, watched them and then read the manga after getting them translated by George," remembers Yuzna.

With the background research on Guyver done, and Yuzna now having a better understanding of this strange but unique property, it was time to meet with Wang, who Tani wanted to bring on as his co-director.

"How I met Steve, is that George brought him over and he showed me his movie *Kung Fu Rascals*, which I thought was really, really great. George is very artistic, like a fine artist and Steve was much more into the action," says Yuzna.

Now that Wang had the sign-off from Yuzna, with both Tani and Wang complimenting each other's work within their respective special effects areas, it was onto developing and writing the script.

"I knew a writer named Jon Purdy and got him to sign up to write the script," details Yuzna. "He basically wrote the story that Steve and George wanted to tell, and I really didn't have much to input into the script. The story they wanted to tell was their business and I was there to help facilitate that, and to make sure the investors and financers got, what I would consider for the money, a first-class movie. Obviously, you're not going to get a $100 million class movie, but it would be a very professional movie for their investment."

With Purdy hired as their script writer – his first credited screen-writing gig – it was down to Tani and Wang to help steer Purdy in the right narrative direction for this live-action adaptation. The three of them settled on telling a re-designed origin story, partly due to it being more cost-effective and partly as a way of introducing a culturally Asian character and idiosyncratic IP to a Western audience.

The first hurdle both Tani and Wang had to overcome was how to make the mythology concise and engaging for the average viewer, without alienating them. It was during the script writing process that issues started to rise for the directors. "I think the writer was hired very close to when I came on," says Wang.

"I remember sitting there and working with Jon Purdy. He was a nice guy, but the problem with writing the script was that Jon kept saying '*I just don't understand any of this stuff*, and I'm like '*Jon, you have to understand it, you're writing this*'. So, to help with the writing process, we had to work very closely with him to at least make it true as possible to the mythology of what the Guyver is and how the things happen. But you can see how difficult that was at the time and I don't blame him for not understanding it," remembers Wang.

"If you look at that big roll up in the beginning - it's like *Star Wars*, it was explaining everything. I'm watching that and I'm thinking to myself, '*is this really necessary? This is so heavy-handed and cumbersome*'. But at that point, he's like, '*well how are you going to explain this?*'", recalls Wang.

"We knew we weren't like master filmmakers. It was our first movie, right, and we had so much to learn. We didn't really know how to tell the story and get all this across in the narrative that we had. So, we just had to resort to, 'Well, here, here it is. Sorry, but you know, just read it.'"

Regardless of the narrative hurdles, the script was finally locked down. The main character of Shō Fukamachi was westernised to be Sean Barker, an unremarkable teenage youth. A major change to the characters came in the form of Shō's best friend Tetsurō Segawa. Instead, he became Tetsu Segawa and the father (not brother) of Mizky (changed from Mizuki). Tetsu also became the reason the Guyver Unit disappears from the Chronos Corporation, with his death setting off the film's events and Sean's becoming of The Guyver to take down Chronos.

A few additions were also made to the gang of Zoanoids that Chronos dispatches to retrieve the missing Guyver Unit. A more comical element was added (much to the chagrin of Guyver fans) to the Zoanoids, particularly their leader Lisker, who in the manga and anime ultimately becomes Guyver II (not a Zoanoid) with the assistance of a damaged unit to take on Shō.

To round off the new inclusions, Purdy would change Chronos co-founder and big bad Hamilcar Barcas to Fulton Balcus (who is closer in persona to the character of Guyot) and give human personas (as opposed to the soldiers of the manga and anime) to Lisker's team. This included, rapping buffoon M.C. Striker; heavy metal biker chick Weber; and the deranged-looking Ramsey.

The final new addition would come in the form of CIA agent and family friend of the Segawa's, Max Reed. When it came to casting, it's fair to say *The Guyver* would have an eclectic mix of character actors drawn from different areas in the industry.

The whole cast would cast its net far and wide from within the B-Movie character pantheon. This included the likes of Wes Craven regular Michael Berryman (as Lisker); Jim Wynorski's frequent collaborator, comedian, and voiceover artist extraordinaire Peter Spellos (as Ramsey); Stuntwoman and body builder Spice Williams-Crosby (as Weber); and *Good Times* (1974-1979) star Jimmie Walker (as Striker). A few Yuzna regulars also pop up for good measure including the late, great, David Gale (Dr. Carl Hill from *Re-Animator*) as Balcus and chewing every ounce of the scenery he's present in, along with Jeffery Combs (Dr. West from *Re-Animator* and its subsequent sequels) as Dr. East – a relation to Dr West perhaps? – and Williard E. Pugh (*Robocop 2* (1990); *Air Force One* (1997)) rounding out the bad guys as Col. Castle.

"I think it was George's idea to have David Gale as the big bad guy," says Yuzna of the casting of the legendary horror character and theater actor.

During the production, the late David Gale was interviewed by *Fangoria* (October 1991, Issue 107) and the actor had this to say about the role and being in the film.

"[…] I'm having a lot of fun with this part, especially since I'm able to do comedy. That was never intended, but the situation demands humour. Monsters and effects are bigger than life, and so is the acting. In theater, you have to extend yourself from the stage without being too large for the audience. But I've already complained to Steve and George that I'm being upstaged by all of these Zoanoids! [….]," said Gale.

In the same interview, the late actor clearly relished being the bad guy once again. His performance, despite the tonal inconsistencies throughout the film, helps add a sense of fun and darkness as Balcus (Gale) chews every ounce of the scenery.

"[…] He's more insidious and mentally together than my other characters, and the only thing that drives Balcus mad is not possessing the Guyver [….]." For viewers, a good example of this madness is during the moment where Lisker (unknowingly) brings Balcus a toaster instead of the Guyver Unit. A superhero film is only as good as its final level boss, and Gale's Balcus elevates each scene he is in and remains one of the strongest aspects of the finished film.

It wasn't just the bad guys who got all the fun casting. Yuzna would also bring in the likes of Luke Skywalker himself, Mark Hamill, as Max Reed. Legendary B-Movie scream queen Linnea Quigley (*Silent Night, Deadly Night* (1984); *Savage Streets* (1984); *The Return of the Living Dead* (1984); *Hollywood Chainsaw Hookers* (1988); and *Night of the Demons* (1988) to name just a few) would also have a brief cameo putting those lungs to good use. And finally, there was up and coming Chinese actor Vivian Wu (as Mizky) and TV Actor extraordinaire Jack Armstrong (as Sean Barker). A true smorgasbord of eclectic talent.

"Vivian Wu and Mark Hamill were passing requests from the financiers, and we got lucky in getting them. I was surprised when we got Jimmy Walker. When you try getting people and say, '*Do you want to be in this kung fu monster flick*' they kind of just glaze over," chuckles Yuzna.

To help Yuzna produce he would bring on ongoing collaborator and future Filmwerks founder Gary Schmoeller as a co-producer on *The Guyver*, with Aki Komine and Yutaka Wada acting as executive producers on the film. Following *The Guyver*, Schmoeller would work on three other Yuzna features – Tony Randel's gloopy body horror *Ticks* (1993); Yuzna's cult classic *Return of the Living Dead III* (1993); and the horror film anthology *Necronomicon: Book of the Dead* (1993).

Schmoeller would have an interesting career as a producer on countless independent genre film productions after branching out on his own; specifically, those directed by late low-budget pioneer and cyborg film auteur Albert Pyun (including such rental classics such as *Nemesis 2: Nebula* (1995); *Omega Doom* (1996); and *Mean Guns* (1997)).

"I met him [Schmoeller] on *Society* (1989)," details Yuzna. "He started as a PA and then became the Production Manager by the time production started on *Society*. By the time *Return of the Living Dead 3* (1993) was shot, he was sharing a producer credit with me. He wasn't from the movie industry originally, but from construction. He's great, a really good producer and I think what makes a good producer is their ability to follow a budget, move pieces around and get things. So, he was a big part of making this film happen."

"It is very complicated having two directors," continues Yuzna. "They have two different styles, there's a lot of effects and puppetry, lots of characters, all of which have to be brought together." With the financing, script, and casting in place for this live-action adaptation, it was time for Wang, Tani, and the rest of the crew to set about designing the impressive creature effects work and Guyver suit, ahead of the shoot. No small undertaking even with the impressive calibre of special effects wizzes working for the two directors; but now the fun was really going to begin.

With the cast in place and the production in full swing, Wang called in some additional help from his *Kung Fu Rascals* cohorts who would support Wang and Tani in various capacities, in an effort to keep costs down and the film on schedule.

Fresh off their stint on *Kung Fu Rascals* and proven assets in assisting Wang with his vision, would be Eddie Yang working the creature shop; Asao Goto also in the creature shop; the late great sculptor and creature designer Moto Hata; Michael Deak (who'd also have a brief cameo in front of the camera with scream queen Linnea Quigley); Aaron Sims; Wyatt Weed and Ted Smith, both of whom would pull multiple duties.

The old adage goes – pain is temporary, but film is forever – and this is absolutely the case with independent filmmaking. Everything is squeezed out of the small amount of time and budget one has to create the ideal vision present in the minds of the filmmakers. There is an element of being a crazed genius to help pull all these varying parts and disciplines into literal Frankenstein's Creature. With so many personalities working different areas, it's a small miracle any films (regardless of the budget) are completed.

Despite having a high calibre of talent at his disposal, Wang was always on hand to perfect details on sculpts, sometimes to the frustrations of crew members. Like Weed has said, it wasn't due to any of the crew doing bad work or even having an ego; it was because Wang had such a distinct vision of what he wanted.

"The first couple of times [when sculpting] he said, '*Well yeah, that looks good*'. But he would then take your sculpting tool and go, '*Okay, but do it like this*' or '*what about like this*'," remembers Weed.

Instead of recreating the Zoanoids from either the anime or manga, Wang and Tani decided to instead create wholly unique Zoanoids that each sculptor was individually responsible for. This would allow the sculptors a chance to showcase their creature skills and designs, while also freeing up Wang and Tani to focus on their respective directing duties.

Eddie Yang would be responsible for possibly the most unique and visually iconic Zoanoid of the bunch – Lisker. Although all the Zoanoid designs have their own distinct characterization, it's hard to deny that Lisker remains the standout within the creature group, particularly in terms of overall design aesthetics. And this is thanks to Wang's trust in Eddie Yang's sculpting and design skill.

"We were given free rein that none of the Zoanoids had to come from the original storyline," details Yang. "Steve really trusted everybody that he put in charge of those characters. You know, Moto was already an incredible artist at the time, but everybody was kind of known for being great artists, as well as being responsible and carrying a project all the way through."

Even though the live-action Zoanoids were given a complete redesign and are wholly separate from the Zoanoids, either the manga or anime, were there any set guidelines at all for Lisker's overall look?

"The only thing Steve told me," remembers Yang, "was him saying '*this is your Predator*'. I was 21 at the time, which was about the same age that Steve was when he did the Predator. So, you know, I just heard that, and it was like a fire in me going '*I gotta make this good*'."

"We all started by doing little designs, like a little head sculpted in a kind of action figure pose, and then we would all sculpt on top of that our ideas and designs so that Steve could see them. All of a sudden, he pointed to one which kind of had this bulge out on its head, and he said, '*Hey, that's kind of cool. You should develop that further*'," says Yang.

"That's how Lisker came about, because Steve was showing me how to choose kind of a unique and original design. So, as an artist, you know, I'm just like, riffing, right? I'm just sculpting, and things just started coming out, you know, here's this head, here's that head, here's a different head, whatever. Your parameters are that the actors and performers have to be able to see and speak some lines, talk or whatever. And by him pointing out a particular one and said, '*You know, I never seen anything like that, it's kind of cool*', it was developed further."

"Back then, as a very young artist, I didn't know what the most unique looking or the most exotic looking thing was. But having the suggestion to go with that design and then further develop it was one of my first lessons, as a designer, as to what to look for in the design. Why should you choose that design and why you should develop it? So, I did what he [Steve] said and developed that sculpture into another maquette and he liked it. And I think from that point on, we all went to the full scale sculpts," remembers Yang.

This part of the sculpting process is where the final look of Lisker would begin to take shape. The kinks and flaws would also be worked out of the design during this period, often through an organic discovery between the sculptor and the clay. While it might sound strangely philosophical, this was especially the case for Yang during the design of Lisker.

"It was just a kind of being in the moment, like, 'whoa', probably how a musician feels when they come up with a song and just keeps adding to it and it just flows," describes Yang. "I felt like I could display it physically because I hated drawing at the time. I made very rudimentary sketches, but I loved sketching in clay. I think I had made something similar to the back of the head and had a direction. And I always felt that when I'm planning it out, whether it be clay or pencil sketch, it always got you a lot further than when you started just sculpting full size."

"The real thing was, like 10 times better, because they had worked out a lot of problems on the smaller version. But Steve did add some things. I think he came up with the hind dogleg idea [for Lisker] and said I should explore that and go with like big wrinkles like turtles have. So that's where all those wrinkles came from on the body."

Working in the creature shop wasn't without the occasional problem. Although it's now looked on fondly, there was a particular issue in workshop during the sculpting and design process, one that affected Yang's own work. "Actually, there was a big accident on that show. It taught me how to deal with those issues as well," says Yang.

"Lisker was the first sculpture to be finished, and we were supposed to mold it. So, it's all ready to go in the mold shop," remembers Yang. While it might have been the first creature sculpt to be finished, disaster was about to strike the work of young Mr. Yang, as the creature creator recalls.

"I had not built the base myself and through many weeks it got really wet and weak and the screws pulled out of the entire body of the sculpture. It was the night before it was supposed to go in to be molded and the whole sculpture fell," remembers Yang.

"Moto [Hata] saw it falling and ran over to me to see if I was okay. Oh man, the whole thing, just the whole body buckled beneath it. The legs flew off and the whole sculpture was dented and everybody's trying to lift it up, but by touching it they left fingerprints. But yeah, these things just happen."

With the Lisker sculpture dented, it would lead to a setback for the final creature rendering and suit creation. Thankfully, Yang managed to salvage a good portion of the sculpture, leading to a slightly quicker repair job. "I had to take another few weeks to fix it, but it wasn't as horrible as I thought."

"You have to be professional, particularly when you get put in charge or are supervising the shops. Artists can tend to freak out and, you know, throw clay across the room, or have tantrums. Artists can be hot-headed, but I tend to be a lot calmer about things," details Yang.

Thankfully, minus the incident with the Lisker sculpture, the creature shop was an enjoyable place to work and create. Despite the long hours, people were still producing creative endeavours, even when it was not part of the production. There was one instance Yang remembers vividly.

"The hours were super long, and people were getting tired. I remember somebody started spray-painting graffiti on the inside studio, and then everybody just started doing graffiti and all of these things," says Yang. "Steve actually stood up for us, saying 'I don't condone it, but I understand it'. To protect us, I guess."

With the Lisker suit now fully designed and fabricated, Wang would put Yang in charge of the suit while shooting commenced; it was Yang's creation after all. This meant making sure the suit performer (in this case Brian Simpson) was cooled down in-between setups; the animatronic head taken off between shots; and various parts of the Lisker creature suit maintained during the course of the shooting, to avoid any physical inconsistencies or to fix the suit where required.

"Steve introduced me to the first assistant director [Tom Milo], and they showed me that we had this little room where we kept everything, in some kind of abandoned warehouse they were shooting in," remembers Yang.

"I was then very much responsible for looking after Lisker and making sure he looked good on camera," continues Yang. "I think at some point, I was helping with the Guyver suit to make sure that got finished in the studio, as well as on set. I remember jumping back and forth between the two because they were the most important, and Steve trusted me. I think being one of the guys with the most experience, besides Jim Kagel, who obviously had a lot, but I don't know if Jim went on set often. So, yeah, everybody was kind of in charge of their own thing. I remember Asao (Goto) just saw us so much. He was such a workhorse and would just crank out suits and then just be on set, working all night. He just didn't sleep."

Wyatt Weed was also busy, as he was just about to finish his stint within the creature shop, having contributed a number of interesting effects for the film.

"I finished the creature shop stint, having done some pretty cool stuff," remembers Weed. "I did a lot of breakaway armour for like the reverse action scenes where Sean turned into the Guyver. It was a lot of these full-size armour pieces that we would we put on the actor [Jack Armstrong] and then we'd pull them off and run it in reverse. I then did the melting Guyver effect, so it went from having very little responsibility to having quite a bit more responsibility."

An early maquette sculpt of a Zoanoid, created by Jordu Schell.
Photo courtesy of Wyatt Weed.

Another early maquette sculpt for one of the Zoanoids,
created by Jordu Schell. Photo courtesy of Wyatt Weed.

An early maquette design of Balcus, sculpted by Screaming Mad George. Photo courtesy of Wyatt Weed.

Another angle of the early maquette design for Balcus, sculpted by Screaming Mad George. Photo courtesy of Wyatt Weed.

A close-up shot of the Balcus Maquette sculpted by Screaming Mad George. Photo courtesy of Wyatt Weed.

Another close-up shot of the Balcus Maquette sculpted by Screaming Mad George. Photo courtesy of Wyatt Weed.

Various sculpting prototypes of the Weber Zoanoid design, all in maquette form and sculpted by Jordu Schell. Photo courtesy of Wyatt Weed.

A half-human/half-Zoanoid transformation maquette, sculpted by Jordu Schell. Photo courtesy of Wyatt Weed.

Another early Zoanoid maquette design sculpted by
Jordu Schell. Photo courtesy of Wyatt Weed.

Another early Zoanoid Maquette sculpted by Jordu Schell.
Photo courtesy of Wyatt Weed.

Original maquette mini bust sculpt of the Guyver's look. Maquette
sculpted by Steve Wang. Photo courtesy of Wyatt Weed.

Steve Wang sculpting the original helmet for the Guyver
Photo courtesy of Ted Smith.

Steve Wang sculpting additional detail onto the
WIP Guyver suit. Photo courtesy of Ted Smith.

Full body shot of the sculpted Guyver suit
sans helmet. Photo courtesy Steve Wang.

Torso close-up of the Guyver suit sculpt. It's easier to see the level
of detail Wang put into the fibrous muscle strands on all the unarmoured
parts. A realistic interpretation of the anime and manga suit details.
Photo courtesy of Steve Wang.

The in-progress Guyver suit sculpt from the back
and side. Photo courtesy of Steve Wang.

Additional close-up of the Guyver suit chest and arms, taken in the creature shop. Those with an eagle eye might spot two creature maquettes in the lower part of the image. Photo courtesy of Steve Wang.

The unpainted Guyver suit worn by Haruo Matsuoka.
Photo courtesy of Wyatt Weed.

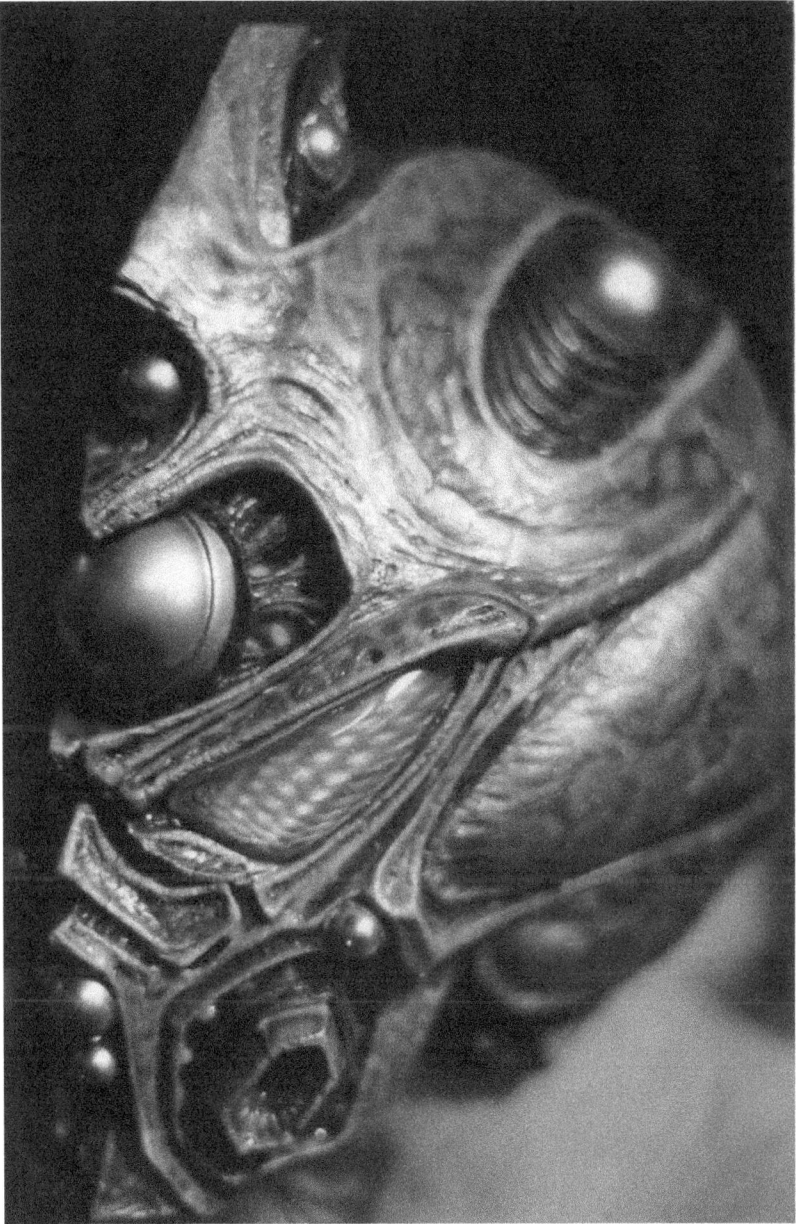

Close-up shot of Wyatt's completed reverse action helmet.
It would split apart in the middle, ejecting away from the actor
on wires. The footage was then run in reverse and at a different
camera speed to give the impression of the helmet engulfing Sean's
face during the transformation. Photo courtesy of Wyatt Weed.

Complete Guyver prop head created by Weed which put his
airbrushing skills to good use. Photo courtesy of Wyatt Weed.

"I made the Guyver blades, those were sculpted and molded. I figured out how to put an aluminium armature in them, along with figuring out how to do like a lock screw, so we could basically put different blades in and then lock them into place. I got to develop all of that."

"They wanted very solid blades so he could come into camera and do a pose and it wouldn't wobble. But then there were other times you want to stunt blade because he was gonna fight people and you didn't want to put somebody's eye out. So, there was a lot of that all throughout the creature shop process," remembers Weed.

The creation of the previously mentioned melting Guyver was an interesting challenge for the young special effects technician. Weed took a shell of a Guyver suit which was built by painting latex into the suit mold. They would then reinforce the latex with a fibreglass cloth. This allowed it to hold its shape and allowed it to be quite flexible. "Some of the pieces, like the feet and hands, were reject casts that weren't being used for some reason," recalls Weed.

"I assembled this Guyver on a board, like a big sheet of plywood. Under the suit, I drilled holes and ran cable from the inside, the upper surface of the suit and then down through the holes and out the bottom, at least a half-dozen holes for each limb, then a few for the body and a few for the head. The cables were all tied to large metal washers, and then the washers were glued down and painted over with latex, so it would grip the suit really well and not pull out when yanked."

"And this was because all those cables were run down to a piece of wood hanging underneath - one piece of wood for each limb, and then one for the body and head," continues Weed. "So, from underneath, you could pull down on these pieces of wood and the Guyver would collapse. You could do them all at once, one at a time, in pairs; however, you wanted it to collapse, slow or fast. Also, the cables were all slightly different lengths, so different sections would pull tight and collapse at slightly different times."

"When we shot it, I seem to remember it was supported on all sides by stage flats, like two-foot-tall stage risers, with the plywood holding the Guyver and placed over a gap between two risers. I spent an afternoon texturing and painting the plywood and flats to look like the regular cement stage. When we actually shot it, I think I had two other people under there with me, pulling on the wood pieces."

"The Guyver Unit being pulled from the head and the chest opening up were shot as inserts with different suit pieces. Those might have even been pickups done later, but my full suit was shot during principle, I'm pretty sure," says Weed.

And what about the close-up head melting? For this, Weed would employ a little *Raiders of the Lost Ark* (1981) magic. "The close-up Guyver head melting in one take was a wax Guyver head that had been built in the mold and then melted with heaters while shot time-lapse." The old and most simple effects really are the best effects.

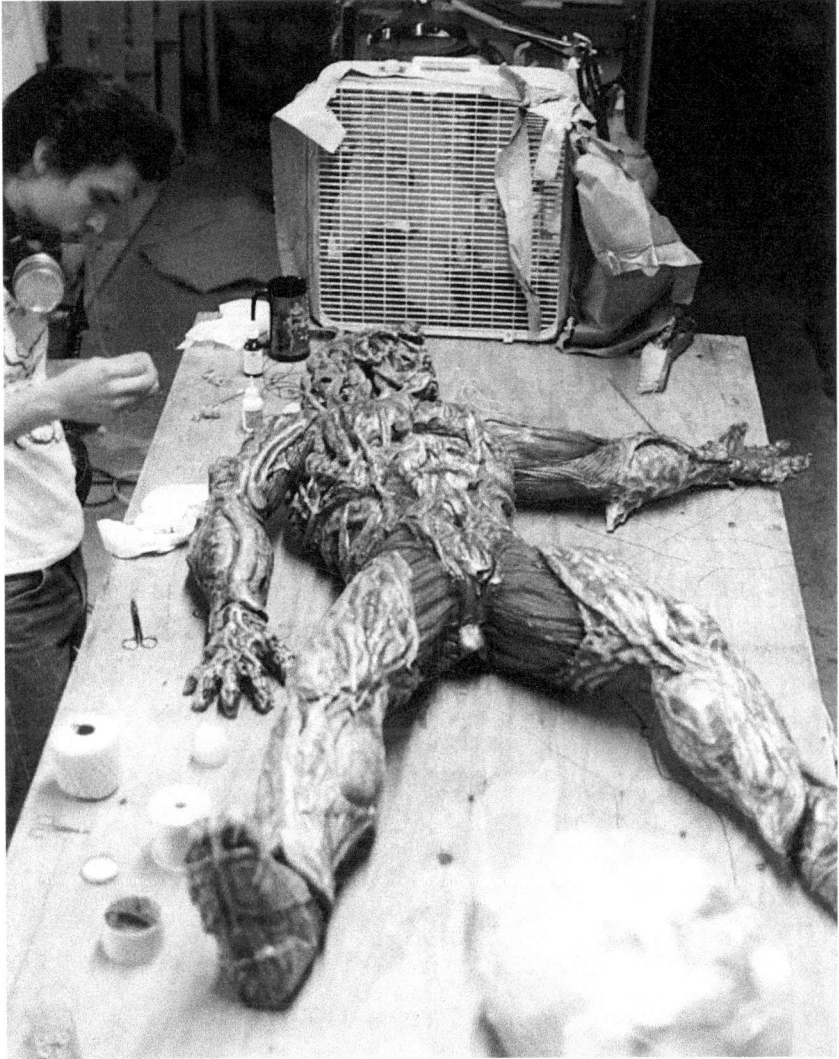

A young, fresh-faced Weed adds melted details to the collapsible Guyver suit. Photo courtesy of Wyatt Weed.

Close-up of melted Guyver hand. Photo courtesy of Wyatt Weed.

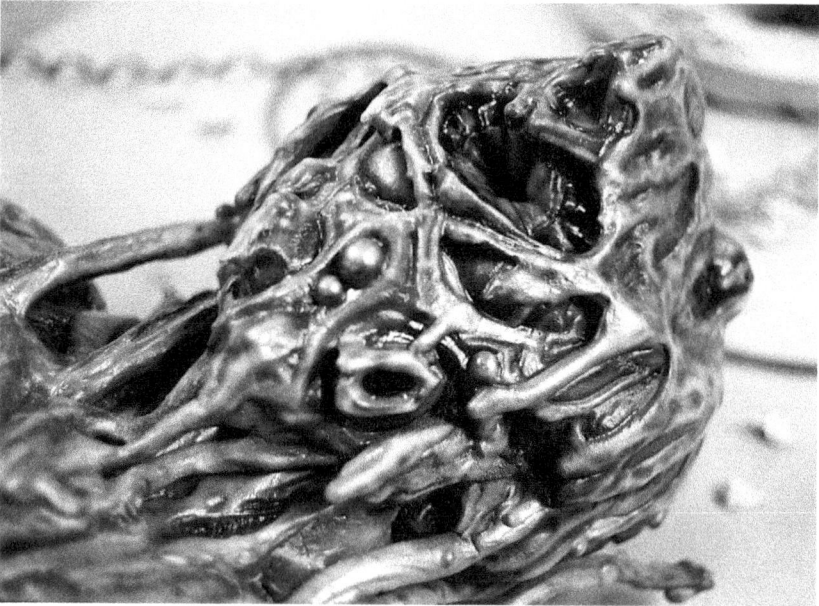

Close-up of the melted Guyver head *sans* control metal.
Photo courtesy of Wyatt Weed.

Close-up of the melted Guyver chest plate.
Photo courtesy of Wyatt Weed.

Full body shot of the Melting Guyver from the Zoanoid Warehouse Fight. The spare Guyver suit was used and retrofitted with foam on top of it to create the melted look. Photo courtesy of Wyatt Weed.

Although he was sharing directing duties with Screaming Mad George (Joji Tani), Wang always had a goal affixed in his sight when directing a project, and those who had worked with the sculpting wunderkind knew just how ambitious of a director he was, particularly after the long journey from the original *Kung Fu Rascals* short, through to its completion as a feature film.

Although Weed was a relative newcomer to the Wang filmmaking consortium, it was clear he understood Wang's passion for filmmaking after working on *Kung Fu Rascals* and for the, then upcoming, Guyver project.

"The way Steve gets stuff done is he's incredibly ambitious and you're either on board with that, or you're not," says Weed. "So, if you're just like a union guy and don't care about Guyver, you're just going to show up expecting to work 10 hours, and if you work overtime, you better get overtime pay. *'But hey, I can't work 12 hours, because that's just ridiculous, nobody works 12 hours!'* Well, you're not on Steve's level then because Steve is willing to go 15, 18, 20, even 24 hours, he's willing to stay up all night and he's going to ask you to stay up all night."

"There's two ways of looking at it," Weed explains further. "Either you're trying to do too much for the budget, and you should scale it back, or work extra hard and wring it for all it's worth and make it the best thing that it can possibly be. Now, me, Steve, Ted, all of us were like, *'Hey, we're young. We're in Hollywood, somebody has given us a couple of million dollars. Let's make this the best thing we could possibly make it.'*"

"Half the crew was like, *'man, six o'clock, I gotta go home'*, so you end up with that clash of styles where you got crew guys sitting around scratching their heads going, *'What the hell are we doing?'* But then you've got those people working with Steve who are huddled around the camera looking at when the effects come off going *'See, that's what we've been doing, that's what we've been working on this whole time.'*"

The *Rascals* crew were *au fait* with Wang's focused and passionate directing style where, regardless of a film's budget, Wang wanted to create the best feature possible. It's easy to see why some crew members not used to this directorial style - having only worked within union rules - might have their noses put out of joint for working longer than their designated hours, particularly someone who's as focused and determined to create a unique vision as Wang.

There is often a fine line as to what classifies a filmmaker as an auteur. Rather interestingly, this concept doesn't seem to be carried over to filmmakers outside of either arthouse cinema or the occasional big-budget feature, with it rarely being mentioned within low-budget filmmaking in recent years. Whether it's something a cinephile or critic subscribes to or not, it does have a place within the micro/low-budget sphere where a handful of directors continue to be creative with minimal finances afforded to them. In turn, they create a very definitive style and aesthetic unique to them, and this is more than clear with Wang and Co's low-budget determination.

"We have jokingly called Steve the bastard child of Jackie Chan and James Cameron," jokes Weed. "And it's accurate, because he can write, he can produce, he can direct, he can do martial arts, he can create creature suits, he can sculpt, he can paint. I mean, there's literally nothing the guy can't do. But it's not like he was kicking back on his throne, with women with fans and somebody feeding him grapes,".

"If you worked 22 hours a day and your fingertips were bleeding, Steve worked 23 hours a day and his fingertips were bleeding. He was always the first one in and the last one home. He always worked harder than everybody else, and he had a high standard. Eventually you got to the point where you knew what his standard was," recalls Weed.

Chapter Three

Crazy Bio-Organic Critters and Other Stories Part Two

Much like Wyatt Weed, Ted Smith was tasked with multiple roles on *The Guyver*. If he wasn't working on various models, prop pieces, or a particular effect, Smith would find himself pulling double duty on-screen; firstly, as gang member Ronnie (who Sean beats up following his initial bonding with the Guyver Unit), and then as the physical creature performer for the Striker Zoanoid.

"During pre-production, I was helping to build the suits and the housing that it comes in, while working in the effects shop. Steve realized we need the Guyver Unit which transforms. He was so busy with everything else, as I'm a model maker he asked me to do it and starts describing all the stuff he wanted it to do. I look back on this by today's standards and I'd start shaking my head like *'you're crazy'*, but I was so young and eager to work and improve myself," says Smith.

"So, Steve's like, *'the Guyver Unit has got a metal in the centre, and it glows. And then it needs to pop open and shoot tentacles out'.* And I'm like *'What?'*, and he just keeps talking and I make all these notes. It was an eye-opening moment for me - just saying what he wanted and then let me get on with it," Smith elaborates.

"As a director [despite his background in effects work] his job is not to make this stuff or figure out how to make it. It's his job to tell you what he wants. That's why you're there, to meet this guy's vision. A director's job is to translate their ideas to you, so you get it and there's no confusion. Just tell us what you want, and we'll do it and that's exactly what Steve said. Then I'm like '*Oh shit, I've just realized it's up to me*', it's not a job where somebody supervises you every day, and Steve just cut me loose to do it."

With Wang trusting him for one of the key props in the film, it was then down to Smith to research what the Guyver Unit was and how it would transition into a convincing live-action interpretation, given this was a fictional alien device which had only been seen in two-dimensional mediums prior to the film.

Both Wang and Smith were conscious to take the known elements – the infamous Japanese tentacles and glowing metal center – but to create their own take on what this unit would be in the real world.

"I looked at the Guyver Unit from the animation and the manga," says Smith. Steve's philosophy was that the unit was a biomechanical alien, and organic. Obviously in the anime and manga it had like a metal casing on it, so he goes '*I want to lose that completely*'. That bothered him, so Steve would go '*I want this to resemble what the Guyver suit is*.' So, when Steve was sculpting, I would just look at what Steve was doing, as reference for the unit. I took that design and made it more organic. Then as we started it, Steve was like '*I want finger-like attachments, like the panels are cool, but these little brackets here, make them like fingers.*'

From there, Smith continued to add more organic elements to the Guyver Unit as it evolved with the sculpting of Wang's suit design. "Steve was like, '*throw me some ideas and show it to them to me*'. I did it under Steve's direction really, but I would suggest ideas," says Smith.

With the outer shell of the Guyver Unit finally taking its more organic shape, all that was left to add was the internal workings.

In the anime and manga, the unit housed a delightfully unsettling and viscus-looking wreath of undulating tentacles; a remnant from Yoshiki Takaya's hentai beginnings, perhaps? Either way, the solution for the undulating living organism beneath the Guyver Unit was impressively low-tech and DIY, harking back to the creative solutions Wang and Co. would use on a micro-budget film.

"Steve wanted the coils to not be perfectly clean and even, so he said, 'use some tubing'. I made a jig, which is like a template, and sculpted this donut-like shape out of clay, and I bought, like, 100 yards of plastic surgical tubing I just spiralled all around this thing to get the texture of it and molded that separately," recalls Smith.

"I really designed this thing to be really elaborate because it's featured so prominently in the movie. We made several different Guyver Units. I had the hero one that was like a rubber cord with fiberglass fingers on it and it had an actual glowing light ball; this was back in the 90s before LEDs. We rigged it with a controlled variac, and I was off camera rotating the variac, making it glow. It was so old school."

Another key moment which involves the Guyver Unit, and one that would etch itself into the minds of many a young viewer - is when Sean, during his tussle with the street gang, falls onto the Guyver Unit causing it to be activated and subsequently bonding with him, resulting in his transformation into the Guyver. Despite it being a brief sequence, it still manages to insight an uncomfortable feeling and overall grossness more commonly found within the body-horror subgenre.

The sequence would be broken down into two specific parts; the on-location section with the actors and then the visual effect section done after principal photography was completed. It's a sequence that morphs from humor to horror in a matter of seconds. In today's CGI enhanced filmmaking landscape and barring a small handful of low budget practical features, you would be hard-pressed to create anything as tangible and viscus as this transformation.

"We were on location with the actor [Jack Armstrong]. When he hits his head on the Guyver Unit, that was a rubber one. And then when he rolls over, it's still the actor holding the Guyver Unit on his face," explains Smith.

"I painted up everything to make it look just like the Guyver suit. The coils on the unit I made from rubber castings, and I took rubber tubing and linked them all together individually."

"I slathered them up with a silicone grease because it was rubber. If we used like an oil-based grease it just would destroy it. Actually, thinking back about it, I could have just used KY Jelly, but we did use silicon grease," remembers Smith.

"I was looking at it; I noticed it was all the same color, and I realized you couldn't see it. Steve's like, '*Yeah, break it up with different colours, like seeds are. Do like light or dark red, stuff like that*'. So, one night we talked about it and kind of worked out the problems."

The shooting of the unit attaching to Sean's head was surprisingly straightforward, as Smith explains.

"It's literally just half of a Guyver Unit, which the actor is holding up in front of the camera with these two strips of rubber and pulleys coming off it. It's all because we know that we just have to show one particular section. So, it was just me, with an AD who called action, and I would just start pulling and turning to make it move. You watch that thing and it lasts like mere seconds."

Despite its mere seconds on-screen, the undulation of the unit manages to lodge itself into the viewer's subconscious incredibly well. Once again, the ingenuity behind a brief sequence like this shows just how creative the Guyver crew was with just a few bits of rubber and string. Low-tech solutions are sometimes the best.

Smith was also responsible for the Guyver Unit taking over Sean's face, leading to his first transformation as The Guyver. "That was my gag," says Smith. "It's actually a puppet head from another movie Screaming Mad George did prior to *The Guyver*."

The movie in question was Frederico Prosperi's in-name only sequel *Curse II: The Bite* (1989). The prop head was used during one of the film's more vomit-inducing moments where J. Eddie Peck's character - Clark Newman - appears out of a sewer duct and proceeds to have a large python vacate his mouth.

With the prop head being masked by the Guyver Unit as it engulfs Sean's head, it only required a few tweaks; namely dyed hair and new teeth, along with dressing the head and shoulders in Sean's clothes. It's an ingenious reuse of previously designed effects to help keep production costs down on such an effects heavy film.

"We had the molds, and we just ran a new foam skin into it," continues Smith. "The head didn't have teeth, so we added those and just stuck a wig on and painted it because since it's covering the majority of the face it didn't matter, as all we see is the mouth."

"So, we did all that and I painted it to match the skin color of the actor. I didn't know how to do makeup flesh tones and it was just me by myself, so Wayne [Toth] taught me his techniques, like, airbrush a little bit light blue, then a thin transparent yellow, then blue; it was basically a really quick skin tone. I was literally painting on set before we shot it," remembers Smith.

"Then we rigged it up, so it hinges open. We had the ribs rigged up on little hinges as well, so it would flip open, and we rigged up pulleys on it. I had all these heavy Teflon lines used to pull it open and airbrushed them black so they wouldn't be seen."

The end effect on-screen is delightfully unsettling and gross as the unit engulfs Sean's head, the unit's organic cables start to undulate, and the viscus liquid starts to pour out of the centre as the Guyver begins to awaken. Despite it only being a few seconds of screen time, it leaves a lasting impression; one that was sure to give nightmares to many a young viewer (and maybe even some older viewers) at the time.

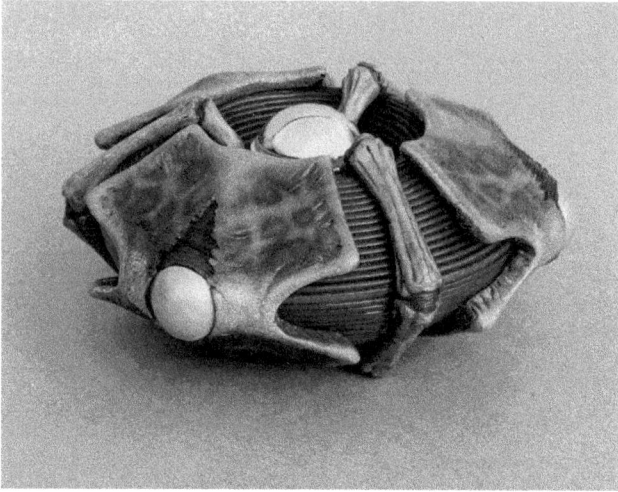

Ted Smith's finished Guyver Unit prop. Photo courtesy of Ted Smith.

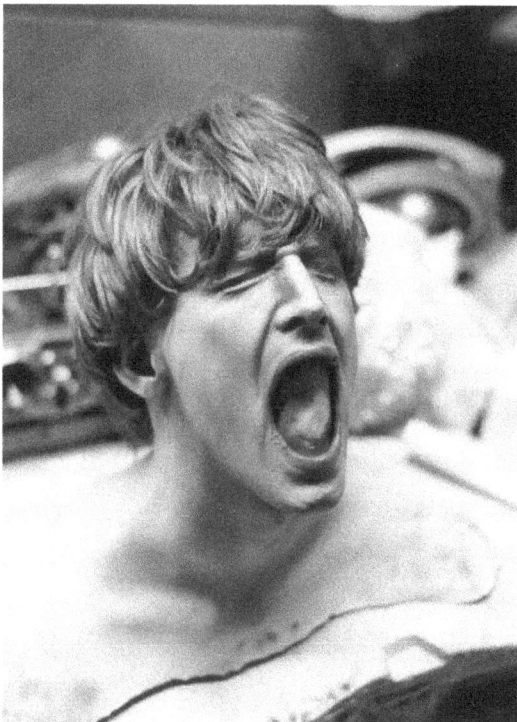

Prop head for Sean based on a head cast from one of Screaming Mad George's prior films, in this case *Curse II: The Bite* (1989). Photo courtesy of Ted Smith.

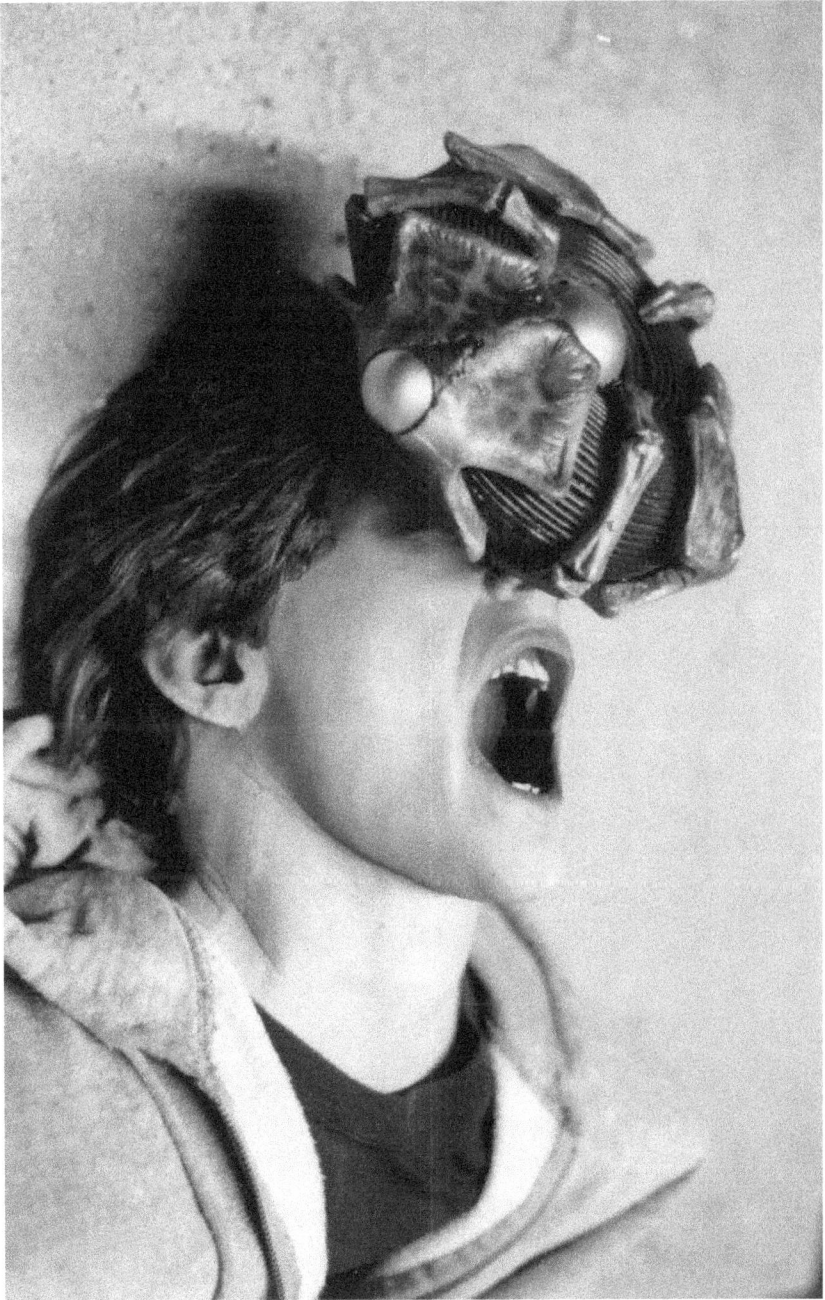

Fully completed Sean prop head with attached Guyver Unit.
Photo courtesy of Ted Smith.

Behind-the-scenes shot of the Guyver Unit taking over Sean's body.
The tendrils were melted plastic and pulled into the center of the unit.
The footage was then reversed and sped up to give the feeling of it
enveloping Sean's face. Photo courtesy of Ted Smith.

When he wasn't creating the Guyver Unit and torturing the poor animatronic head of Sean, Smith would spend his time in the physically restricting Striker Zoanoid suit. For the complex animatronic head that Smith would be wearing, Wang and Tani would call in the creative genius of FX industry legend Jim Kagel, who would design and operate the complex animatronic head for Striker.

Although the name of James Kagel won't necessarily be familiar to the average viewer, the films he has worked on will be familiar, particularly with his extensive work on a vast array of creature features such as Alex Winter's cult classic *Freaked* (1993); *Stargate* (1994); *Tremors II: Aftershocks* (1996); *The Abyss* (1989); *Big Trouble in Little China* (1986); and *Deep Rising* (1998).

Prior to getting the heavy animatronic head on, Smith had to first have his body cast, so he'd fit within the Zoanoid suit. "Steve liked working with me and my performance, so he figured, what the hell, I should play the character of Striker as I could do really animated characters," says Smith, having demonstrated his experience doing so while they both worked on *Kung Fu Rascals*.

"They were doing the body molds at the time," remembers Smith. "So, Steve got them to do a full body cast on me for the Striker suit. That's when I learned about the whole science about monster suit making and the work that goes behind it. They make you put a spandex suit on, and they literally slather you up with Vaseline," details Smith.

"Then they take plaster bandages and make a two-part body cast. So, you're in a position where they put sticks underneath the arms to hold your arms up, because it starts to get heavy, and then you're tilted slightly back so they can make a particular mannequin form of your body with the intention of sculpting it, so when they made the rubber suit, it fits you exactly. It was such a learning curve to watch these guy work," Smith recalls.

"I had an absolute blast on set, and I realize now looking back on it what an opportunity it was. Brian [Yuzna], the producer, loved my performance, and I would make the crew laugh on set. I would do a scene and people would just crack up and start laughing during a take," remembers Smith.

"I was always class clown when I was a kid. So, this time I was able to do it and perform a character. One thing I learned really quickly was, when you're acting in a monster suit, some of your gestures get lost, so you have to over-animate or overemphasize things. I knew Striker's eyeballs were positioned on my forehead while wearing the creature suit and I realized that if I looked, where my eyes I looked out of (in this case out of the creature's mouth) I was seeing anybody's chest, but the creature head looking at their eyes."

"So, I learned really quickly where my eyes were so every time I would perform, I always made sure Striker's eyes are either facing toward the camera or looking at people. I'd be very conscious of that. I was very over-animated, too, particular with the fingers or big claws. I'd always hit the mark and over-gesture or do a big comical move," details Smith.

"It's kind of like you're doing theatre and I'd notice what the other guys were doing as well, particularly Brian Simpson who played Lisker. Brian was really great and passed a lot of his knowledge of suit performance onto me during the shoot."

It seemed that for Smith, the advice from Simpson would become invaluable and helped breathe even more life into the former's creature performances during *The Guyver* and beyond. "I learned a lot from him [Brian]. So, when we were doing a scene together, he was a really big help. We actually had a monster class where we'd all hang out and try out our mannerisms and movements," recalls Smith.

"As Striker, I always lent my chest forward along with my hands, and I'd keep my arms back and would roll my fingers. I always made sure to do quick head movements, especially when I came 'round a corner, I'd make sure to snap my head really quick."

Ted Smith (along with Striker head) poses with animatronic, and creature effects legend Jim Kagel, in-between takes on *The Guyver*. Kagel was responsible for Striker's complex inner workings. Photo courtesy of Ted Smith.

Ted Smith models the latest in Zoanoid fashion with the Striker suit (sans animatronic head) on *The Guyver* set. Photo courtesy of *Wyatt Weed*

From left to right, Ted Smith (in Striker suit), Doug Simpson (in Ramsey suit), and Eddie Yang taking a break between filming *The Guyver*. Photo courtesy of Ted Smith.

"We all had our individual movements," remembers Smith. "Because Lisker was so big, he was always chest forward, rolling his body to move around. We always kind of stayed behind him, so whenever we moved, we couldn't get in front of him. Like *'Don't get in front of this guy because he's the boss'*. We'd have a gag where I'd walk up next to him, and he would raise the back of his hand ready to smack me for getting out of line. We would play with that all the time, it was fun."

Watching how the other Zoanoids interact with Lisker, its clear to see this monstrous hierarchy, which Smith and the rest of the suit performers put into their characters, in full force. It helps add an extra layer to the overall performances and turns the Zoanoids into much more than just cannon fodder for The Guyver to maim and mutilate.

One area that was problematic about the suit for Smith was getting in and out of the Striker costume. "I was usually in it for around 16 hours. When you're in it, you are in it. I always kept thinking I have to urinate, but you sort of have to just sweep past it. But it's a whole process of getting into that suit. The biggest pain in the ass was the neck piece," remembers Smith.

"That would come down and it would then have to be blended into the body. So, I'd essentially be glued in from the collar bone. They would then have to feed me a straw through Striker's mouth, so I'd get to drink in-between shots. They did sculpt the suits so we could take the hands and feet off between shots. They were like gloves, and you'd just slip them on, and the seams would blend nicely. So, between shots we'd take our heads and hands off because nothing holds heat more than your hands."

"The feet were easy as well; basically, they were built-in shoes that they'd sculpt the feet around. Steve was like *'Let's get some nice form-fitting tennis shoes and then sculpt round those'*. So, when they called action, you'd be able to start up relatively quickly, but in-between takes we'd be able to kick back for a little bit, get rid of the feet, hands, and head. It wasn't totally uncomfortable to perform in it, but you are wearing a rubber suit, day after day and for like weeks on end."

"We had two heads, one was the hero head, and the other was the rubber one," recalls Smith. "The hero head had the mechanics in it, like all of the servos and was a little bit heavy. It had a fiberglass skullcap that I'd wear which had like an elastic strap that I could adjust once it was on. That went around my jaw so I could open and close Striker's mouth from the inside. So, all the jaw movement was me".

This would leave the rest of Striker's facial moments, such as the eyes and ears down to Kagel to perform off-screen.

George Tani (Screaming Mad George) sculpts a full-scale Balcus head in the Guyver creature shop. Photo courtesy of Ted Smith.

Although mostly shot as a miniature rod-puppet, there was still a call for the Balcus creature to be a large-scale head in shots during the film's climax; and this hulking monster head would be sculpted by Tani. Despite its relatively brief inclusion, the Balcus head and elongated neck are truly a sight to behold and as per Tani's usual standard of work, is incredibly detailed.

Tani would also sculpt the whole creature in miniature from clay, and it would remain his main Zoanoid design contribution to the film. Much like the rest of the Zoanoid troupe, the design of Balcus is unique and wholly original which once again distinguishes itself from the manga and anime source material. Tani's overall design concept behind this imposing big bad villain was an interesting one.

"You know, next to the other Zoanoids and with it being the Lord, it had to be something bigger," describes Tani.

"The driving-force behind the style was that it contained elephant-like legs and a bunch of different animal types. Parts in the body have some more organic looks, like the back section and a tail, which is like a dragon, but then it has these human-like forearms. It's just not a normal four-legged creature you know? And I thought that would be a nice change."

With Balcus dragon-like aesthetic, a potential homage to oriental folklore, Tani would add a few extra attributes to his gigantic creation, such as Balcus's array of protruding horns, resembling a crown of sorts which further confirms his lordly status? "Yeah, not really." chuckles Tani. Well, at least that interpretation has been debunked.

"When I designed it, I just I thought this would be cool," continues Tani. "I just kind of drew the whole creature and made the horns untypical, like a twisty type. I wanted to have, like a fleshy look to everything; keep it organic. I avoided anything harsh or robotic."

While the full-scale Balcus head would only be briefly seen, it still allowed for some fun moments during the final fight sequence as it went toe-to-toe with the miniature Guyver puppet. More on that later.

While Tani and Steve Wang had a dedicated crew of consummate professionals within the makeup and special effects department, it didn't stop them from occasionally reaching out to fellow colleagues when they needed a little extra help, due to the increasingly complex nature of the shoot. Both men were pulling in as many favours as possible from any SFX colleagues who could lend a hand to this FX heavy feature.

The inclusion of legendary FX artist Gabe Bartalos to the effects crew – as a favour to effects friends Wang and Tani – remains an interesting addition, despite only contributing a small percentage of work to *The Guyver* creature shop.

"What's really cool about the makeup effects community is it is, in fact, exactly that, a community. This was especially the case more than 30 years ago, now," says Bartalos.

"Steve Wang is a super likable guy and has terrific energy and is a really good artist. I knew George as well from New York even before I moved to Los Angeles. They were making the film independently and making it happen on the goodwill of a lot of people and getting resources where they could," remembers Bartalos.

"John Carl Buechler was, I guess, letting Steve use the MMI studio for spill over work and a suit that I was involved in was built there. I came in for a few days during a crunch period and helped lay down some paint or airbrush paint on it."

"I was more than happy to jump in and help. A lot of the creature suits were sculpted and molded in a traditional sense, while some of the other suits were made with what's called foam fabrication, whether its sheet foam built from scratch or pre-made pieces, they are glued together and assembled. And there was one of those characters like an insect thing [the Max Zoanoid created by the late Moto Hata]."

In fact, Hata's insect-cum-cockroach creature that Max (Mark Hamill) disgustingly transforms into is a unique creation in its own right. It had various stages of transformation, each requiring a different angle to achieve the look of a painful on-screen transformation, ultimately becoming the most unsettling for any of the characters. Bones twist, snap and contort. Max's body warps in on itself and his facial features distort and change during the course of several shots. It's a decidedly stomach-churning experience, not just for our hero's companions, but for the viewer as well.

Given his prior insect transformation experience on *A Nightmare on Elm Street 4: The Dream Master* (1988), Tani would be responsible for shooting this twisted body-horror sequence. For the first part of the transformation, a conveniently placed Guyver suit performer stands in the centre of the frame/front of the camera to conceal the crew puppeteering the in-human breaking of Max's legs under false flooring, which helps to hide Hamill's body and sell the transformation illusion. For the second part of the transformation, the camera would shoot a close-up of Hamill's head in full mid-transformation makeup. Ahead of the cameras rolling, he would insert a mouthpiece full of insect pincers to complete the unsettling look. To achieve the elongation of Max's head and neck for the final part of the transformation, Hamill would position himself in a small, cut-out section of the floor, moving under the staging on an office chair. Like many of the effects in *The Guyver*, it's wonderfully simplistic in its execution and much like a good magic trick, is a clever visual deception.

Through the various stages of makeup, a lot of KY Jelly, and Ted Smith in the full Max Zoanoid costume (albeit briefly), the unsettling transformation was complete. Even with all these combined elements, the action only happens for a handful of seconds, but it's no less effective despite the on-screen brevity.

A number of creature effects crew get Ted Smith zipped into the Max Zoanoid insect suit, which was sculpted by the late Moto Hata, for the climax of the film. Photo courtesy of Ted Smith.

It's not just the effects work where *The Guyver* looks more expensive than its meagre budget would suggest. In fact, one area which makes *The Guyver* look about several million dollars more than its actual budget is in the impressive and timeless visuals from fabled genre cinematographer Levie Isaacks, who gives the aesthetics a, at times, hyper-realised comic book vibe with its distinctive lighting and camera angles.

At the time, Isaacks had just come off two features from the late Tobe Hooper. The first was an under-appreciated sci-fi tale about governmental conspiracies, *Spontaneous Combustion* (1990), followed shortly thereafter by the TV Movie *I'm Dangerous Tonight* (1990). Before this, Isaacks had worked with British director Anthony Hickox on his vampire-comedy-cum-western, *Sundown: The Vampire in Retreat* (1989).

Although he'd never set out to be a cinematographer for horror or sci-fi features, the genre quickly became synonymous with his name and anyone who grew up in the 1990s VHS rental era would almost certainly recognise Isaacks' work.

Outside of the previously mentioned titles, working on the likes of *Children of the Corn II: The Final Sacrifice* (1992), *Leprechaun* (1993), and *Texas Chainsaw Massacre: The Next Generation* Aka *Return of the Texas Chainsaw Massacre* (1995), along with 16 episodes of *Tales from the Crypt* (1989-1996) including William Malone's "Only Skin Deep" (1994), Gregory Widen's "Half-Way Horrible" (1993), and Martin von Haselberg's "The Assassin" (1994).

Isaacks would also find himself working with Brian Yuzna again several years after his stint on *The Guyver*, where he'd lens the killer cavity horror *The Dentist* (1996).

After adding a touch of visual class to a multitude of horror titles, Isaacks applied his craft to a number of TV productions; most notably *Malcolm in the Middle* (2000-2006) and *Dawson's Creek* (1998-2003), before returning to the DTV sequel sphere with *Bring It On: In It to Win It* (2007), *Road Trip: Beer Pong* (2009), and *Mean Girls 2* (2011).

It'd be the 1990s though where Isaacks' work would be most fondly remembered and even now, some 30-plus years later, his visuals for *The Guyver* and the films pre- and post this sci-fi action mash-up still hold a unique aesthetic to them; full of dark hues and an almost dreamlike quality which separates them from a lot of their contemporaries at the time.

What ultimately lead to his inclusion on this bizarre creature feature? "Brian [Yuzna] had seen my reel and knew I'd done those pictures with Tony [Hickox] and Tobe [Hooper]," remembers Isaacks. "I thought it was kind of an interesting thing to work for two directors. I mean, Steve [Wang] did most of the direction, but Screaming Mad George certainly had a lot to do. They really collaborated with each other," says Isaacks.

Coming up with the overall visual look and cinematography for *The Guyver* was an interesting process as well, according to Isaacks.

"Really, we worked it out as we went along," remembers Isaacks. "A lot of what a DP does is just problem solving such as *'How do we get this done? Where do we put the lights etc.'* So, for this particular movie, a lot of it was just keeping the light out of the shot, which was difficult as George wanted to see these rubber suits."

Thankfully the lighting chosen by Isaacks (and his team) meant the audience would see the suits in the most atmospheric way possible, with dark hues and smoky aesthetics highlighting and accentuating the impressive sculpting work done by the skilled creature effects crew.

Consistency was also key, which is something that's hard to keep track of while shooting multiple units at once. While shooting on the main unit, how did Isaacks keep visual consistency between all the different crews, such as the second unit, which the late Thomas C. Rainone was responsible for?

"I've had that go wrong before on previous films," remembers Isaacks. "I would make them take an image of the scene, so if I'm using a cool backlight with warm side light and white fill, I make them use the same lights and the same colouration so they can see what was done and mimic it."

Clearly this process worked for Isaacks as the visual consistency between first and second unit are indistinguishable from each other; a testament to Isaacks' professionalism and planning.

Working with two directors, a first for Isaacks, was an interesting experience in of itself, but was never difficult as one may initially think it would be. "They were really easy to work with," describes Isaacks. "I thought *'They know exactly what they want'* and had it planned out very well." It also seemed that Wang was always keen to learn, even while making his first feature film.

"One of the things that Steve wanted to do was a one frame swish pan, so he'd ask, *'How do you do that?'* So, I said, *'Here, you take the camera, you do it'* and I let him operate those shots," remembers Isaacks.

Despite his prior work, Isaacks credits *The Guyver* as an interesting learning experience, particularly in regard to his cinematographic craft.

"I look at that movie now and, you know, my ability has gone way beyond that," says Isaacks. "I mean, it's one of the shows where I really learned how to cut light. Even in some of those backgrounds I think there's too much light going on, you know. I'd want to take it down so that the characters kind of pop out and that sort of thing. So, it's come a long way from The *Guyver.*"

"But you know, I didn't know that at the time. I mean, I changed the soft light on a TV series in the early 90s, and lighting for a TV series is a whole different ballgame. And I think it's really one of the things I've learned from European productions, because in a lot of Europe they're using single sources. It's a much better look for film and so I started really going in that direction with using soft light," recalls Isaacks.

Looking back at his work, it's clear anyone *au fait* with European cinema will spot the late 1980s and early 1990s visual sensibility where soft light contrasts against the characters on-screen, giving the shots a distinct, aesthetically pleasing feel and making each character look stunning, regardless of who or what is in the shot.

For Isaacks' work, there always seemed to be a soft haze or smokiness which fills the frame, only adding to its nightmarish, dreamlike quality, and this is particularly the case with visuals in *The Guyver* playing more into an otherworldly realism. Take a single shot or still from *The Guyver* and it very much feels like a comic book panel come to life.

It could be argued that this particular aesthetic misses the point of the manga it is based on, a bombastic and noisy visual image which has been filtered through a western lens to make it feel closer, tonally at least, to an American comic book. That isn't too far from the truth, particularly given how unique a western live-action adaptation of an Asian property was at the time; but it also makes it a visual treat to revisit even with these flaws.

Whereas the script and acting can be below par at times and the narrative isn't particularly interesting (and in retrospect it's easy to see why this is the case), *The Guyver* stands head and shoulders next to the prior and ultimately more expensive comic book films such as *Dick Tracy* (1990) and *Batman* (1989), by really leaning into its unique visuals to create a truly engaging viewing experience, even if other areas (such as silly comedy and bad acting) cause the film to stumble more than once.

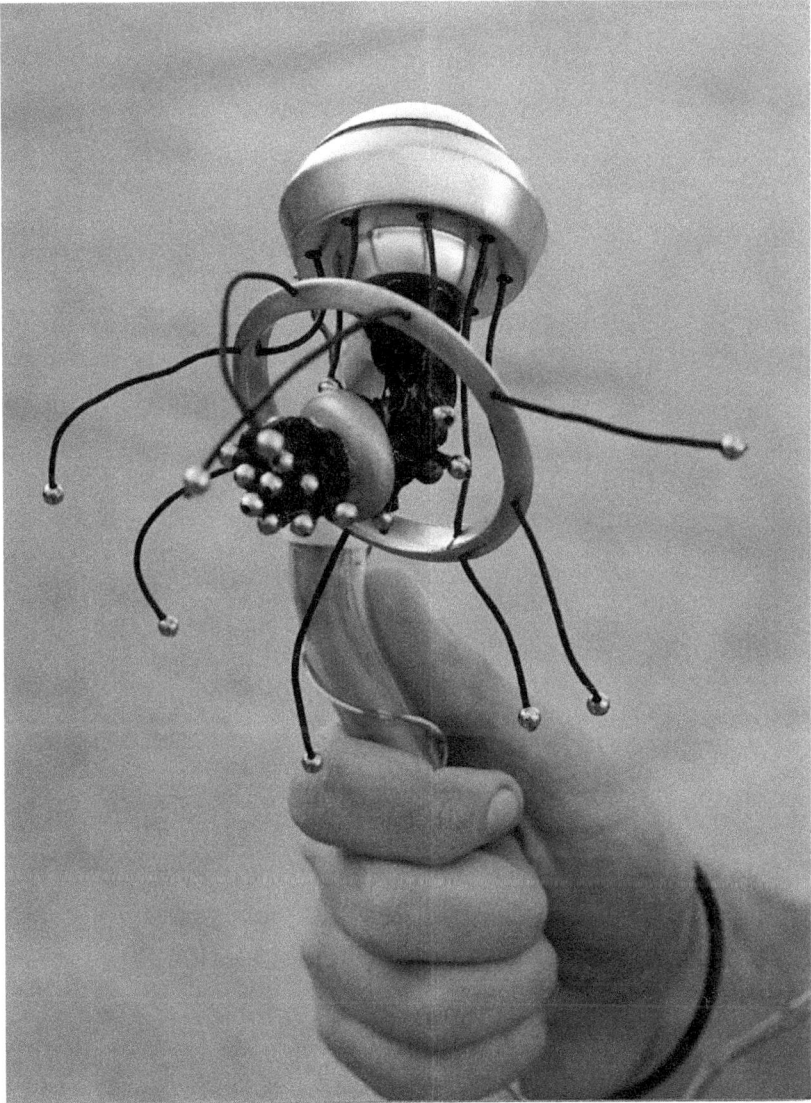

The reverse action growing control metal. The tentacles would
extend and wrap around the hand of Vivian Wu's stand-in.
Photo courtesy of Wyatt Weed.

Another close-up shot of the growing control metal with the tube hidden behind the hand. Photo courtesy of Wyatt Weed.

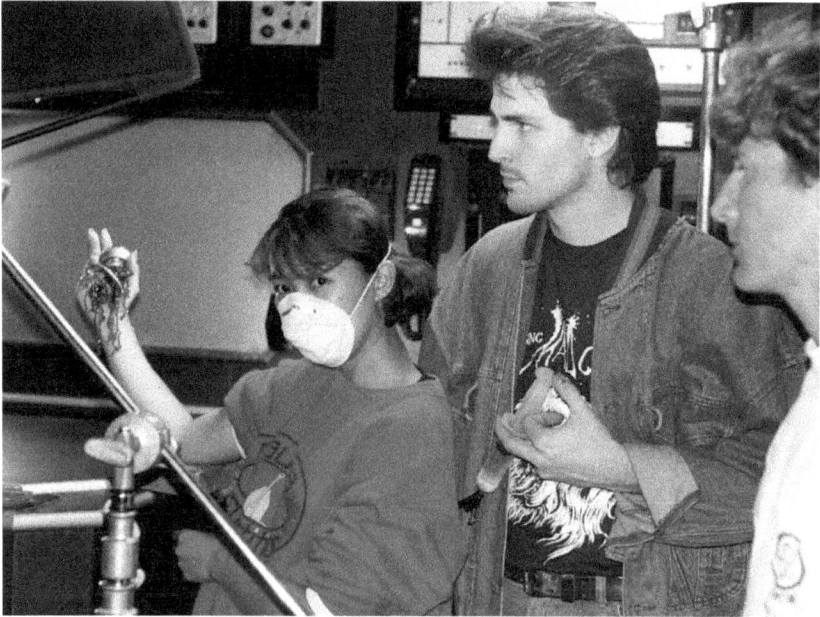

Vivian Wu's stand-in with Wyatt Weed on the lab set, operating the reverse action control metal. Photo courtesy of Wyatt Weed.

The late David Gale and legendary character actor Jeffery Combs pose for a photo in-between setups. Photo courtesy of Ted Smith.

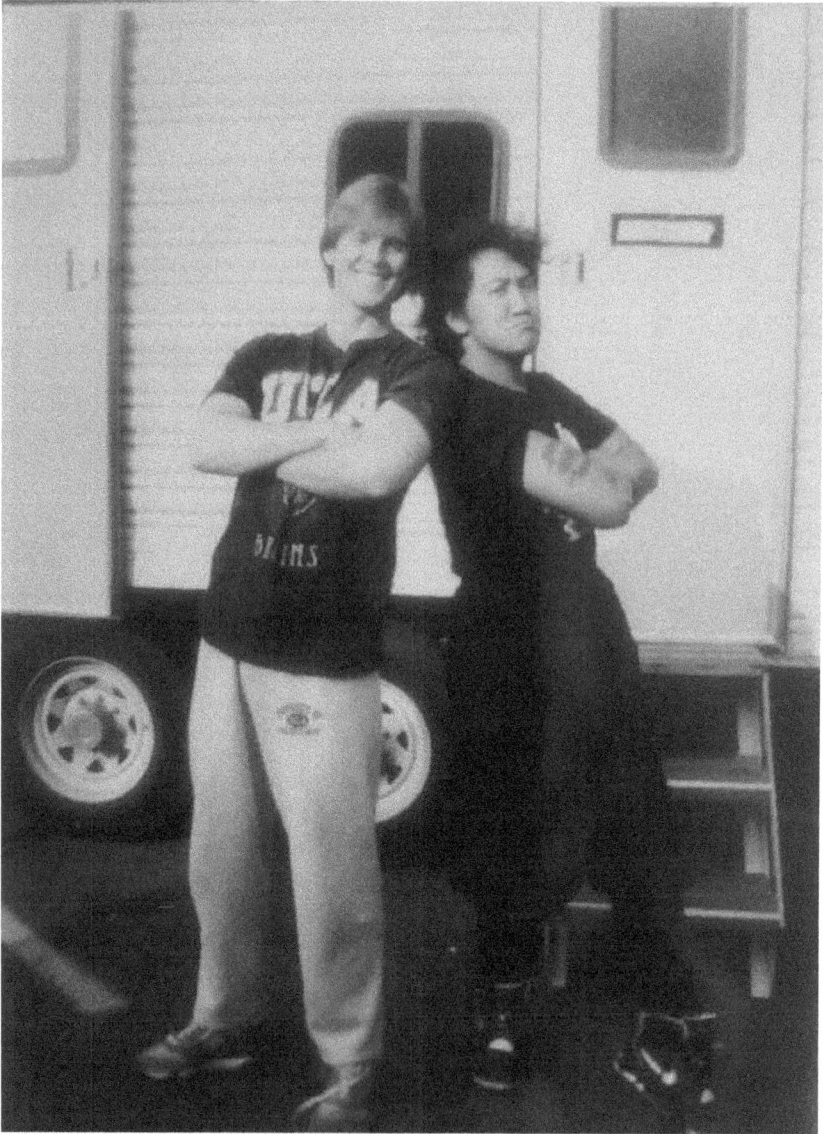

Johnnie Saiko and Jack Armstrong goof around between shots on *The Guyver*. Photo courtesy of Johnnie Saiko.

Behind-the-scenes shot of actor Jack Armstrong shooting the pre-Guyver transformation. Photo courtesy of Wyatt Weed.

A close-up shot of Jack Armstrong striking the Guyver transformation pose. Photo reference of this sequence would later be used to sculpt the realistic looking stop-motion puppet for the wide-shot transformation. Photo courtesy of Wyatt Weed.

Chapter Four

Hard Knock Life

One of the many areas where *The Guyver* did falter, and faltered hard, with fans and viewers alike, was the level of action and martial arts on display. Or rather, the lack thereof. It's hard not to make comparisons to its creature feature contemporary *Teenage Mutant Ninja Turtles* (1990), whose action and fight sequences remain some of the best action showcases for suit performers.

The Guyver, despite its best intentions, was often lacking in this department. The fights feel restrained and often fail to insight any form of excitement, a shame given how impressive the production design and suit work remains.

With its successor opting for a more Hong Kong wirework (or Wuxia) approach to the action and fisticuffs – ultimately giving it a high-energy appeal and sense of danger – this first entry took a more realistic approach to the martial arts, much to the detriment of the director's decision to include it. In the late 1980s and early 1990s, aikido was the martial art *du jour* due in large part to the sleeper success of Steven Seagal's arrival on the big screen. His triple threat of bone-crunching action thrillers *Above the Law* (1988); *Hard to Kill* (1990); and *Marked for Death* (1990) would catapult the unique Japanese martial art into the mainstream consciousness of the time.

Above the Law would become notable as being the first western film to prominently include aikido. Tani was practicing aikido at the time and, being from Osaka himself, was particularly taken with this martial art, quickly seeing an opportunity to include it within his directorial debut. "I had been studying it for a long time, and that's why you saw it in *The Guyver*," details Tani about his aikido learning.

"When I moved to L.A., I went looking for a dojo where I can, you know, study aikido. In Hollywood, where I lived, there was one close to a barber. So, I went into the dojo and found it was run by Steven Seagal," remembers Tani.

"That was before he [Seagal] was doing any movies and he was just a very good aikido teacher. I went in and that was the first time I sat in his dojo. As he sat next to me, he began speaking in Japanese to me in an Osaka-ben, which I found very surprising and welcoming, as I'm from Osaka myself. I then saw his demonstration, and it was incredible. I'd never seen the actual demonstration using a real-life knife. This is where I first saw Sensei Matsuoka."

After taking up aikido, Tani would ultimately convince Wang and Yuzna to hire Seagal's instructor - Haruo Matsuoka - to don the iconic Guyver costume and to add a unique, otherworldly movement to the Guyver's characterization. Unfortunately, there is a reason Seagal's features quickly descended into tedium following his early big screen ventures. Aikido, as interesting and mindful as it is to practice, doesn't really have the cinematic oomph to hold the attention of an action audience. Holds, wrist locks, and throws don't scream cinematic excitement at the best of times. This all led to its martial arts sequences, despite the inclusion of an aikido sensei, becoming more laughable than exciting.

Barring the occasional Seagal feature, aikido fights have a rather uninteresting visual aesthetic for the average viewer, often causing the fight choreography to feel less fantastical than a character like the Guyver should ultimately display. Even with these flawed fights, however, it still has a certain uniqueness which separates it from other comic book movies and that includes its successor.

"Well, I think the decision for *The Guyver* was to try to emphasize aikido as self-defence; it's not like just a fight for fighting's sake. It's not your aggression, you know, it's much more positive, a more spiritual and the centered thing," explains Tani.

"Instead of him [Sean] trying to do something strong, like in regular karate, I felt it should be a little deeper," continues Tani. This is probably where the clash in styles took place between Wang and Tani, as the former would be the one to ultimately direct the action. "Most of the fight sequences are done by Steve anyway," says Tani. "Steve is more, you know, keen on Jackie Chan style action. So, it has much more impact."

As the film progresses towards the explosive climax, the Guyver ultimately begins to opt for a less defensive and more offensive fighting style. Despite this slight style change, it still comes across as a 'what could have been'.

Ultimately, if the decision is made to use a limited martial art – which is great during a one-on-one encounter but less impressive as a visual spectacle with multiple assailants – the action, no matter how well shot it is, will feel unengaging. With *The Guyver* being closer in style to a Japanese Tokusatsu production, it requires martial arts action that is as bombastic as the creature and superhero design.

While aikido is great for realism – that's why early Seagal still feels unique as it's brutal, direct, and efficient – it lacks the superhero element that other martial arts can be easily adapted or retrofitted into.

Imagine if *Kyōryū Sentai Zyuranger* or its American equivalent *Mighty Morphin Power Rangers* had all five characters perform aikido instead of a mixture of various martial arts styles and gymnastic feats. It would admittedly be quite dull to watch, and the fast-paced action would slow to a snail's pace.

It's easy to see why Wang injected a little more humor into each of the fights, along with more physical impact during specific encounters, particularly as aikido is known to involve minimal strikes (punches or kicks) during an attack. Even with these action flaws, Tani was happy they used Matsuoka as the Guyver.

"He's [Matsuoka] a very nice guy, you know, he doesn't have like any huge ego," says Tani. "He was like '*Oh, of course. Yeah, I can do it*' when we asked him to do things. So, he was very, very good, I love him."

This would be the first and last time Matsuoka would be in a creature suit and given his past stunt experience within the industry being in a handful of Seagal features, it must have been a unique experience for the sensei, particularly with the limited vision of the Guyver helmet.

In an interview with *Fangoria* (October 1991, Issue 107) when the magazine conducted an onset visit during production, Matsuoka would describe his process for the Guyver's fight movements. "I combine punching, kicking and throwing [....]," said Matsuoka during the interview. "[…] I watched the *Guyver* cartoons to understand his movements, and I've been concentrating on grace instead of making him look like a fighting machine."

"He's not a big guy, he's rather small and skinny," says Tani. "That's perfect for, you know, being a guy in a creature suit. And then he can move, but his movement is not typical like you know power kind of things, it was more of a fast and was able to move and fight with lots of people around him. So, I think he was a good choice for that," remembers Tani.

"When we had his head and body cast, he was very skinny," remembers Tani. "By the time that we are going to film, he'd gained weight, so the suit was a little bit tight. That was really funny, but he still managed to do everything," chuckles Tani.

Haruo Matsuoka in the fully completed Guyver suit while on set shooting the 'Warehouse Fight'. Photo courtesy of Wyatt Weed.

Haruo Matsuoka (in Guyver costume) and Spice Williams-Crosby (in full Weber Zoanoid costume) during the latter's back ratchet stunt.

Despite the lack of truly engaging action – one of the key improvements made later for *its follow-up* – the stunt work was still dangerous for the suit and stunt performers. Although the stunt crew was predominantly male, there was still one tough chick that could take the hits as good (if not better) than the next guy.

The lady in question would be martial arts defense teacher and stunt woman extraordinaire Spice Williams-Crosby. Prior to getting the gig to play Weber in *The Guyver*, Williams-Crosby would become most well-known to *Star Trek* fans as the imposing Klingon Vixis in William Shatner's (much derided) *Star Trek V: The Final Frontier* (1989).

Even with the film's less than stellar critical reception, Williams-Crosby's Vixis would remain a highlight of the film due to her imposing screen presence. Post-*Guyver*, Williams-Crosby would turn up in a slew of action-packed features ranging from: Richard Pepin's budget cyborg actioner *T-Force* (1994) for PM Entertainment; in *From Dusk Till Dawn* (1996) she donned a set of fangs as one of the Titty Twister's vampiric dancers; and she would also pop up in films as varied as *Crank: High Voltage* (2009) and *Terminator Genisys* (2015), through to Syfy schlock like *Mega Python vs. Gatoroid* (2011).

Suffice to say, Williams-Crosby's credits range wide and far within the stunt field. While the actor-stuntwoman was no stranger to prosthetics, *The Guyver* would be one of the rare (and possibly final times) she would do any creature suit performance.

However, this wouldn't be the first time that Williams-Crosby had to wrangle herself into a creature suit; in fact, she was adamant to never do it again after her first instance for 1987's little-seen, trippy sci-fi feature *Stranded* (1987).

Despite swearing against yet another restricting suit performance, when the role of Weber came up and she found out it would be a dual role of sorts, Williams-Crosby was determined to give it her all yet again. "I did this movie with Maureen O'Sullivan, who was awesome. We filmed this way back in 1986," details Williams-Crosby.

"It was about these aliens who crash down near this small cabin ranch, and they wind up getting into this house. I played one of the aliens and was outfitted head-to-toe in this rubber suit and blackout glasses. It took at least six hours to get into this costume and during the day it was incredibly hot."

The process, it seems, was less than ideal given the sweltering conditions, which were only exacerbated by the amount of hassle it took to get into the full suit.

"They would have to put lubricant on me to shine me up," continues Williams-Crosby. "They'd also have these packs of paint to make sure no holes could be seen in the outfit once it was sealed up – it was basically like plastic paint and then I had the lenses and everything. So, I had a fight, I had to hit my mark. Fall down, whatever, get shot. There was a lot of stuff going on. And I literally had to be walked around with Kevin Westmore because I couldn't see where I was going, and even need to take me to the bathroom. He'd just stand outside, maybe hang on to my hand, just so I didn't fall over."

"I'd be working all day dying from the heat, and then when working at night I was freezing because we're out in Monrovia, which a mountainous area in Los Angeles County. I almost beat up the director on that one," chuckles Williams-Crosby. "I swore when I got done with *Stranded*, that I'd never do another suit again."

After that uncomfortable and awkward filming process, it was understandable for Williams-Crosby to be hesitant to get back into a creature suit of any kind. In the years between *Stranded* and *The Guyver*, Williams-Crosby honed her stunt and acting experience further.

"You have to be a good actor if you're doubling someone," describes Williams-Crosby. "You've got to watch how the individual moves, how they walk, how they flip their head, how they move their shoulders. Are they old? Are they young? and then you've got to be able to play the pain, you know, make it believable, because when somebody punches you, they're not really hitting your face, you're at least a foot apart, so once that happens, you've got to play that pain. You have to be able to bring what's happened to you in your own life. It's not the whole kit and caboodle but it is one ingredient."

With that philosophy in place, it's easy to see why Williams-Crosby gained so many credits to her name (in both acting and stunt work) over the years. Despite swearing off doing suit or creature work again, she found herself drawn to *The Guyver* for one specific reason; she wanted to challenge herself in a dual role. "I went to audition for the female part [Weber] within the Zoanoid group. I got the part, and then found out she mutates into this hairy red beast with big boobs," chuckles Williams-Crosby.

With Williams-Crosby having bagged the part of a pre-Zoanoid Weber, what caused her to put herself forward for the Zoanoid version of Weber and go through the demanding rigours of being a suit performer again? Particularly one that would be even more complex when compared to the skin-tight rubber alien suit from *Stranded*? It seems Williams-Crosby wanted to inhabit every aspect of her character and that included both human and inhuman versions of Weber.

For Williams-Crosby, it was the most logical choice for both aspects of the character to be played by her, especially given her extensive stunt work, and acting. Now, she just had to convince the directors. "I thought, '*Well wait a minute if that's me as Lisker's girlfriend who mutates into this red hairy beast with big tits, that should be me too*,'" smiles Williams-Crosby. "So, I said, '*If you want me as an actress, you got to take me as a bundle*' and they agreed."

With the dual-role of Weber now secured, Williams-Crosby would face an additional set of challenges while in the Weber Zoanoid costume. Even with such a high calibre of Hollywood stunt men on a shoot, there's still likely to be the occasional issue or accident, no matter how much is planned or rehearsed. Other environmental factors, for instance, heavy practical creature suits, can also exacerbate potential issues or risks - such as overcompensating for the force of a ratchet gag due to the weight of the creature suit. This was especially the case for a stunt Williams-Crosby had to perform while in the full Weber suit.

"The ratchet back into a cement wall was not a fun job. I remember I was jerked and pulled six feet off the ground and 30-something feet across and then slammed into cement with a big 'ol costume on with the mechanical head which would flop back and forth," the veteran stuntwoman recalls.

"I remember when I got out of the suit and was taking the pads out, I kept telling my stunt coordinator 'Get that pad out from my back'. I'm not even kidding, there was a big giant bubble of fluid, and you could see the imprint in my skin from the sacrum."

The back injury wasn't the only instance where Williams-Crosby encountered a painful mishap during the filming of the warehouse sequence.

"During the ratchet, when I hit the wall, my neck snapped back due to the force. I remember getting out of bed the next day; I had to use both my hands to pick my head up off the pillow. Most likely because it was a severe whiplash. Within the suit as well there was a metal bar, which kept cutting into my nose," remembers Williams-Crosby.

Regardless of budget, careful preparation and doing the stunt as safely as possible - whether it's for themselves or others - is of paramount importance for a stunt coordinator. Stunt safety for crew members participating in a stunt has changed significantly within the last 30 years in and outside of Hollywood. Hong Kong cinema of the 1980s and 1990s, for instance, is one such example of an almost lawless Wild West approach to filming action set pieces. Filmmakers and performers schooled in martial arts and gymnastics would do everything they could to create engaging and breathless action sequences.

Granted, many of those stunts have reached legendary status among audiences (and for good reason), but they were not without incredibly high-risk factors for the stunt person involved. Accidents will inevitably happen to stunt performers regardless of how much rehearsal time is put into a sequence, but thankfully serious injury has been reduced in three decades.

Despite the uncomfortable nature of the Weber suit and the discomfort from the ratchet stunt, it remains an impressive set piece in the film; particularly with the impactful sound design added in post-production. The painful set piece looks impressive and within a narrative context shows the physical power of the Guyver's abilities.

Outside of Williams-Crosby and the extensive stunt team, a few of the actors and non-stunt suit performers would also get in on the action, albeit in a less risky form. Although relatively small-scale in comparison to the wire-rigging, back flips, and aikido, Ted Smith and Mark Hamill would engage in a rather hilarious round of fighting for a scene where both Striker (Smith in costume) and Max energetically wrestling, or so it would first appear. Filmmaking, regardless of budget, is essentially an elaborate sleight-of-hand, a modern-day magic trick with illusions to fool viewers into thinking a scene or stunt is more dangerous than it might ultimately be.

Smith recalls a funny moment of improvisation while shooting the warehouse fight, and his first interaction with star Mark Hamill, all while Smith was suited in full Striker makeup. It was certainly an interesting experience. "When shooting The Guyver we were at the warehouse during the scene where Guyver melts after the Zoanoid fight, and I have to jump on Mark Hamill," reminisces Smith.

"So, this is where I first met Mark and finding out that we were going to be interacting with each other, and I'm wearing this giant Striker suit. Now, the only way I could see anything was out of my mouth, so my visibility is limited, and I always know, when in a creature costume, to look at the guy's chest through the suit's mouth. I had these Striker hands on, which were full rubber, but they also had long nails which were made from acrylic, so were really expensive. I mean, they had finger cups inside, which went over my own fingers, so the creatures could touch and grab things," recalls Smith.

"Steve wanted me to knock Mark to the ground and wrestle him, and I just thought '*Oh shit*'. I told Mark, '*Hey, I gotta knock you to the ground and wrestle you with these acrylic nails on, then when you get to the ground, I'm supposed to hold you down or choke you.*'"

With visibility being limited and Striker's claws at risk of both breaking and potentially causing a little bit of damage to Hamill due to Smith's limited visibility, caution had to be taken. Both Smith and Hamill were able to be cautious without compromising the drama of the moment, which according to Smith, involved Hamill's previous creature experience. This would ultimately allay Smith's initial fears of causing injury to the star.

"Mark's like '*I'll grab your wrist and hold onto it. At that point, once you feel me grabbing your wrists, make your arms go limp like noodles and I'll puppeteer you,*'" says Smith. Despite only being seen ever so briefly, the human puppeteering worked out well for both Smith and Hamill with no damage to either actor.

Spice Williams-Crosby (in pre-Zoanoid Weber costume) sweeps
Ted Smith off his feet in-between shots on *The Guyver*.
Photo Courtesy of Ted Smith.

A classic cinematic motive that is present in many a superhero or comic book film, revolves around the hero first discovering their powers. This is usually followed by their first fight or action sequence as they adjust to this new-found prowess. *The Guyver* is no different, except perhaps for the overly comical way it's displayed.

This uneven tone became something of a known criticism for *The Guyver* after its release and even during more recent years. The sequence where Sean (Jack Armstrong) is bullied by his Dojo peers – played by Johnnie Saiko, Ted Smith, Brian Simpson, Doug Simpson, and stuntman Dennis Madalone – is tonally bizarre to say the least and certainly boarders on more broad comedic tones, akin to Hong Kong action comedies of that era.

What starts with the gang bullying Sean, quickly descends into full body-horror once our hero falls onto the unit and it attaches itself to his body. Once fully transformed, the action is set back to a comedic overtone, which remains jarring. Smith remembers the shooting of this sequence, while playing gang leader Ronnie.

"Troy Fromin [Lao Ze] from *Kung Fu Rascals* was originally going to play Ronnie, the gang leader," says Smith. "He was going to play Ronnie, the gang member in the alley, but what happened was, he got a job on a Ford truck commercial. So, he dropped out and we needed a last-minute replacement."

The story goes that it was Brian Yuzna's idea to quickly cast Smith in the role of Ronnie, and thus one of the more bizarre moments of the film was born, purely from Smith's improvised nonsense. According to Smith, it was Yuzna's idea to add a bit more personality to the gang members, to make them a bit wackier and sillier than their initial conception. As they were losing time to get all the shots, there wasn't much either Wang or Smith could do differently, so the choice was made to keep it intentionally ludicrous.

"There was very little time to get something serious or polished," remembers Smith. "It was easier to just keep the shoot moving quicker if we just made it campy. So, Steve asked what am I going to do? And I just started doing this thing with the knife, so he's laughing at it and seems to like it. Then I get these foam nunchucks and just kept being silly. Steve said, '*That's great*', and we just stuck with it. This was literally five minutes before we shot the scene, and all the dialogue itself was just improv of me talking smack and getting my ass kicked. Then the Guyver grabs me, throwing me into that five-gallon drum," chuckles Smith.

It wasn't just as gang leader Ronnie where Smith would have his ass handed to him. At one point during an action sequence, Smith (while in the Striker costume) would have to do a particular move as directed by Wang. It was ultimately decided that Smith was too valuable of a creature performer to put through the vigorous stunt work, despite Smith being willing to take part.

"When the Guyver grabs me by the feet, swings me around and slams me into the pole, that was me after the dummy that was used for the swing shot, so I hit the pole and spun round. Steve kept going '*Yeah hit it, but I want you to jump and hit sideways, so you turn in mid-air,*' and I'm like '*What*'? So, I had to literally jump up sideways and hit the pole, like Jackie Chan-style while my body was up in the air, so partially my body would spin a little bit before I hit the ground. So, I did that, that was my stunt," remembers Smith.

"But Striker being shot through the air on the air-ramp, that was a stunt guy. I was going to do it, but Steve's like '*You're our performer, if you get hurt then we're screwed. Like I know you probably want to do it, but let's get a stunt guy to do it*'. So, we had a stunt suit made and a stunt man performed that one. Basically, anything that could involve me getting hurt or being put out of commission, Steve would go, '*Yeah don't do that*', but all the fights in the lab at the end were me."

"Actually, that was my only injury I've ever had on any film," says Smith. "We were running out of time to shoot, so we were choreographing a fight scene with Steve, and he was pretending to be the Guyver while we rehearsed. He was going '*Okay, you're here and you're there*, moving people around. So, as we're rehearsing, I charge (as Striker) at Steve, and he does a spinning roundhouse kick into my chest."

"Now, there's two forms of fighting. When you're stunt fighting you use your toes, but when you're really fighting you use your heel, because that's really got the momentum. So, Steve's absolutely in the zone and has hit me square in the chest with his heel, and I just stopped and dropped to the ground. And he was doing that half-speed, and I kept thinking *'If that was for real, a roundhouse kick with a heel would bring you down'*, and at the time, Steve could fight and he knew martial arts, so he was still in the zone in his head. It was very funny," reminisces Smith.

While much of the action and stunt work is strangely lacking the excitement that one would associate with a character like *The Guyver*, it does have moments of Tokusatsu-inspired silliness which adds to its overall schlocky charm, ultimately giving it a unique cinematic flavor compared to similar features of this ilk.

Even when viewing these action sequences with the best intentions, it's clear, no matter how much of a staunch defender the viewer may be, they are still a disappointment.

The action would be further compounded, albeit retroactively, following the release of its successor-come-reboot, which elevated the fight choreography (on a substantially lower budget) to God-tier status among action fans and would set a new standard for low-budget action cinema at the time.

While the martial arts action and fight choreography in *The Guyver* would be at a disappointing minimum, the intricate miniature effects work which appeared on-screen would be in plentiful supply.

Chapter Five

Miniature Madness

One of the key (and standout) components of *The Guyver* is the sheer number of practical effects on display. The inclusion of in-camera effects and visual trickery puts other low-budget features from the same timeframe (such as *Teenage Mutant Ninja Turtles* or *Spaced Invaders*) to shame in some respects.

Where *The Guyver* separates itself from its fellow 1990s superhero film peers, is in its use of extensive miniature effects work; a filmmaking skill that feels almost (if not completely) disregarded in an age where CGI and green-screen set extensions can be created relatively quickly within the computer, especially when compared to the time-consuming skill needed for matte-paintings.

While CGI was present well before *The Guyver*, such as the stained-glass knight from *Young Sherlock Holmes* (1985) (the first fully CG character seen in a feature film) or the visual spectacle of the (still impressive) water tentacle from James Cameron's *The Abyss* (1989), it wouldn't be until *The Lawnmower Man* (1992) (a year after *The Guyver*) where smaller films would begin to use it more extensively. Granted, *The Lawnmower Man* had a significantly higher budget than *The Guyver* ($10 million compared to $3 million), but this would be a starting point for future low-budget films to experiment with CGI animation alongside practical effects.

Although far removed from being a budget film, the melding of CGI and practical effects would reach its tipping point with *Jurassic Park* (1993), where it would engrain itself into the cultural zeitgeist. The CGI dinosaurs melded with practical effects would be such a jaw-dropping experience that it would create a technical revolution within the film industry.

Despite this, miniatures would still be an integral component for both large and smaller films as the years rolled on, even with the cost of the software dropping. Before *Jurassic Park* went full-CGI for some dinosaur action, the legendary animator Phil Tippett would create stop-motion puppets for the dinosaurs. The stop-motion movements were ultimately used as a reference point for the animators at ILM (Industrial Light & Magic). Physical miniatures would still serve a purpose, even in this new CGI-led world.

Looking back at the miniatures in *The Guyver*, be it the use of small-scale sets or for puppetry, they remain a time capsule for a pre-CGI era of filmmaking, where budget constraints bred creative solutions and in-camera trickery would be harnessed to achieve the director's intended vision. While this may come across as disregarding CGI technology and suggesting their creative practitioners are less skilful due to creating effects within a computer, that couldn't be further from the truth.

These animators are highly skilled in creating intricate visual effects and even whole fantastical worlds; many of which could not have been achievable without this technology. When used sparingly, CGI can heighten existing practical effects work and even, in some instances, help to complement the makeup effects to push past any previous physical limitations. While CGI is an impressive advancement in filmmaking (particularly in the right creative hands), it still lacks the more visceral and inherently tangible look that a painstakingly handcrafted effect can create or the wondrous reaction it can elicit. It's the sort of work that captured the imaginations of cine-philes, most likely during their formative years.

Stop motion pioneers such as Ladislas Starevich, Willis O'Brien, Ray Harryhausen, Lou Bunin, and Phil Tippett, along with miniature effects artists such as Martin Bower; Reg Hill; Gerry Anderson; David Mitton; and more recently John Dykstra, would go on to inspire countless generations with their ground-breaking effects work and will most likely continue to do so for generations to come.

Looking over the staggering amount of miniature work for *The Guyver*, it's clear the visual effects crew had honed this once abundant craft to a fine art. With crew members such as Wyatt Weed, Asao Goto, Joanne Bloomfield, Ken Tarallo, and miniature director of photography Ted Rae behind these complex and often time-consuming sequences, it helps provide a deeper insight into how small-scale effects work can, in retrospect, be seen as a love-letter to a bygone era of effects filmmaking.

Throughout the film, there are miniature sets, stop-motion animation, full-scale models, and puppets, often working in conjunction to create the action on-screen, even if it's only for a matter of seconds. *The Guyver* would be an incredibly complex shoot (despite the relatively low budget) due to the sheer number of different effects techniques needed for specific sequences. Crew members such as Wyatt Weed would perform multiple roles behind the camera, often coming up with creative solutions to avoid running over budget.

Although it appears on-screen for a matter of seconds, the stop motion miniature of Sean transforming into the Guyver during the warehouse sequence stands out as a pivotal moment within the film. The miniature Guyver and Sean armature was skillfully created by Weed (from photographic elements of the actor on set).

Even with the multiple behind-the-scenes roles under his belt, Weed was keen to expand on his previous miniatures work experience from *Kung Fu Rascals*. *The Guyver* used every in-camera trick in the book (particularly in an era where CGI was costly and not readily available). To achieve its distinct visual style, Weed and the effects crew would use a multitude of filmmaking techniques to create several fantastical moments seen on-screen. These included using miniatures, false perspectives, rod puppets, and stop-motion animation.

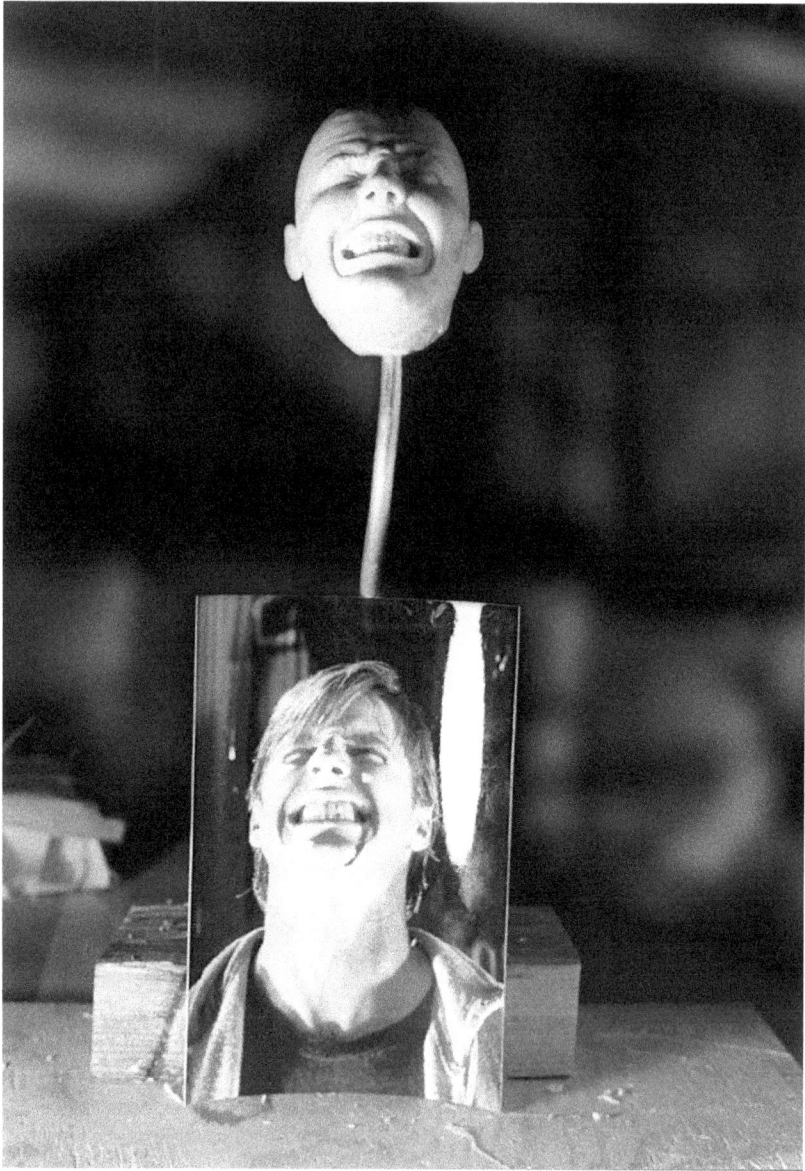

The beginning stages of Wyatt Weed's head sculpt of actor Jack Armstrong for the Sean puppet pre-Guyver transformation. All done from a set photograph. Photo courtesy of Wyatt Weed.

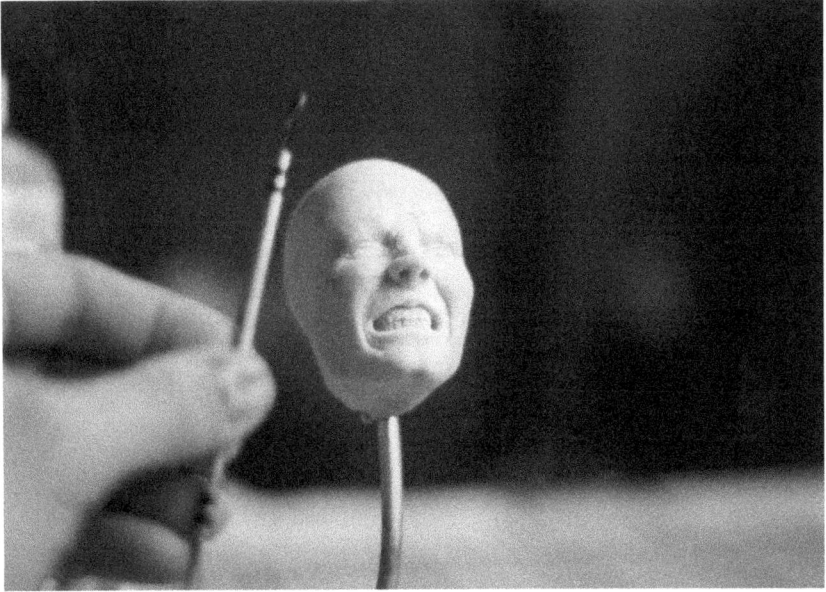

Close-up of Weed's miniature head sculpt of Jack Armstrong.
Photo courtesy of Wyatt Weed.

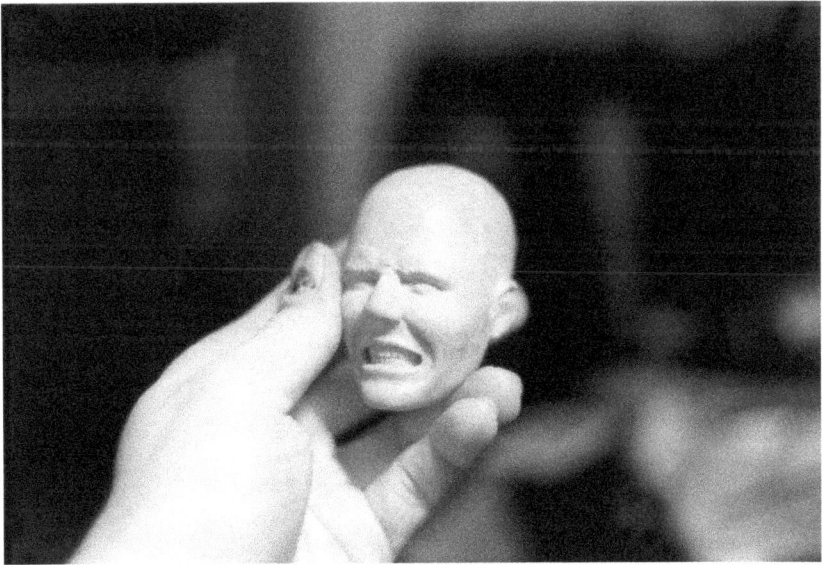

Another close-up of Weed's exceptionally detailed head sculpt.
Photo courtesy of Wyatt Weed.

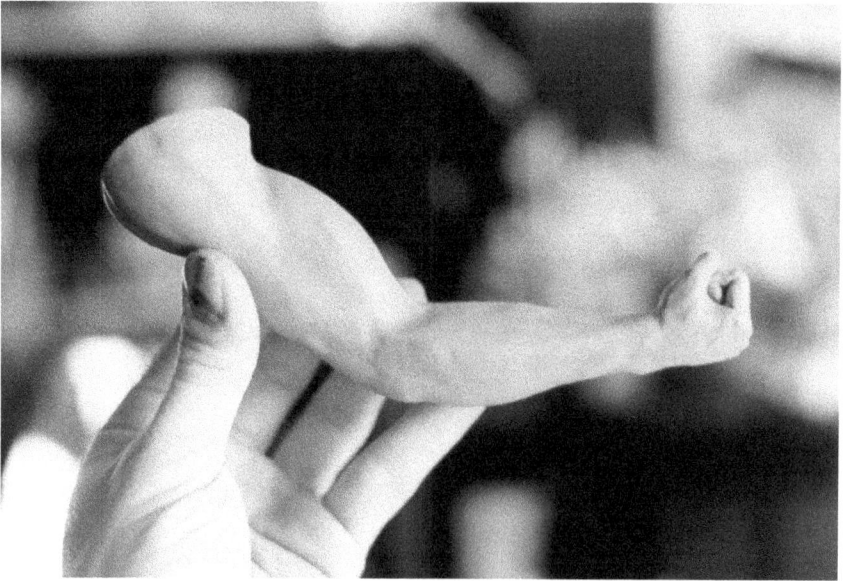

Close-up of outer arm sculpt for the Jack Armstrong puppet.
Photo courtesy of Wyatt Weed.

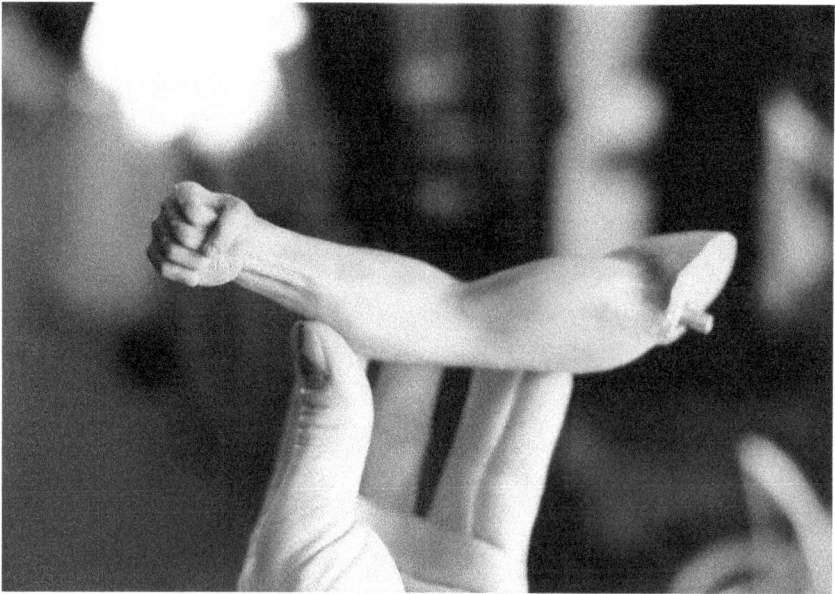

Close-up of the inner arm sculpt. Photo courtesy of Wyatt Weed.

The original Guyver puppet (standing at around 14" inches tall or 1/5th scale) prior to painting. Photo courtesy of Wyatt Weed.

Front close-up of Weed's sculpting detail for the Guyver puppet.
Photo courtesy of Wyatt Weed.

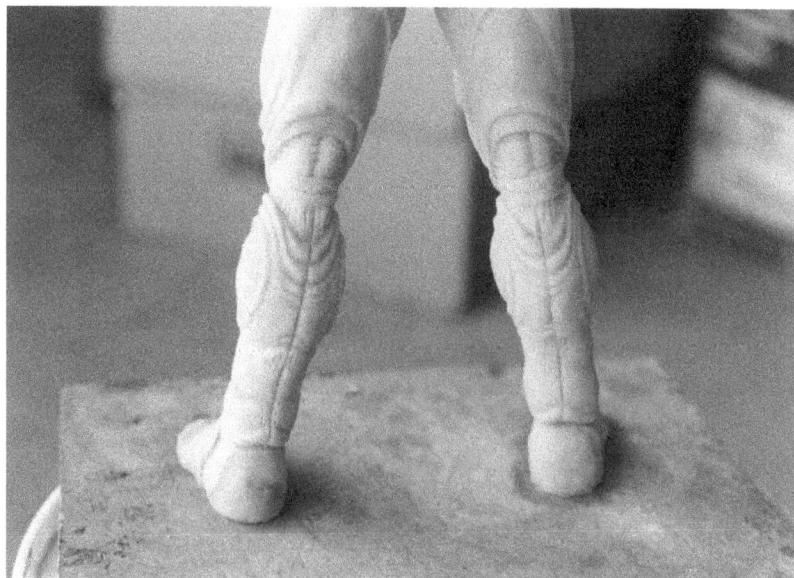

Close-up of Weed's sculpting detail on the back legs of the
Guyver puppet. Photo courtesy of Wyatt Weed.

A Guyver puppet hung to dry after being underpainted.
Photo courtesy of Wyatt Weed.

Weed posing with a posed and fully painted Guyver puppet.
Photo courtesy of Wyatt Weed.

Weed saw another chance to gain valuable industry experience with some of the best creatives in the field, but despite his prior work on *The Guyver*, he still had to prove and pitch himself for the role. "Once shooting began, I was lobbying to do the miniatures, because a lot of what I got to do on *Rascals* was make models for things," details Weed.

"Steve knew I had a passion for models, but again, I still had to prove myself because I really had to sell myself to the producers, so I had to put a budget and a proposal together and show them my portfolio, which included the other stuff I'd done for Steve."

"I got the miniature gig and went, almost, right from creature shop work into the miniature work. As a matter of fact, I made a deal with Screaming Mad George to do the miniature work in one of his shots. I pretty much got to ride out that entire project from start to finish doing effects work."

Weed was also on location a handful of times during the shoot, although it was in a smaller capacity when compared to his other work. "I got to visit the set, but it was more to coordinate special effects and take measurements for miniatures and reference photos for the end showdown between Guyver and Balcus, like the laboratory so we could duplicate that in miniature form. We did that whole miniature sequence in the film," recalls Weed.

"What was interesting, though, especially coming from *Rascals* to *Guyver*, was that we could take a whole day to do something on *Rascals* with the Super 8 camera, like setting up foreground miniatures and doing force perspective tricks," remembers Weed.

"Sometimes Steve would be over here shooting martial arts fights, and I'd be off with my own camera, spending hours setting up foreground perspective stuff and all kinds of tricks. And we just worked until we got it done. It was much more of an Asian cinema filmmaking approach. In Asian cinema, there's not as much of a schedule as there is for American filmmaking. The former works until it gets done. So, on *Kung Fu Rascals* we'd work until it got dark."

Various camera tricks were also brought across to the *Guyver* production, anything to reduce costs and create interesting moments within a smaller budget. As Weed explains, forced perspective shots and miniatures would again be used to create a sense of scale.

"On *Guyver*, Steve had plans for force perspective and miniatures," recalls Weed. "So, for instance, shooting in a warehouse and then floating a miniature on the top part of the frame to make it look like something else."

"He [Steve] wanted to do all these really elaborate things. But there was never time and never enough extra money for a camera that allowed for a setup of shots like that. We had the creature effects side, the stunt side and then we'd have had these elaborate floating miniature effects, it was just the Steve Wang mentality," says Weed.

Although Wang and co-director Tani would have to compromise on the vision they had in mind for a number of the shots; a hanging miniature (although less elaborate) would still be used in the climax of the film and Weed would be the one to create it.

With Tani having created a large scale Balcus head, was it always Wang's intention to use miniature puppets in the final showdown, in conjunction with the large-scale head prop?

"Steve, I'm sure he could already see it in his head, like *'This is going to be the Guyver, this is going to be the puppet,'*" says Weed. "I think he probably had to sell it to Brian [Yuzna] and the other producers. I think in Steve's mind, yes, it was always going to be miniatures, and at the very least the producers knew, okay we're gonna blow up the laboratory at the end but we're not gonna blow up the full-size lab, it'll have to be a miniature lab."

"At one point in time, Steve was trying to sell them on the Zoanoid Growth Chamber, a hanging miniature where it was a corridor that was ten-feet long and five-feet wide," remembers Weed.

"The actors would walk down the centre of it, and they were full-size, but like 50 feet in the background. I think Steve did a sketch and showed it to production; they were like, *'Well, we can never afford that'.* At which point Steve was like, '*We can do a foreground miniature'.* So, I think there was a little bit of negotiation."

"Steve had me create a 'hanging miniature' that was closer to camera with the actors in the background, appearing to walk past the chambers. I designed it, then we split it in half and shot the end explosion," says Weed.

"There was a little bit of trepidation until the first shots got done. And then they were like, '*Oh, okay'.* So, once we showed them what we were talking about, they were completely cool and went '*Okay, we get it, we get it',*" recalls Weed.

A Guyver puppet miniature would be used for the final climactic fight between Guyver and Zoalord Balcus for several shots. "when he's fighting Balcus there are shots of a poseable puppet. It was essentially a floppy puppet," says Weed.

"When Balcus is riding around and Guyver is on top of him holding on to his horns, that was just a floppy puppet that we just glued the hands [of the Guyver] on to the horns. We shot the puppet and then ran it in reverse."

"It then almost looks like Guyver is pulling his head. And then there are other shots in the movie where you'd see the Guyver standing there and that was the puppet with a wider armature so that we could pose it," says Weed.

These shots would only happen for a handful of frames and a viewer would have to be incredibly eagle-eyed to spot them. It's really a testament to the craftsmanship of the miniature puppet that one's eye is fooled long enough to not spot it, at least on a first viewing.

It wouldn't be the only time a miniature puppet would be used in a shot. Another armature was used during a more extensive sequence earlier in the film.

Although it's only on-screen for mere seconds, Weed was also responsible for the Sean puppet-armature, when the character transforms in dramatic fashion in front of the Zoanoids and Mizky.

For the puppet, Weed would sculpt the head from photo references of the actor, Jack Armstrong.

To achieve the life-like accuracy, Weed would visit the set to get photos of Armstrong, along with having reference details such as a full body shot of Armstrong in the pose in just boxers and tennis shoes, to get as much detail as possible for the puppet-armature.

"I got to visit set a lot," says Weed. "But that was more to coordinate special effects, take measurements for miniatures and take reference photos, stuff like that."

"That photo reference of Jack [Armstrong] was taken by me on stage during production," details Weed. "About the time the warehouse fight was being shot. To cut down on distortion, I rented a zoom lens for my 35mm still camera, like a 300mm zoom, and got way back on stage and zoomed all the way in to 'compress' Jack so there would be no distortion. If I had used something standard, like a 25mm or 50mm and only been back five or 10 feet, the proportions wouldn't have been true."

"I cut Jack out of the photo and enlarged it to the exact size that the puppet needed to be and then used that to guide my sculpting. Then I would estimate the entire puppet took about two months to create with all the sculpting, clothes, hair, and painting done," recalls Weed.

"I sculpted the body, head, and arms of the Sean puppet and that took about a month. The body and head were made with Super Sculpey, and the arms were Roma clay. There was no neck as Ted [Rae] would create a foam neck because he wanted the head to tilt back during the transformation. The arms were going to be cast in foam and then have armatures for animation. The body would be used as is and remain rigid," describes Weed. This would allow for less issues while animating, particularly during a tight deadline.

Although Weed was responsible for the main bulk of the miniature's creation, he states that Asao Goto was responsible for the clothes the miniature Sean (pre-Guyver transformation) would wear. Given Goto's extensive work in creating miniature special effects, before and after *The Guyver*, it makes logical sense he would be the one to craft these detailed pieces of mini clothing and hair.

"Asao created the clothing and probably the hair," recalls Weed. "He also created the miniature set, using the template I built. Andy Clement painted the hands and face of the Sean puppet."

"When you see Sean say '*Guyver!*' and the camera pulls back and you see all those little armour plates fly out, they were castings off of all my little plates from the original mold. The Sean armature was like 14-inches tall, I don't remember the scale we were working, but in I think we were working in 1/5 scale," recalls Weed.

"I was also in charge of creating the miniature set," details Weed. "I created a mold/template for scale corrugated metal, with the idea to either vacuform plastic or rub heavy foil into the form to create scale metal walls for the background."

Weed constructing one of the Growth Chamber tube miniatures.
Photo courtesy of Wyatt Weed.

Behind-the-scenes for the in-camera set of the extended Zoanoid Growth
Chamber. Photo courtesy of Wyatt Weed.

A close-up shot of the hanging miniature Growth Chamber.
Photo courtesy of Wyatt Weed.

The small bit of full-scale set for the actors to interact with, before the
hanging miniature helped to artificially extend the Growth Chamber
in-camera. Photo courtesy of Wyatt Weed.

Wyatt Weed stands at the end of the false perspective hallway.
Photo courtesy of Wyatt Weed.

Close-up of Weed in the hanging miniature hallway.
Photo courtesy of Wyatt Weed.

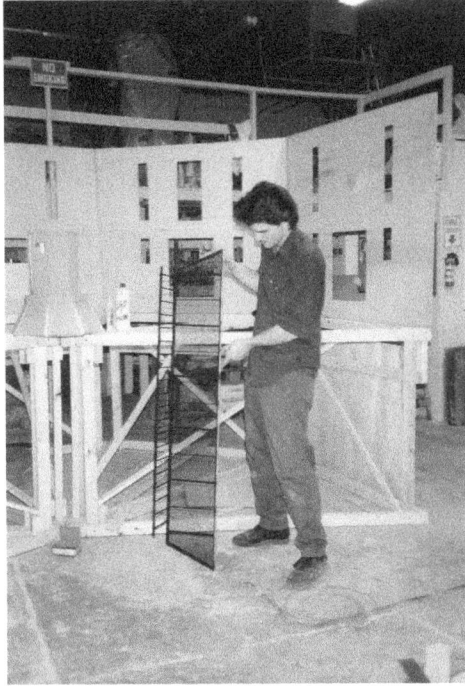

Wyatt Weed arranging the miniature Chronos set for the action-packed and explosive finale between Guyver and Balcus. Photo courtesy of Wyatt Weed.

Wyatt Weed constructing the miniature Chronos lab set.
Photo courtesy of Wyatt Weed.

Additional shot of the wooden set construction.
Photo courtesy of Wyatt Weed.

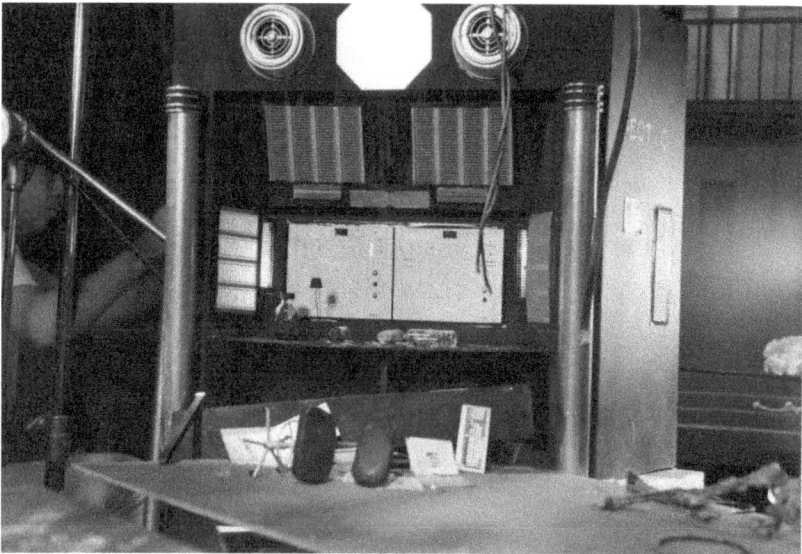

Another shot of the Chronos set post-fight (note the miniature skeleton in the right-hand corner). Photo courtesy of Wyatt Weed.

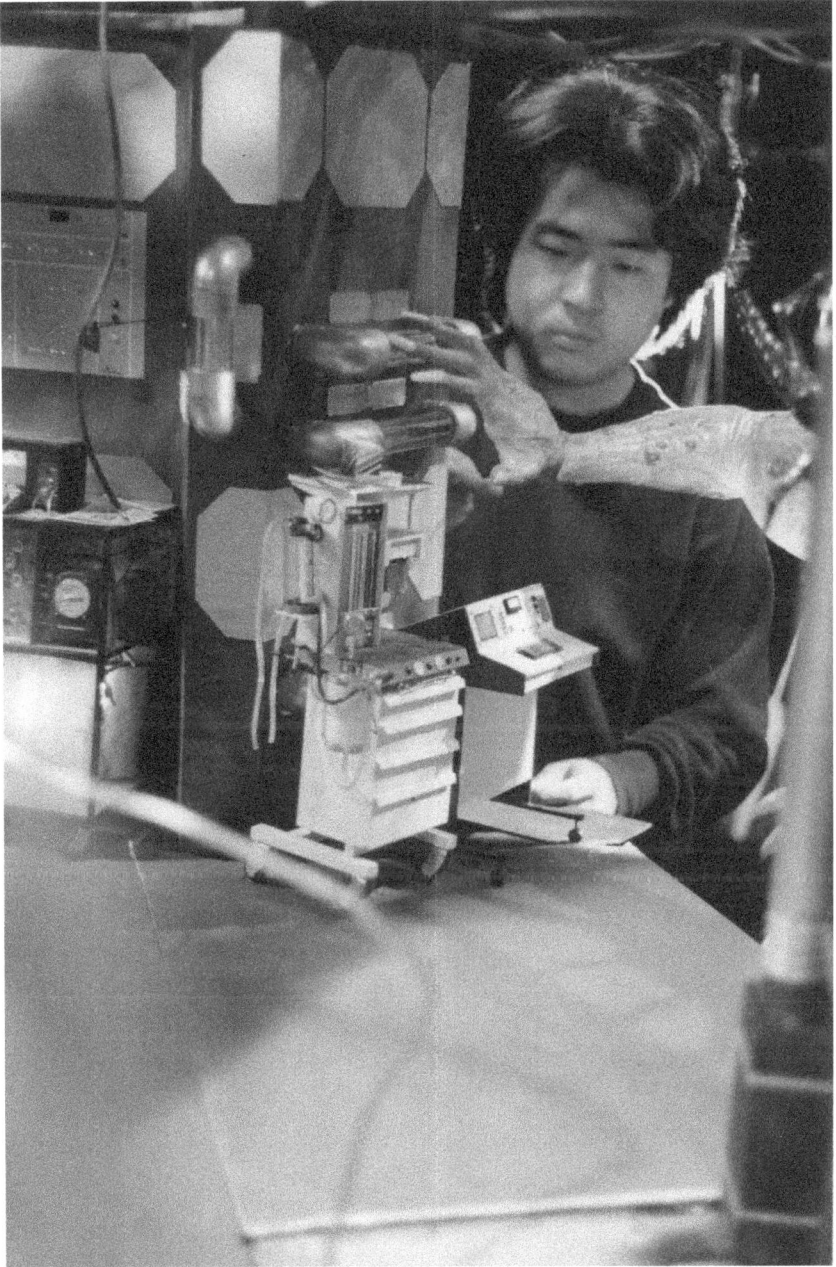

A crew member on the miniatures unit oversees the placement of the
Balcus puppet arm. Photo courtesy of Wyatt Weed.

Model maker Jeanna Crawford with the Balcus puppet.
Photo courtesy of Wyatt Weed.

Model maker Jeanna Crawford caught off-guard with the camera, with the
back end of the Balcus puppet in view. Photo courtesy of Wyatt Weed.

The Guyver puppet on set during the climactic battle with the rod-puppet Balcus. Hands of Asao Goto posing Guyver below the floor set. Photo courtesy of Wyatt Weed.

The Guyver puppet takes a small breather in-between takes on the miniature Chronos lab set. Photo courtesy of Wyatt Weed.

Shot of Guyver posed on the miniature Chronos lab set,
with the Balcus rod-puppet looming ominously in the background.
Photo courtesy of Wyatt Weed.

Ted Rae filming the Balcus puppet. Balcus was a rod and cable puppet
operated from below the miniature set. Photo courtesy of Wyatt Weed.

Close-up of the Balcus rod puppet. Photo courtesy of Wyatt Weed.

"I'm ready for my close-up, Mr. Wang." Close-up shot of the Balcus puppet in the miniature lab set. Photo courtesy of Wyatt Weed.

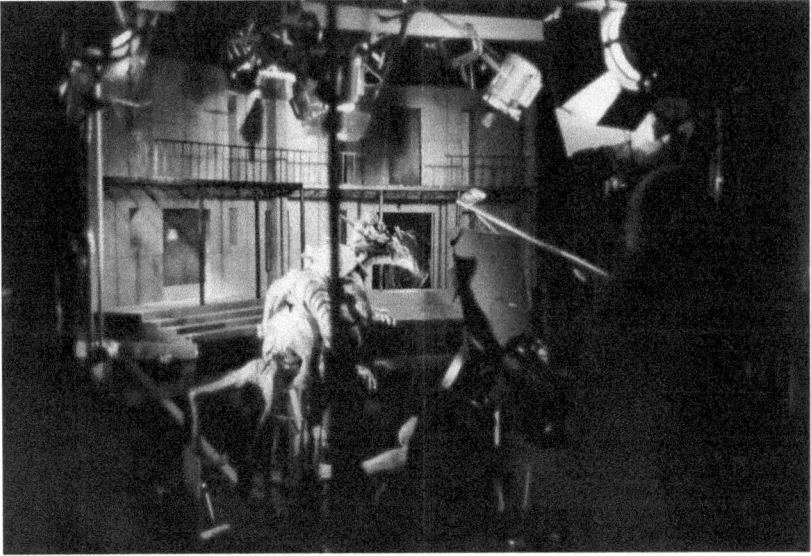

Another behind-the-scenes shot of the miniature effects crew shooting the Balcus puppet. Photo courtesy of Wyatt Weed.

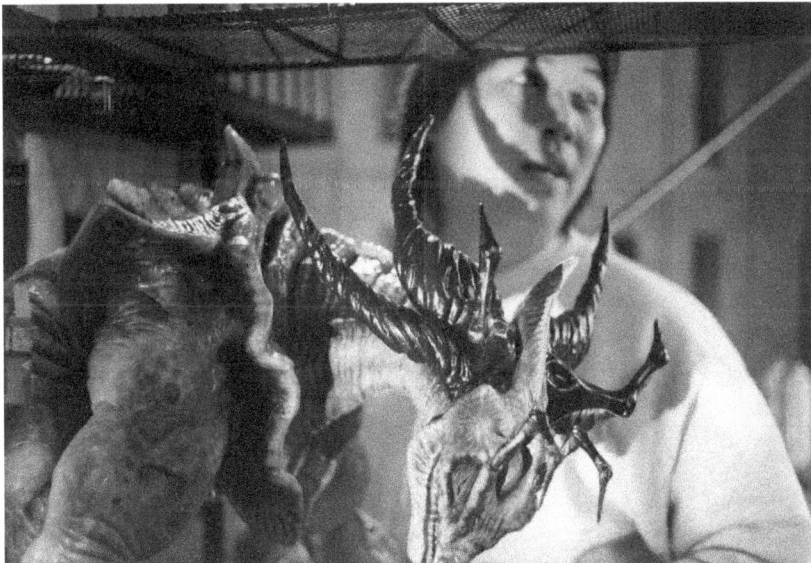

Steve Wang in the Chronos miniature set with the small-scale Balcus rod puppet. Photo courtesy of Wyatt Weed.

Setting up the corridor miniature for the explosive finale.
Photo courtesy of Wyatt Weed.

The Balcus puppet is prepped for its final on-screen moments.
Photo courtesy of Wyatt Weed.

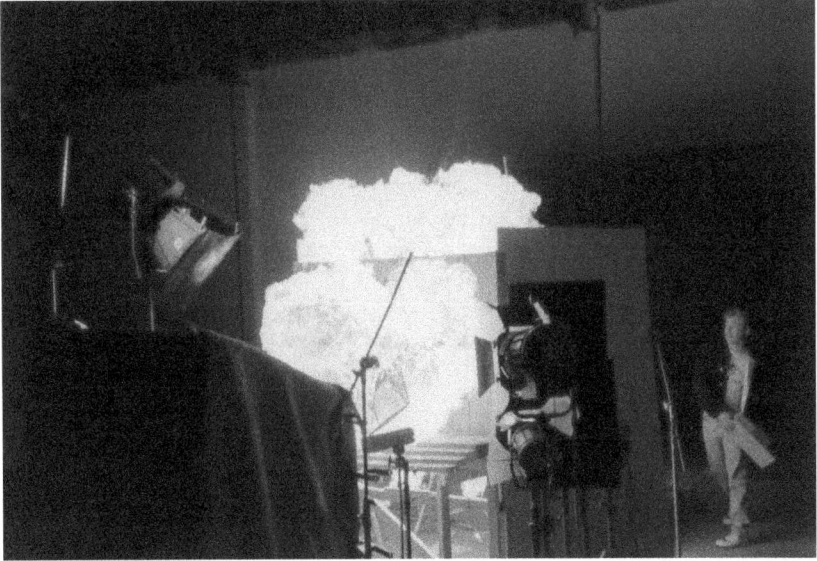

Fire in the hole! Photo courtesy of Wyatt Weed.

Another angle of the explosive shot. Photo courtesy of Wyatt Weed.

Asao Goto inspects the charred aftermath of the Growth Chamber explosion. Photo courtesy of Wyatt Weed.

Looking at each of the miniature sets and puppets (such as Guyver and Balcus) and the level of detail that went into each of those elements is truly a sight to behold. Like many of the effects used in *The Guyver*, despite their brevity, they are impressive enough to trick the mind's eye (if only for mere seconds) due to the extensive level of detail put into the miniature sets.

For instance, in the Guyver transformation sequence, the same graffiti and lighting seen from the live-action footage is an exact match (or as close to) for that scene, thus essentially being a condensed version of Levie Isaacks' impressive cinematography from the original footage. While this could now be done in potentially less time with CGI in a modern filmmaking landscape, the sheer level of labour and small details that went into these shots, which mixed different filmmaking techniques into one sequence, is astounding.

Goto and Ted Rae, with his miniature effects photography, would bring the stop-motion transformation of Sean to life. Goto would even be responsible for building the miniature warehouse set and matching the lighting with its full-scale counterpart.

"It was pretty much Ted Rae and me doing that shot. I was responsible for taking care of the puppet, animating it and the lighting," remembers Goto.

There were still challenges to animating the Sean armature, as Goto describes. "You just have to be patient. You know smoke is so hard to control with animation because 12 hours in at the same density, it ends up becoming like a swamp. I was sitting there. Not eat anything, and we just had to keep going."

During the shoot of *The Guyver*, Rae spoke with *Cinefantastique* (February 1992, Volume 22, Number 4). In the behind-the-scenes interview, Rae would go into detail about the stop-motion and how they made sure the full-scale sets, the actor and the miniatures transitioned as seamlessly as possible between each other.

"[…] Pre-stop-motion with Jack Armstrong (before cutting to puppet) was shot at six frames per second, which is why it has a stilled movement to it. Pre-recorded vocals from Armstrong would then be played back (at one-quarter speed), which he would lip-synch to. The shot to the stop-motion puppet - which Goto animated – would then be blended with the shot of Armstrong by dissolving it optically [....]," described Rae in the interview.

Although it suffers from being a little rough-and-ready, the effect is still impressive, possibly even more so in this more digital and less analogue age of filmmaking. What sells the shot is Rae's impressive camera tracking, the atmospheric lighting, and Goto's stop-motion animation of the tendrils and Guyver armour jutting out of Weed's sculpted miniature of Armstrong.

Chapter Six

Synthphonic Zoanoids and Post Release Woes

Several decades on, the score for *The Guyver* - composed by Matthew Morse - remains as unique as the film it accompanies. That's the thing about musical scores from 1990s comic book films; they always had a distinctiveness and individuality to their soundscapes, particularly when compared to more recent counterparts.

We currently live in an era of the oversaturation of comic book movies and cinematic universes. And while the popularity of comic book movies isn't anything new, the slew of movies associated with the likes of big hitters in the comic book world – apart from the occasional film – feel as though they're treading water, mass-produced on a studio conveyer belt. The same can be said about their scores, which lack a distinctiveness to them, all feeling entirely too uniform for their own good.

Whatever faults viewers might have with pre-cinematic universe features from the 1990s through to the early 2000s, they all had their own unique theme and score. *The Guyver* is no different, as it manages to create an infectious theme tune full of otherworldly heroism, and this is thanks to Morse's musical background.

The journey to creating *The Guyver*'s otherworldly score is quite fascinating. It begins in Soul music before moving into digital frequency modulation because prior to getting into composing for films and commercials, Morse would be a touring musician.

"I had been a bass player with Ray Charles and a few other people, before deciding to come off the road," recalls Morse. "To be honest, the bass is pretty limited, so I thought, '*Well, I'll start playing keyboards*' and just got into that. I got one of the very early DX7 keyboards from Yamaha."

The DX7 was Yamaha's first digital synthesizer to be a success for the company and would become a mainstay within the music industry throughout the 1980s. Often, it could be found on the backing tracks for countless pop and power ballads.

At the time of its release, analog was the dominant synthesizer on the market and within the music industry, and with the arrival of the DX7, came a new wave of digital sound.

It's easy to see why it'd become so popular among music professionals throughout the decade, and despite its difficulty to programme on (it was notoriously hard to master due to its level of complex menus), it would be ideal for creating ambient soundscapes and otherworldly sound design. Clearly the perfect combination needed for the composer of a sci-fi film.

Morse would soon find himself working on a number of projects involving his cherished DX7 keyboard. "I'd started doing some commercial work for the likes of Toyota and was living in Nashville," says Morse.

Morse would be ultimately perusing a well-known publication during the early 1990s when he happened upon *The Guyver* being in production. "I would often get *Variety* magazine as I decided I'd wanted to work in film. So, I'd just page through it and see what was in production or about to go into production."

"Often, they'd say which star was attached to the project and who's going to direct it. I would go down the list and call every one of those people and just be absolutely relentless," recalls Morse. "And eventually someone called Brian Yuzna answered his phone."

"I didn't know who Brian Yuzna was. I maybe had seen *Re-Animator*, but I wasn't familiar with him. I saw he was producer on this *Guyver* film. He was saying something, I don't remember what, but I do remember I wasn't gonna take no for an answer. I'm gonna really do this film," remembers Morse.

"He [Brian] had spent some time growing up in Asheville, North Carolina. I said, '*I'm not from there, but my wife was from North Carolina*'. I'm grabbing any kind of possible straw I can. Brian said, '*Well come on out*'. He introduced me to George and Steve, and we hung out." Persistence and a hunger to do something different was a key component of Morse getting the scoring gig.

Like many of the cast and crew, Morse was also not familiar with *The Guyver* prior to signing up to the project. "The manga hadn't come to the States, and I don't think there was really anything about it here yet. In fact, when we first met, Steve and George talked about the backstory of it, and I noticed there was a lot to it, and I didn't really know what it was about," says Morse.

"Internally, I was thinking I would do it, no matter what the story was. I later found out the tone of the manga is completely different from the film."

Despite the unfamiliarity with the source material and unsure as to what Morse was getting himself into, he nevertheless began forming a good relationship with the two directors, especially with Tani, prior to signing on to doing the film's score.

"They're both really great guys," says Morse. "George would take me to dinner, or we'd go to a bookstore, and he'd show me Joel-Peter Witkin photos and artwork. He also took me to his studio and when we got there it was like '*Okay, you're going to do the film*'," chuckles Morse.

"But what really sold it was something I usually do for people. So, I'll write something so they can see what the score might look like, because you can talk about music all day long. But until you hear something, you're either going to like it or hate it. And that part isn't really that much up to me; it's like, I'll do the best I can and hopefully, they liked it."

"Thankfully, they both liked the theme. So, from then on, I was in. I just mentioned to Steve recently and said, '*Do you remember the lyrics that you wrote to the theme?*' because he would sing '*Guyver… na…na…na…na…Guyver*' as he went around the studio," laughs Morse.

Was the theme always this distinctive, or did it evolve and change into the theme viewers now know, from something else? "Well, it didn't morph into the theme from anything," remembers Morse. It seems composing is, much like directing, a creative skill where the individual becomes a mad scientist, in the best possible way.

"This is gonna seem crazy, but sometimes things come to me. After I've spoken to people and gotten the info or the brief, in just a matter of seconds, I can plan the whole thing in my head. Then I just have to write it out. All the parts are there, it's almost like a taster, it just happens," explains Morse.

"You know, I haven't done that many feature films," says Morse. "But when I do, I like to work thematically. Different situations can also have a theme as well as the main title. Sometimes I use the chord structure and change them around or elongate them for the scene, etc. But the main title itself was pretty much verbatim from how I thought of it," details Morse.

With the theme pretty much done, and Morse happy with it, it was then onto composing the rest of the score for *The Guyver*. But there would still be one or two teething issues while trying to find the rest of the source's sound, which is to be expected during such a creative process.

Just a few years prior to *The Guyver*'s release, cinemas would have a brief influx of live-action comic book adaptations, with the likes of Tim Burton's gothic blockbuster *Batman* and then Warren

Beatty's visually scrumptious *Dick Tracy*. Both films have huge, rousing scores full of personality, excitement, and energy; thanks in large part to eclectic composer Danny Elfman having worked on both films.

Because each have thematic similarities running throughout their scores, was this something Morse leaned into for his own score to *The Guyver*?, and were there any requests from either Wang, Tani, or Yuzna to lean into what Elfman had successfully done with his entries in the comic book movie landscape?

"What's funny, is that I had a conversation with Steve Bartek [Danny's orchestrator]," recalls Morse. "It was really just about how he worked etc, and he told me a story about how *Dick Tracy* was done."

"For this particular score, everything was written on paper, which I've done too in the past. I mean, I've written for the London Philharmonic Orchestra and it's all on paper, you know. You might be able to hear it all in your head, but for anyone else to hear it they need a sheet of music," chuckles Morse.

He continues. "He [Steve] was telling me that during *Dick Tracy* they had a big fight scene to perform with the whole orchestra, who were out there ready to do it, with all the music written out," remembers Morse.

"Well, in the previous session, without anyone knowing, the editor had taken alternate frames out of each punch, so they look faster. Well, any cues or any accents, or articulations are off three frames on the first punch. Now it's off six frames, now it's off nine frames, and then 12 for every punch in a whole scene, in a matter of seconds."

Thankfully, Morse wouldn't encounter anything as dramatic which befell his fellow composer, with the scoring process being relatively straightforward for the most part. He did come up against one minor challenge, though, one that was wholly unique to a film with two directors who'd have slightly different approaches to the same source material.

"Steve and George are two different people," says Morse. "There were times where I'd read a queue and, you know, I think it's probably safe to say that maybe George who'd have the most fanciful approach about it, and Steve wanted it closer to the manga flavour it was," recalls Morse.

"So, there are two directions here, and they're both equal, so you have got to listen to both. Something could be too much on the one side, and we'd have to discuss it and either make it more serious or go a completely other way."

"What I wanted to do was create some pieces that could be pulled out and placed elsewhere. They would signify different situations. The main beat I would sometimes use that just as a sort of an under carriage on another track. So, the viewer would know, 'Oh, so now we know we're talking about the Guyver', and it's like, you know that the predatory shark is coming."

What is most astonishing is just how many minutes of actual score was composed and created for *The Guyver*. "I think it was 80 minutes altogether," recalls Morse. "Yeah, 80 minutes' worth of music, but I believe the CD only had 45 minutes on it when it was released."

The CD in question would be the Japanese score release – which used the original poster artwork for its cover – and would be the only physical release of Morse's score. That was until media company, Terror Vision, put out a remastered vinyl and Cassette Tape release of Morse's eclectic score.

Thankfully the scarcity of Morse's score (which was becoming more difficult to own and listen to) has been remedied and is now readily available for Western audiences and fans of *The Guyver*.

The score manages to combine the otherworldly with the zany. It is at once heroic, comedic and unsettling, creating a truly idiosyncratic soundscape. Unlike its operatic counterparts released during the 1990s, *The Guyver* has a distinct and almost chaotic nature to its themes. This makes for a great representation of the Guyver suit's unpredictability, the alien-like physicality of the Zoanoids, and the sense of otherworldly wonderment found within classic sci-fi scores.

Given that Morse had to work with two talented (but creatively different) directors, what he created effectively straddles the fine lines between each of their distinctive filmmaking styles and aesthetics.

With the score fully created and ready to add to the film, it was just a case of finishing the final edit to lockdown the picture, but there were more than a few hiccups during the editing process as Steve Wang would explain. "We had an editing assistant, who was ultimately hired to edit the film," recalls Wang.

"So, he cut together that whole scene in the warehouse in the middle of the film and it was just incomprehensible. I got a call and saying, '*You guys got to get in here, right now, this is a disaster*'. And I'm like, '*What's going on?*' George and I went in to look at that whole sequence, which was a 10-minute sequence, and I'm like, '*What, who edited this? It doesn't make any sense whatsoever*', so I said, I'll cut it myself."

"It was a Friday afternoon, and I was told I wasn't going to do it. I said, '*I'm not asking permission, I'm telling you, I'm going to do it. So, you give me an editing assistant to teach me how to use all this stuff, and how to find all the footage*'. The producers agreed and let me get on with it."

Clearly, nothing was going to stop Wang from addressing the editing issues and jumping feet-first into fixing the mess which had been created. His determination had served him well on previous projects and he knew how to do basic editing after working on his own little films prior to *The Guyver*.

"I sat down the editor and started asking questions. I say, '*Okay, how do you sync this up?*' '*Okay, how is the script corresponding with the way we catalogue all the raw footage?*' '*Okay, how do I find this?*' After an hour of it I said, '*Go home*', and they're like '*Oh, no, no, no, my instructions were to...'* and I slam the door, lock them out and I just say, *'Bye, have a good weekend',*" chuckles Wang.

What followed would be an intensive weekend for the film-maker, so determined was he to get the film right, regardless of how long it would take.

"I was in there from Friday afternoon until Monday morning, re-editing this entire 10-minute sequence in the warehouse. That weekend was like, the most ridiculous comedic shtick you could ever imagine," remembers Wang.

"It's like 3am, I'm tired, I'm grabbing and covered with rolls and rolls of film. I'm trying to find the sound; things are going out of sync and I'm trying to find out how many frames are out of sync so I can get it back in sync."

"I grab 1,000 feet of film; I pick it up and the whole thing drops underneath me and starts to uncoil down the entire hallway."

"And I'm chasing it down the hallway, it's like the worst disaster you get to think of, but I've got to get it done. I finished it at like 8:45am or 9am, the producers came in, you know, and just said, *'Show me what you got'.* I put it on, put some music to it, sync'd it all up, and played it. And it was just silence for 10 minutes," remembers Wang.

"As we're watching this, I'm thinking, *'I wonder if I'm going to get fired now, you know?'* And to my surprise, at the end of the 10 minutes they said, *'Great. Why don't you look at some of the other stuff and cut those scenes too?* So, I ended up editing about 33 minutes of the actual film myself, uncredited, but I did edit all this stuff."

The Guyver would be released (in limited form) on 18 March 1991 but would also be screened at Los Angeles' Comic Book and Science Fiction Convention on April 14, 1991, on a 35mm print.

It would be the last film shown during the day following screenings of the two- hour *The Flash* TV Pilot, and Mark Goldblatt's cult comic book feature *The Punisher*. The original advert for the convention would state the following about *The Guyver*: "*The Guyver* is a fun super-hero action film that features *incredible* monster effects. Based on the Japanese comic book character".

Despite the 35mm screening, *The Guyver* would ultimately be relegated to the direct-to-video (DTV) aisle after being distributed by New Line Cinema, the independent company responsible for the *A Nightmare on Elm Street* series (1984-2010), the first four *Critters* films (1986-1992) and the most successful independent film at the time, *Teenage Mutant Ninja Turtles* (1990).

Sadly, *The Guyver* would also suffer a DTV fate outside of the U.S. as well. In the character's homeland of Japan, it would also be released straight-to-video, whereas throughout U.K. and Europe it would make its way to rental stores under a retitled name in attempt to appeal to the *Teenage Mutant Ninja Turtles* demographic.

The new title would completely ignore any ties to *The Guyver* and instead market itself as *Mutronics: The Movie*. Unlike the U.S. cover art, which incorrectly or rather falsely advertised that Mark Hamill would be The Guyver, his face half-spliced with the mask, the *Mutronics* title leaned heavily into its mutant creature aspect, with the Zoanoids and the Guyver suit on the cover, front and centre.

In retrospect, despite the title change, it would be a clearer indication of the film's content and thankfully lacked incorrect advertising. Interestingly, the title wouldn't be the only thing to change on each release as the taglines would also be reformatted for the different titles.

The Guyver would have the tagline of '*Part Human. Part Alien. Pure Superpower*', which gives a fair indication to a perspective viewer as to what this comic book feature might entail. *Mutronics: The Movie* on the other hand went with the rather confusing '*Some Mutants Are More Equal Than Others*'.

In Germany, they made the Zoanoids the key focus, posing in a humorous way (reminiscent of 1980s comedies) and used the tagline '*When Robocop Meets Predator*'.

Confusing marketing and advertisement aside, *The Guyver* was met with middling reviews. The acting, bizarre tone and action was the most heavily critiqued by reviewers and fans, with the creature designs and effects work being the only positive seen by many critics.

Despite its tonal inconsistency, with the movie often leaping from broad comedy into dark body-horror, usually within the same sequence, and the action which lacks any genuine excitement, threat, or sense of danger, it has gained something of a cult following due to fans whose parents mistakenly thought it might be something more akin to *Teenage Mutant Ninja Turtles*.

The Guyver was clearly a learning experience for all involved and should be commended for the things it does do right, such as the aforementioned miniature and creature effects work, which captured the imagination of fans the world over and no doubt led to their own careers within the film or television industry.

Despite the challenges the directors and crew faced during production and in post-production leading up to the film's release in 1991, there remains a lot of warm feelings towards this sci-fi oddity.

"Everybody was so dedicated in the film," says Eddie Yang. "Everybody just worked so hard on it because they really loved and cared about Steve for it to be successful. And George was just awesome as well."

There's one particular memory which has stuck with Yang all these years later. A lot of the time, prior to creating Zoanoid suits which had removable hands and feet, the actors would be sealed in, often meaning all of the sweat would accumulate during a day's shooting.

"I remember they were shooting a lot with these particular suits," recalls Yang. "Ted Smith had to do something where he jumped, that guy was just so dedicated. So, he jumped and all of a sudden felt something in his feet."

"Basically, it was a cold, wet, congealed mush, that was an accumulation of baby powder and sweat. And the alcohol they used to clean up just mostly spread this mixture of cold gelatinous sweat and baby powder all over him. I'll never forget that because I remember looking and was like, '*Oh my God*'! I don't know why that sticks out," chuckles Yang.

"Everybody put blood, sweat and tears into this production. So, you know, it wasn't luxurious by any means."

Producer Brian Yuzna also has fond memories of the film's production, given the complexity of the shoot and what was involved to create this rather gonzo creature feature, and it being a little disappointing for him due to the lack of reach for audiences at the time.

"I haven't seen it in a while, but for me, I'm still disappointed that it didn't get the push it needed to be discovered by a wider audience," laments Yuzna. "Because the miniatures, stop-motion animation and effects work really is brilliant stuff. I'd like to think it'll start getting rediscovered over the coming years."

For Levie Isaacks, it remains an interesting experience, particularly given it's the only time before or since where he'd work with two directors at the same time and despite its tonal inconsistencies, it appears Isaacks still finds a lot to enjoy about the film, particularly in recent years. "It's still a very funny movie," says Isaacks, with it remaining a positive working experience for the seasoned cinematographer. "We did have fun shooting that, and I'll always tell people I never worked a day in my life, it was just so much fun to do."

For Ted Smith, *The Guyver* was an interesting experience, full of multiple roles both in front of and behind the camera and making friends with legendary space wizard, Mark Hamill.

"Yeah, so when we were filming, Mark invites me to his trailer to have a cheeseburger. It was surreal, I was in Mark Hamill's trailer eating cheeseburgers and he's watching cartoons. If someone told me when I was 12 or 14 that at 25 years old, I'd be sitting in a fucking trailer with Luke Skywalker eating a cheeseburger, I would tell you you're a liar," chuckles Smith.

Long after *The Guyver's* release, Smith would find himself doing props for *Wing Commander III* (1994) and would once again bump into his old cheeseburger buddy.

"I worked on one of the *Wing Commander* games and had to build some pilot helmets," remembers Smith. "They're super low-budget vacuform pilot helmets and my friend Michael was making these giant creatures with big giant animatronic heads. Then one day I see Mark here and very sheepishly walk up to him."

"I go '*You may not remember me* […]' and then he just goes, '*Ted!*' I'm like '*What?*', it's crazy he remembered," reminisces Smith.

Johnnie Saiko also looks back fondly on the film's making, and specifically enjoys all the effort, time and skill that went into making the impressive effects work.

"You know, I still like it because it has great practical effects and all the puppeteering stuff. Like the Guyver transformation, that sequence has a great, weird look to it. But while it's happening, it's so fucking cool. You know what I mean? It's like you're seeing a Ray Harryhausen film. And even though we know it's stop motion; it just looks cool."

Given the amount of work, time and effort Wyatt Weed also put into a lot of the behind-the-scenes miniatures and various effects work, how does he feel about it now?

"I do really like the film as it stands," says Weed. "I spent some time working with Clive Barker after *The Guyver*. I worked on *Lord of Illusions* (1995) and then we interacted on some other stuff later on down the line," recalls Weed.

"I remember when I told him [Barker] I'd worked on *The Guyver*. He said, '*Oh, I quite liked that movie. Rather a lot of large rubber monsters smacking into walls wasn't there?*' I was like, '*Pretty much, yeah'.* So that was Clive Barker's take on it, it was a lot of monsters smashing into walls."

It's disheartening to think it's still Tani's only directorial feature film several decades later, with his only other directorial credit being for the short film *The Boy in the Box* (2004), a body-horror art film that is so quintessentially Tani.

During its brief runtime, the viewer's senses are assaulted visually, and audibly as nightmarish and surreal imagery appears without a moment's notice. It's a mind-altering ride. It was easy to see why Tani has continued to work within the experimental art-space and why he continues to evolve with his art exhibitions. He's a creative powerhouse who works best within shorter narratives, where he can go full tilt with his wonderful surrealism.

For co-director Tani, it's clear *The Guyver* still retains a special place in his heart, flaws, and all. "It was a long time ago, you know," chuckles Tani. "That was my first, you know, really big feature directing job. I learned so much just by doing it and by applying some of the effects that I had in my head."

"Being in the director's shoes, you find certain things are just impossible or it's hard to do. I can remember when I was watching the movies, I'd be saying, *'You know, it should be done this way or that way'* but this is slightly different when you're directing. That's why I learned so much with it and I really had the greatest experience directing *The Guyver*," reminisces Tani.

Are there any particular moments or instances which still really resonate with him, decades later? "I mean, I like a lot of things in it," says Tani. "The fish costume at the beginning, or the scene with Michael Deak directing Linnea Quigley for a B-Movie and then Striker falls into the scene. I still think that was one of the funniest sequences and one of my favourites of the movie."

Since the release of *The Guyver*, Steve Wang has been vocal about his disappointment with how this first film turned out, despite softening towards it over the years. Granted, if Wang wasn't disappointed in this experience, audiences might never have gotten the subsequent sequel/reboot, where he'd ultimately rectify the creative frustration he experienced with the first.

With that said, what are Wang's views on the film several decades later?

"My feelings haven't really changed; it's not my favourite film. Everybody did their best and I appreciated that. I was thinking, if nothing else, it was more of a commentary on myself that I just was not in a position to make something that I felt I needed it to be."

"Still being so new directing back then, I don't think my skill and experience level was adequate enough to make something better," laments Wang. "I apologize for the first *Guyver*. I mean, we didn't know what the hell we're doing, we just did our best."

While it's not always possible for a director to come back and redo their past films, would Wang do anything differently with this film? Given that both his and Tani's idealistic creativity wasn't, at times, enough to create a cohesive whole despite the hard work put in by everyone involved.

"I would have started from the ground up and I think the script would have been very different. I don't think the story that we told was necessarily the best story to sell the Guyver in the real world."

"I think I would have restructured it, gotten rid of that roll-up in the beginning and try to get that information through the storytelling. Having the experience that I have now, I think I would know how to do that. At the time it was a complicated concept to get across to people.", says Wang.

"To tell this origin story again, it would be much easier to do than it was 30 years ago. I definitely would have opposed the comedy much stronger than I did back then. It just was not the film I wanted to make. But you know, I was a kid, I was 24 years old, and it was a great opportunity."

Strangely for an independent film, two cuts of *The Guyver* would ultimately find their way to home video throughout the years. The original VHS release would include several moments of Zoanoid gore and dismemberment caused by the Guyver during a few action sequences, while shortening some dialogue scenes.

When VHS started to become an obsolete home format, and it came time to move to DVD (then later Blu-ray), all the versions (regardless of region) would become the Director's Cut. This version adds the additional (slightly) extended scenes missing from the VHS version, but at the same time, it bizarrely removes those three moments of gore. Aside from these extended moments and a flashy comic-book-themed scene transition, this new version feels sub-par without the delightfully fun moments of gore.

The only exception to this Director's Cut being completely R-Rated was for a Steelbook Blu-ray release from Germany in 2015. This limited-edition version would include the missing gore and the previously mentioned extended scenes but was only limited to 1,000 copies. All future high-definition Director's Cut releases used the less violent version.

While the missing gore only equates to a few moments, it is enough to lessen the impact of the Guyver's power, further neutering the tonally inconsistent feature. Ultimately, this makes the Director's Cut feel more like a marketing gimmick rather than a new and improved version. Thankfully, the source elements for these gorier scenes were located, restored, and put into a new release, meaning that fans can now see a version of *The Guyver* in its most complete form.

Ignoring the nostalgia one might hold for a particular film they grew up with, it is hard to deny that several decades on, *The Guyver* still has its fair share of flaws and tonal inconsistencies. Imperfections and faults aside, there is still plenty to enjoy and respect about *The Guyver*.

More than 30 years on, it still gives many modern sci-fi films a run for their money due to the tangible effects work. With awe-inspiring miniatures, inventive stop-motion animation, exquisite cinematography, and impressive creature design, *The Guyver* is wholly unique with its sense of style and ambition on a limited budget. While it might have alienated fans of the source material and is lacking in several fundamental areas, it remains an interesting curio from a more practical effects-driven era of high-concept filmmaking.

While *The Guyver* may never gain a broader audience due to its many idiosyncrasies, it does continue to thrive and garner respect within specific cult film circles, and among fans of absurdist cinema. In 1993, Portuguese film festival Fantasporto would include *The Guyver* (under the title of *Mutronics*) as a nominee for Best Film, but it would ultimately lose out to Peter Jackson's gory, stomach-churning magnum opus – *Braindead* aka *Dead Alive* (1992).

Despite only having a passing resemblance to Yoshiki Takaya's manga, fans did not have long to wait before another adaptation hit VHS rental stores. A few years later, Wang and Co. would set out to create a more tonally faithful adaptation of Takaya's work on a larger scale than the original film, but first, they had to deal with a significantly reduced budget and resources before filming even commenced.

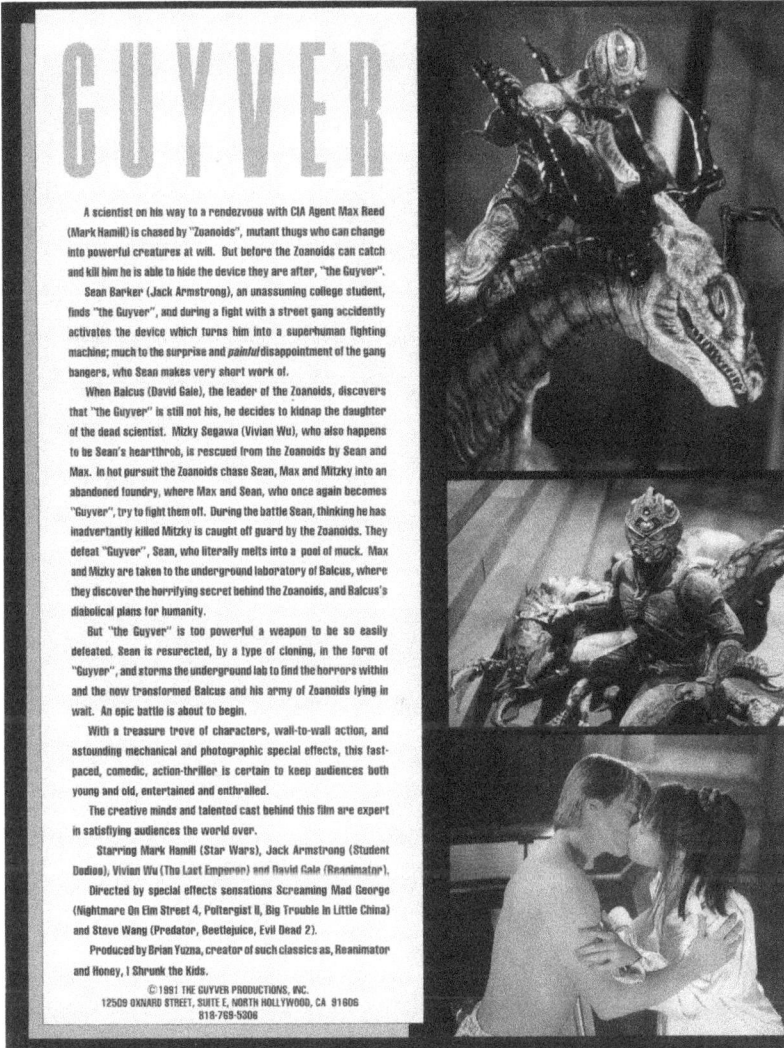

A scientist on his way to a rendezvous with CIA Agent Max Reed (Mark Hamill) is chased by "Zoanoids", mutant thugs who can change into powerful creatures at will. But before the Zoanoids can catch and kill him he is able to hide the device they are after, "the Guyver".

Sean Barker (Jack Armstrong), an unassuming college student, finds "the Guyver", and during a fight with a street gang accidentally activates the device which turns him into a superhuman fighting machine; much to the surprise and *painful* disappointment of the gang bangers, who Sean makes very short work of.

When Balcus (David Gale), the leader of the Zoanoids, discovers that "the Guyver" is still not his, he decides to kidnap the daughter of the dead scientist. Mizky Segawa (Vivian Wu), who also happens to be Sean's heartthrob, is rescued from the Zoanoids by Sean and Max. In hot pursuit the Zoanoids chase Sean, Max and Mitzky into an abandoned foundry, where Max and Sean, who once again becomes "Guyver", try to fight them off. During the battle Sean, thinking he has inadvertently killed Mitzky is caught off guard by the Zoanoids. They defeat "Guyver", Sean, who literally melts into a pool of muck. Max and Mizky are taken to the underground laboratory of Balcus, where they discover the horrifying secret behind the Zoanoids, and Balcus's diabolical plans for humanity.

But "the Guyver" is too powerful a weapon to be so easily defeated. Sean is resurrected, by a type of cloning, in the form of "Guyver", and storms the underground lab to find the horrors within and the now transformed Balcus and his army of Zoanoids lying in wait. An epic battle is about to begin.

With a treasure trove of characters, wall-to-wall action, and astounding mechanical and photographic special effects, this fast-paced, comedic, action-thriller is certain to keep audiences both young and old, entertained and enthralled.

The creative minds and talented cast behind this film are expert in satisfying audiences the world over.

Starring Mark Hamill (Star Wars), Jack Armstrong (Student Bodies), Vivian Wu (The Last Emperor) and David Gale (Reanimator),

Directed by special effects sensations Screaming Mad George (Nightmare On Elm Street 4, Poltergeist II, Big Trouble In Little China) and Steve Wang (Predator, Beetlejuice, Evil Dead 2).

Produced by Brian Yuzna, creator of such classics as, Reanimator and Honey, I Shrunk the Kids.

© 1991 THE GUYVER PRODUCTIONS, INC.
12509 OXNARD STREET, SUITE E, NORTH HOLLYWOOD, CA 91606
818-769-5306

Scan of the promotional flyer that went out to potential distributors. A custom artwork tube was also created which contained the promo materials. It had an outer tube that when turned, would show the characters transform into their Guyver or Zoanoid counterparts (apart from Balcus who remained a mystery). Photo courtesy of Ted Smith / The Guyver Productions, INC

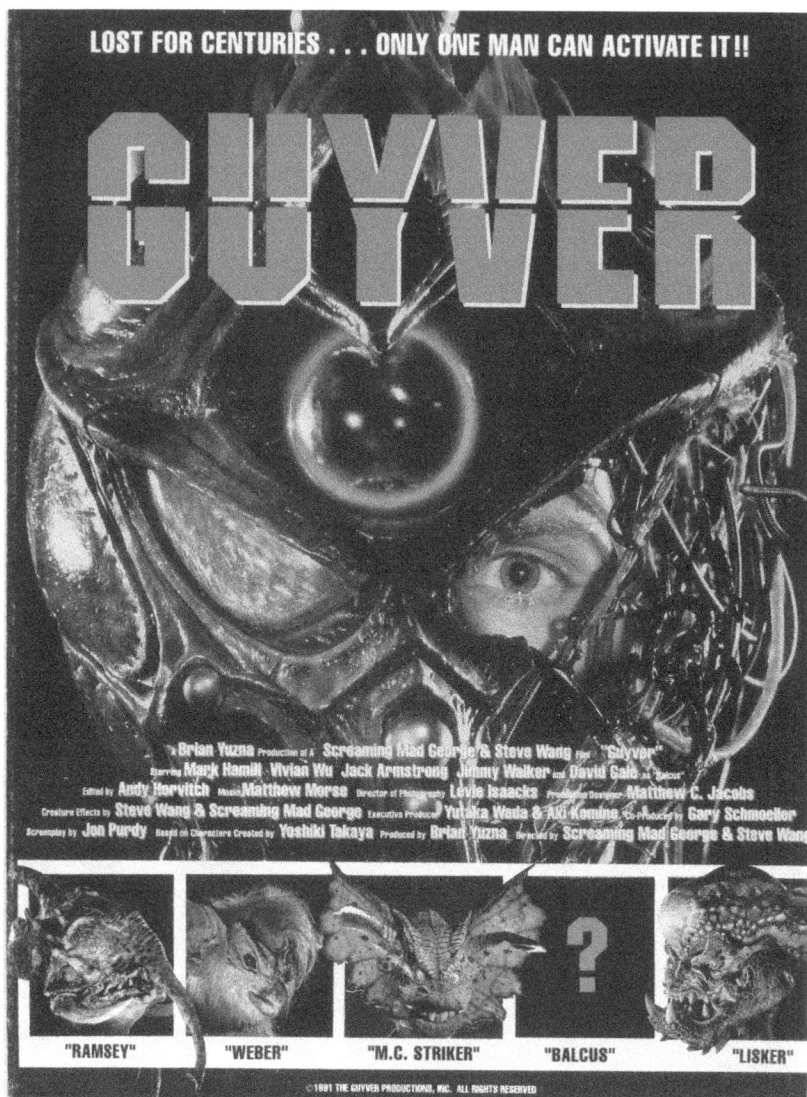

A scan of the original promotional poster which was sent out to potential distributors. Note that the final Zoanoid form of Balcus remains a mystery to audiences. This cover image was used for the Japanese video and laserdisc releases, along with the Japanese CD release. Sadly, in western territories this particular design was dismissed and ultimately changed in a number of ways. Photo courtesy of Ted Smith /The Guyver Productions, INC

Mark Hamill and friend pose for a promotional shot for *The Guyver*. A different image (Hamill and the Guyver back-to-back) would ultimately be used (prominently on the back of the U.S. DVD cover) instead of this one, which didn't help the misunderstanding of people thinking he was playing the Guyver. Photo courtesy of Steve Wang / The Guyver Productions, INC

Advert from an early April edition of *LA Weekly* advertising a local comic convention and a rare opportunity to see the world premiere of *The Guyver* in a 35mm print screening at the Shrine Auditorium Expo Center. Note the screenings of feature length *The Flash* TV Pilot and *The Punisher* (1989).
LA Weekly

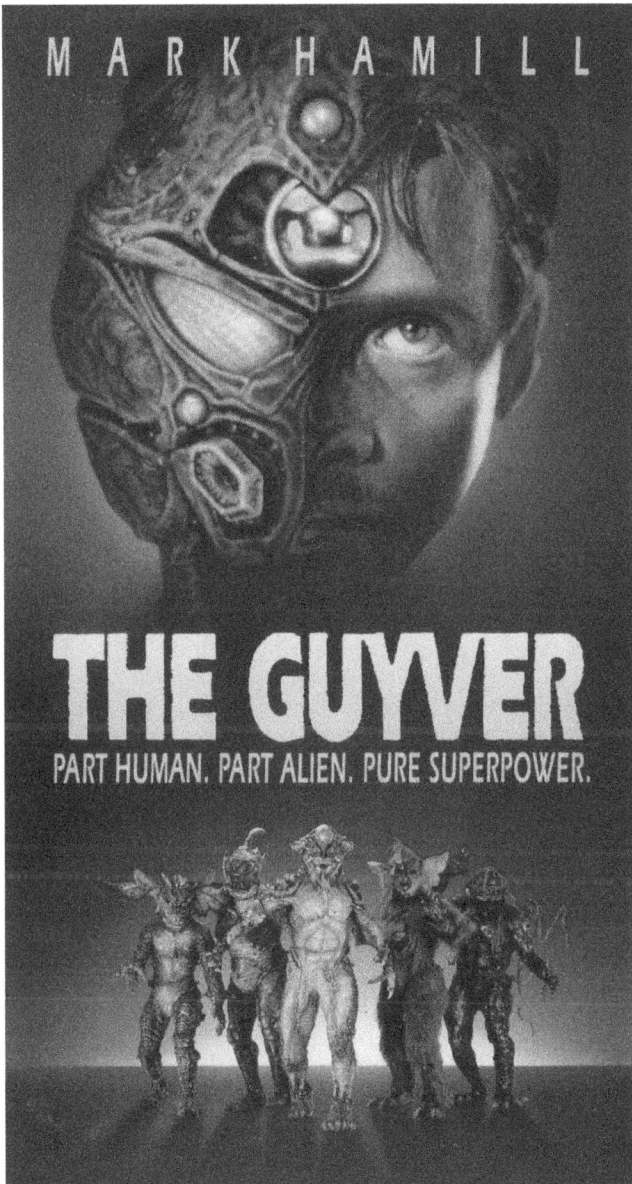

The VHS front cover art for *The Guyver* released by New Line Cinema for the U.S. release. It infamously and rather egregiously dangles the prospect of Mark Hamill as The Guyver. Cue mass disappointment from renters and fans alike. New Line Cinema / The Guyver Productions, INC / Turner Home Entertainment. Photo courtesy of Wyatt Weed (from his personal collection)

The VHS back cover art for *The Guyver* released by New Line Cinema, which takes shots at the two biggest comic book heroes at the time – Batman and Superman. New Line Cinema / The Guyver Productions, INC / Turner Home Entertainment. Photo courtesy of Wyatt Weed (from his personal collection)

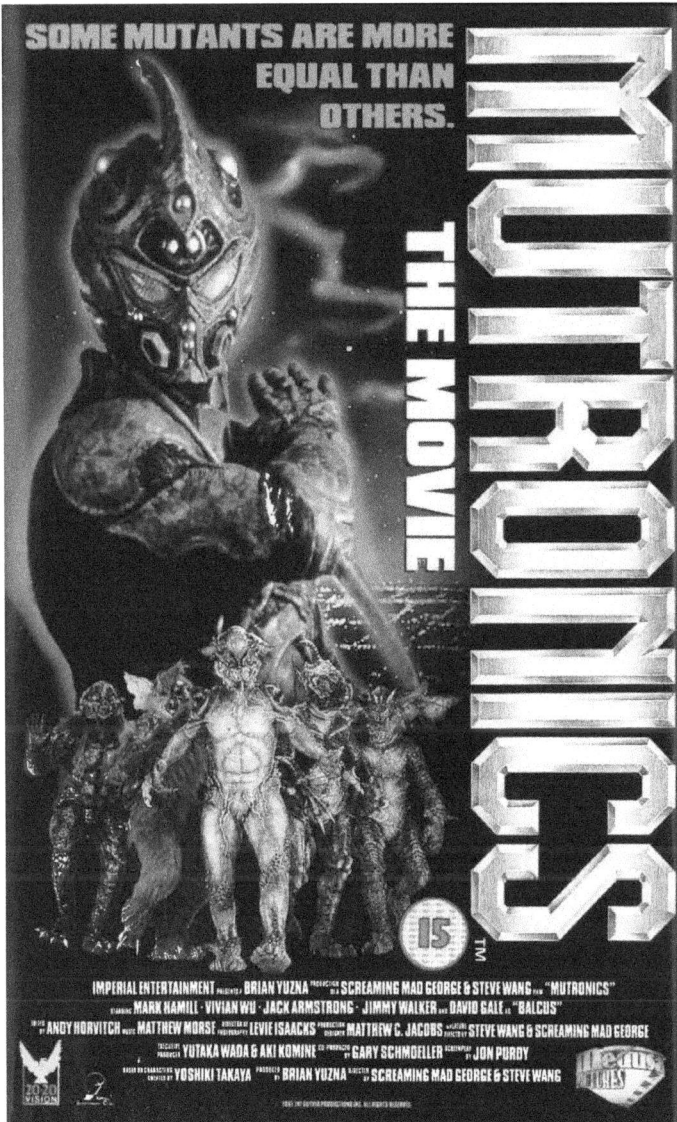

U.K. Rental and Retail VHS cover of *The Guyver*, with its strange name change of *Mutronics: The Movie* and confusing tagline, an attempt by the distribution company 20•20 Vision / Imperial Entertainment to piggyback off the independent success New Line had with 1990s *Teenage Mutant Ninja Turtles*; despite the BBFC rating being too high for its target demographic. 20•20 Vision / Imperial Entertainment Corp/ Medusa Pictures. Photo courtesy of Peter Hayward-Bailey

Yo! Certains Mutants sont plus "frappés" que d'autres...

MUTRONICS LE FILM

METROPOLITAN FILMEXPORT ET IMPERIAL ENTERTAINMENT PRÉSENTENT "MUTRONICS LE FILM"
AVEC MARK HAMILL • VIVIAN WU • JACK ARMSTRONG • JIMMY WALKER ET DAVID GALE DANS LE RÔLE DI BALCUS
MONTAGE ANDY HORVITCH MUSIQUE MATTHEW MORSE LA DIRECTEUR DE PHOTOGRAPHIE LEVIE ISAACKS DÉCORS MATTHEW C. JACOBS
CONCEPTION DES CRÉATURES ET DES EFFETS SPÉCIAUX STEVE WANG ET SCREAMING MAD GEORGE SCÉNARIO JON PURDY
D'APRÈS LA BANDE DESSINÉE DE YOSHIAKI TAKAYA CO-PRODUCTEUR GARY SCHMOELLER PRODUCTEURS EXÉCUTIFS YUTAKA WADA ET AKI KOMINE
PRODUIT PAR BRIAN YUZNA RÉALISÉ PAR SCREAMING MAD GEORGE ET STEVE WANG

French poster for *The Guyver* (entitled *Mutronics – le film*. The Mutronics title appeared throughout Europe). Although they are not pictured, the French release of *The Guyver* also had a set of promotional lobby cards during its theatrical release in 1992 Interestingly, there's not a single shot of the Guyver on this poster, but the Zoanoids are front and centre. Again, this was an obvious ploy to appeal to the *Teenage Mutant Ninja Turtles* demographic. The same image was used for the German VHS (but with the image flipped). Metropolitan Filmexport / Imperial Entertainment Corp

Rare video shop standee promo used to advertise the film during its U.K. release in 1991. From the personal collection of Adam Muir. 20•20 Vision / Medusa Pictures / Imperial Entertainment Corp. Photo courtesy of Adam Muir (from his personal collection)

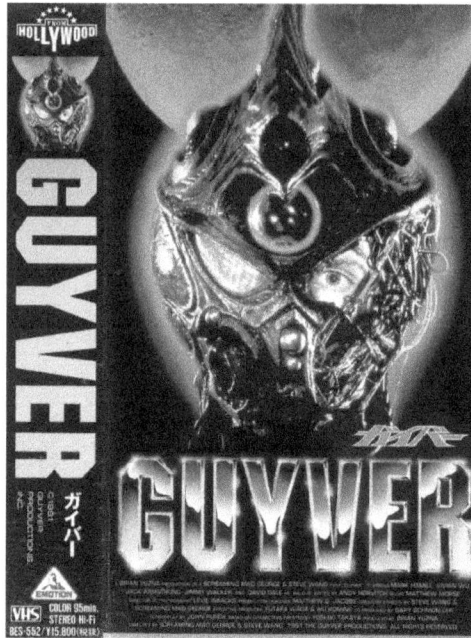

Front cover for the Japanese VHS release of The Guyver which used the
original promotional artwork and was more in-line with the manga artwork
with the torn and broken face covering, revealing the host's face. From
Hollywood / Emotion / Bandai

Cover for the French press release for *Mutronics le film*. Metropolitan
Filmexport / Imperial Entertainment Corp. Photo from Author's Own
Collection.

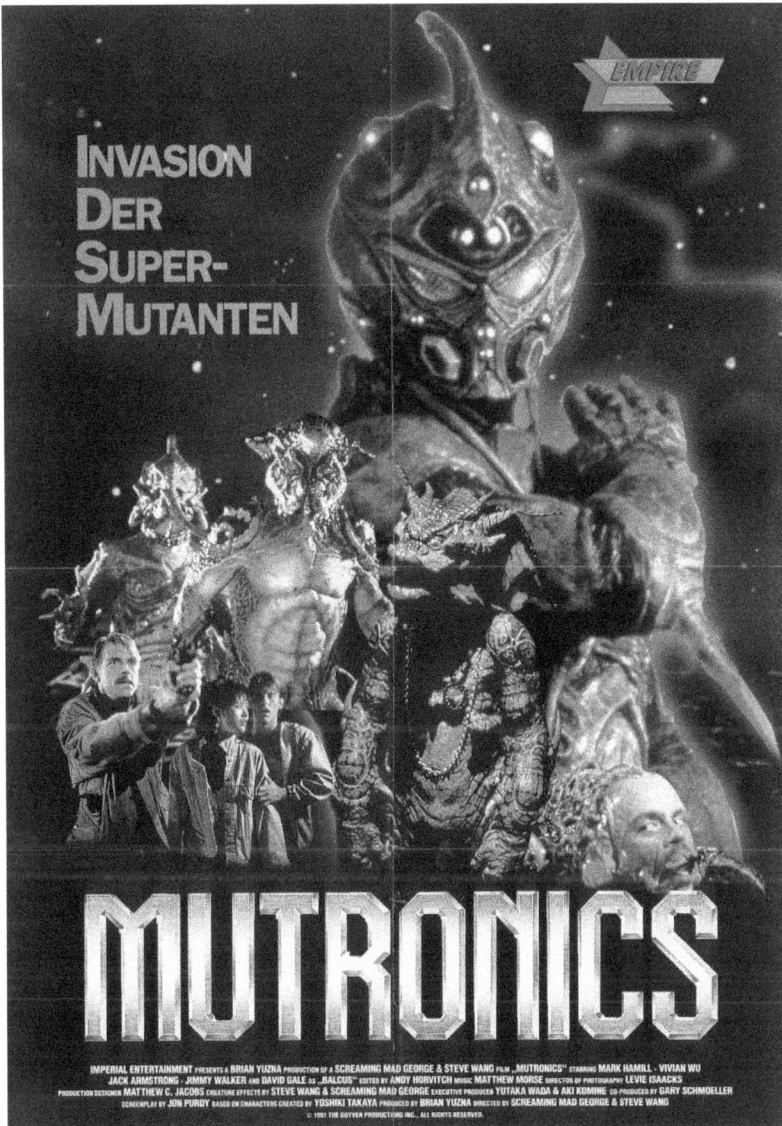

German poster for *The Guyver*, which also uses the *Mutronics title with a little bonus. Mutronics - Invasion der Supermutanten*. Much like the other European covers and releases, it highlights the Guyver and Zoanoids as the key attraction (along with a spoiler of Max's sad fate). Empire / VPS Film-Entertainment

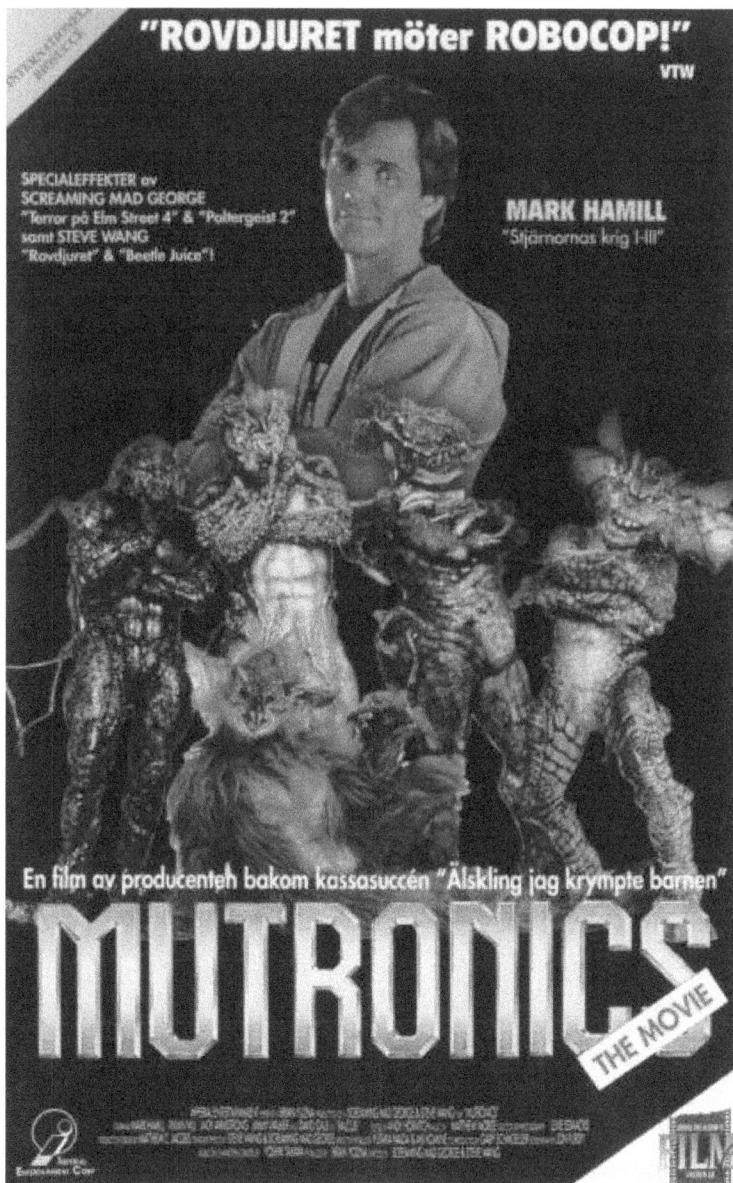

"ROVDJURET möter ROBOCOP!"
VTW

SPECIALEFFEKTER av
SCREAMING MAD GEORGE
"Terror på Elm Street 4" & "Poltergeist 2"
samt STEVE WANG
"Rovdjuret" & "Beetle Juice"!

MARK HAMILL
"Stjärnornas krig I-III"

En film av producenten bakom kassasuccén "Älskling jag krympte barnen"

MUTRONICS
THE MOVIE

Swedish VHS cover which uses elements of the European posters for the Zoanoids, but also has a promo image of Sean (Jack Armstrong) positioned above the Zoanoids. The end result is the implication this is a college comedy with a human trying to control a fraternity of mischievous mutants.
Filmco Sweden AB / Imperial Entertainment Corp

Interlude I

It is not uncommon for ideas, sequences, and whole set pieces to come and go during the script-writing process. It's the very nature of filmmaking that elements change or evolve from the central script. The finished film will differ from the original script and sometimes beyond if it's re-cut from the director's original vision. Before the advent of special features on DVD releases, the tie-in novel would often contain a treasure trove for fans to pour over, often delving into different scenes, cut characters, or unused ideas missing from the final product.

Before the DVD boom in the early 2000s, books like Alan Dean Foster's tie-in novels for *Alien* (1979), *Aliens* (1986), and *Alien 3* (1992) all gave fans a little something extra on top of their theatrical viewing experience. Each of these novelizations would contain cut content from each of their films, so before the arrival of feature-length behind-the-scenes documentaries and Director or Extended Cuts, it was the only way to enjoy the variable differences between the two mediums.

Sadly, with *The Guyver* being an independent film, it would not warrant a movie novelization, meaning subsequent content from the script which was either not filmed due to budget and time constraints or removed from additional script drafts, would not be seen by audiences. Sometimes the cut content can be a fascinating insight into what could have been.

Although minimal content would be removed from the final print of *The Guyver* – the R-Rated cut being filled with slightly more shots of gore than the Director's Cut – in a version of the script it did have one interesting sequence which sadly never made it into the final film, due to either budgetary constraints or lack of time (or both). In both the R-Rated version and Director's Cut, Max's death is an uneventful sequence, making the bone-breaking meta-morphosis and body-horror he goes through to become a Zoanoid feel all for nought.

The following script excerpts, from a draft dated September 24, 1990, shows an entirely different and more tragically heroic death for Max, along with a little more Guyver-tinged violence for good measure, and the original Japanese manga spelling of Chronos (written as Kronos).

The GUYVER

Screenplay by

Jon Purdy

A-Page Revised Draft
9-24-90

Producer - Brian Yuzna
Directors - Screaming Mad George
&
Steve Wang

copyright @ 1990   The GUYVER Productions
12509 Oxnard Street Suite E
North Hollywood, CA. 91606
(818) 769-5306

Front cover of the 1990 revised draft by Jon Purdy. The location listed for
The Guyver Productions is now a parade of shops and leasable offices in
California. Photo courtesy of Stan Giesea

THE GUYVER A-PAGE REVISION 10-14-90 PURDY   , page 87

INT. KRONOS LAB, OUTER RING OF LAB - DAY   202 *

Max and Mizky run back and forth with Zoanoid Saurus chasing
them intercut with Guyver fighting Lisker Zoanoid.   *

Finally Max trips trying to run away from Zoanoid Saurus. *

Mizky looks back in fear as Zoanoid Saurus lumbers over Max
ready to kill him.   *

In a panic Mizky grabs the Black Microscope and hits Zoanoid
Saurus on the head.   *

Nothing happens. At first.   *

Zoanoid Saurus shifts his attention to Mizky as if he is
going to attack her.   *

Mizky is frozen in fear, the microscope over her head.

Then, in a delayed reaction, the blow to his head finally
reaches his feeble dinosaur brain and he falls over
unconscious.   *

A BEAT AND PULL BACK to reveal that Max has rammed a metal
rod into Zoanoid Saurus, killing him.   *

Max and Mizky look at each other.   *

                    MIZKY   *
          Nice work.

                    MAX   *
          I was just doing my job.

Mizky looks at her microscope and drops it.

INT. KRONOS LAB, SECTION A - DAY   203

Guyver shoves Lisker Zoanoid back with a mighty burst.

They exchange a number of blows and kicks.   *

Lisker Zoanoid FALLS on his back, but takes Guyver with him.

They roll on the floor and bash against Section D.

Lisker Zoanoid is on top of Guyver.

Lisker Zoanoid strains for the Control Metal, trying to rip
it out of his head again.

Guyver cuts Lisker Zoanoid's chest with elbow blade.

                                        (CONTINUED)

Script page 87. Photo courtesy of Stan Giesea

CONTINUED: 203

Guyver roars and grabs Lisker Zoanoid's head with both hands.

                     GUYVER
          There's an old saying about
          paybacks!

Lisker Zoanoid and Guyver lock eyes.

                     GUYVER
          They're a bitch!

Guyver TEARS OPEN Lisker Zoanoid's brutish rhino head with
his bare hands, as if he were tear a loaf of bread.

Lisker Zoanoid drops to the ground.

Guyver stands up. Max turns to Guyver.

                  MAX   *
          You're pretty good.

                 GUYVER   *
          So are you two.

Guyver turns to Mizky.

Mizky looks at Guyver for long moment.

                 MIZKY
        Sean?

                 GUYVER
        Mizky.

She hesitates.

Suddenly, before Sean and Mizky can embrace, Max grabs his
head in pain and drops to his knees.

                 MAX
        Oh my God!

Mizky turns to him.

                 MIZKY
        What's wrong?

Guyver kneels down next to Max.

Max begins to SHAKE and SWEAT and grit his teeth in pain.

Max falls to the floor.

Script page 88. Photo courtesy of Stan Giesea

THE GUYVER A-PAGE REVISION 10-14-90 PURDY   page 89

SCENES 204 THRU 207 OMITTED.

INT. KRONOS LAB, MAX TRANSFORMATION - DAY   208

Suddenly his <u>legs and torso contort and bend</u> as if they were
their own creature.

Max looks back in terror as he sees his LEGS transform into
the form of a huge <u>ant-like creature</u>.

INT. KRONOS LAB, BETWEEN SECTION A & D - DAY   209

Mizky reacts in horror at the bizarre transformation.

INT. KRONOS LAB, MAX TRANSFORMATION - DAY   210

CLOSE ON Max as he turns to Guyver and pleads with him.

                    MAX
          Please! Don't let me become one
          of them!

INT. KRONOS LAB, BETWEEN SECTION A & D - DAY   211

Guyver turns to Mizky.

                    GUYVER
          Don't look.

Mizky steps back from Max as his horrid transformation
unfolds. <u>She moves toward the shadows that hide Balcus.</u>

INT. KRONOS LAB, MAX TRANSFORMATION - DAY   212

Max's shoulders and arms BULGE and WARP as they become part
of the insect corpus.

Max's head is the last part to change.

INT. KRONOS LAB, NEAR ZOANOID CORRIDOR ENTRANCE - DAY   213

His cry of pain chills Mizky's blood.

She backs up. In the background <u>Balcus can be seen sending
his telepathic messages.</u>   *

INT. KRONOS LAB, BETWEEN SECTION A & D - DAY   214

Max Zoanoid gives into Balcus' telepathic command and ATTACKS
Guyver.

Max Zoanoid strikes a pathetic, but ruthless attack. Guyver
avoids Max Zoanoid's spear-like arms and refuses to fight
back.
                                        (CONTINUE

Script page 89. Photo courtesy of Stan Giesea

THE GUYVER   A-PAGE REVISION   10-14-90   PURDY   page 90

CONTINUED: 214

Max Zoanoid attacks again and this time gets Guyver in the
clutches of his many legs.

INT.   KRONOS LAB, NEAR ZOANOID CORRIDOR - DAY   215

Balcus emerges from the shadows and grabs Mizky.

He holds her with both hands, for the moment stopping his
telepathic commands.

INT.   KRONOS LAB, BETWEEN SECTION A & D - DAY   216

He drags Mizky out toward Max and Guyver.

                         BALCUS   *
              Pitiful creature. He wasn't left
              in the soup long enough. He'll
              never survive.

Balcus holds Mizky.   *

Max Zoanoid continues his attack on Guyver, but then he pulls
himself back.

                         MAX ZOANOID
              No!

He turns the sharp pointed ends of his front legs on to
himself and plunges them into his insect body in a vain
attempt to take his own life.

Max Zoanoid's eyes beg for the mercy killing.

                         MAX ZOANOID
              Kill me. Please, Sean, don't let
              me end up this way!

Guyver hesitates, holding Max's pleading head.

Just then he feels something at his feet.

Guyver looks down to see Lisker Zoanoid holding onto to
Guyver's leg.

Somehow Lisker Zoanoid has managed to recover and crawl over
to attack Guyver again.

Max cries out in pain. Guyver looks back at Max Zoanoid.

                         MAX ZOANOID
              Please, kill me!
                                                    (CONTINUED)

Script page 90. Photo courtesy of Stan Giesea

THE GUYVER 9-19-90 PURDY   page 91

CONTINUED: 21(

In a fit of frustration, Guyver snaps Max's neck, killing him
instantly.

Max Zoanoid collapses to the floor.

Then Guyver turns and STEPS ON Lisker Zoanoid's head.

The sound of a disdainful grunt rise out of Guyver's throat
as he GRINDS his foot into the head, CRUSHING it into a pulp.

He stares down at his foe, in a daze.

Mizky breaks free from Balcus and shouts.

                    MIZKY
          Sean! Help!

He turns to see Balcus holding Mizky.

Balcus smiles at Guyver.

                    MIZKY
          Sean, he's the one, he murdered my
          Father!

                    BALCUS
          You are even more gifted and
          powerful than I had hoped.

                    GUYVER
          Let her go!

Balcus smiles with great equanimity.

                    BALCUS
          Gladly, if you give me back what you
          stole from me!

                    GUYVER
          What do you mean?

                    BALCUS
          The Guyver Unit. I give you the
          girl, you give me back the Guyver
          Unit.

                    GUYVER
          It is no longer mine to give. I am
          the Guyver!

                              (CONTINUED)

Script page 91. Photo courtesy of Stan Giesea

Part Two

Guyver: Dark Hero
aka
Guyver 2: Dark Hero
(1994)

Chapter Seven

Play it Again, Steve!

Despite receiving a lukewarm critical reception, *The Guyver* managed to gain something of a cult reputation among young monster fans, the whole world over. In the United States it was regularly broadcast on HBO, while in Europe and the UK it was often the talk of the school playground – only under its alternative title, *Mutronics: The Movie*.

Tonally, the first live-action Guyver movie was far removed from its original Manga, OVA (Original Video Animation), and Anime series, catering more to the younger demographic found within the *Teenage Mutant Ninja Turtle* crowd and straying from its source material of violent Seinen monsters and gore-soaked excess (which was comparable to Go Nagi's ultra-violent *Devilman* (1972-1973)).

It was an attempt to craft a more palatable superhero saga for the masses. Even with its niche popularity among creature feature enthusiasts, it still felt like a missed opportunity in doing creator Yoshiki Takaya's work justice. It was a classic case of trying to appeal to everyone and only really appealing to a devoted few.

Even with great memories associated with the first entry, director Steve Wang knew it fell short of what could be achieved. When the opportunity to make a sequel arose, Joji Tani was again sought out to be the director, Wang recalls.

"Screaming Mad George was actually offered the second film, but they only offered him $1.5 million to do it, which was only half of the original *Guyver*. George turned it down because it was hard enough to do the first one at just $3 million, especially with all of the monsters and practical effects."

With Tani deciding to bow out due to the lack of funding for effects work, Wang saw a chance to take a crack at the property solo and got in contact with his old friend and co-director. "I heard about it, so called George up, I said, "*Hey I heard you turned this down - if you don't want to do it, do you mind if I talk to the Japanese company (Kadokawa Corporation - formally Kadokawa Dwango Corporation) and see if they'll let me do it?*' He said, '*Yeah go ahead*'," recalls Wang.

With Tani's blessing to take a solo crack at the sequel, it was now down to Wang to convince Kadokawa Corporation (who own the rights to the manga) that he was the right and only guy for the job. "I had a meeting with them and said, '*I want to do this film, let me produce and direct it*'" The original conditions which George had been offered, were a little incorrect, as Wang quickly found out.

"I asked if the budget was still $1.5 million, but it turned out to be $800,000. So now it was less than a third of the original budget! I thought with that low amount of money, what are you expecting?" says Wang.

"They said, '*To be honest with you we just want one monster, one cute girl, and you can do whatever the hell you want*'. So, I thought, okay great. I got in contact with my friend Ray Cecire - who's a producer for a lot of super low-budget films - to come together and make the movie." Wang was right to call on Cecire, as the producer had a pretty stellar track record of producing some impressive low-budget features.

Cecire would help produce the likes of Scott Pfeiffer's *Merchant of Evil* (1993), starring William Smith (who appeared in cult classics such as *Action U.S.A* (1989) and Donald G. Jackson's *The Roller Blade Seven* (1991))), and *In the Dead of Winter* (1993), that Wyatt Weed would coincidently act in (before re-teaming with Wang shortly after for *Dark Hero*).

Wang was determined to give fans what they wanted - a darker, more serious tone in line with the original manga, despite the challenge of a significantly reduced budget. Although he'd been granted creative freedom by the film's financers, there was only one other individual with whom Wang wanted to discuss the project with, ahead of pre-production.

"I went to Japan a couple of times and met with (Guyver creator) Yoshiki Takaya to discuss the script and a lot of different story points. We agreed that the film universe should be different from the manga, especially because we have budgetary constraints. I said, *'Let me tell a small story within the continuation of the first Guyver but let me change the tone to be more faithful to the manga'*, which he was really cool with."

After gaining the approval from the Guyver's creator to adapt the story for the budget and setting, Wang set about discussing his solo take to Takaya-San.

"I introduced the whole Guyver Zoanoid thing, which at first, he was against me doing because he wanted to include it in the manga. I told him he should still do it, but I think given the low budget of the film we have to bring something new; we have to offer the fans something. He reluctantly agreed, but I think in the end he really enjoyed it a lot and he loved the film."

Despite the initial reluctance from Takaya-San, he would ultimately allow Wang to have carte blanche to create something interesting for *Guyver: Dark Hero*.

With pre-production fast approaching, it was clear where Wang wanted to focus his attention, particularly given his time on *The Guyver*. "The way I'd divide it up was we had a three-month pre-production time, so the first two months was only creature effects. Additionally, during this time, I was still writing the script with Nathan Long and working in the creature shop. We'd coordinate to get all of the creatures built in time for the shoot."

Wang was split in multiple directions during this pre-production phase, so determined was he to make this something the fans would appreciate while reducing costs on the shoot. The first stage was to get the script finalized and ready for shooting. Gone was the complicated and oft-convoluted origin story of the first entry, and instead, Wang and Long would treat *Dark Hero* as both a reboot and sequel, allowing the film to stand on its own without prior knowledge of the first film, with occasional references to past events being brief – essentially making *The Guyver* a past event that wasn't all important for the story.

At the time, the *Dark Hero* script was Long's first foray into a feature film; his working relationship with Wang was built around a love of comics and Hong Kong martial arts films. "I was working at Golden Apple Comics at the time, and it was one of the biggest comic book shops," says Long.

"There was this guy called Chris who used to come in and shop there. He was an editor and publisher for a low-budget film magazine called *Film Threat*. I'd also written an article for them about Hong Kong martial arts films, so I knew Chris pretty well," remembers Long.

"He published an issue with Steve Wang on the cover, featuring *Kung Fu Rascals*, because that's what Steve had just done. And I was like, '*I have to meet this person, I have to meet the guy who made this because I want to write movies that look like this*'. So, when Chris came into the store one day, I said I wanted to meet Steve and we ended up having a four-hour phone conversation about all the stuff we liked," remembers Long.

"After that we decided we were going to work on a movie together." At the time, *Guyver: Dark Hero* wasn't in production yet, so Long and Wang would end up collaborating on another project first.

"I had an idea that was this sort of horror martial arts movie, and we started working on that together. We started writing the script and I started going out to the effects shop Steve was working in at the time, which was Screaming Mad George's shop in the San Fernando Valley. I didn't have a car at the time, and I didn't know how to drive, so I would take the bus out to George's shop. While there, Steve and I would sit around while he sculpted, and I worked on the script. We'd shoot the shit and figure out ideas," says Long.

"This film never went anywhere," he continues. "But Steve and I became good friends. And when he got the opportunity to do *Guyver: Dark Hero*, he called me up and said, '*Hey, do you want to write this?*' '*Yes, yes, absolutely, I want to write this*'. So, we began working on the scripts. It got me my first car and I was able to drive out to his house."

"My first driving experience was getting on the freeway and going north to Steve's house and being absolutely terrified of the freeway traffic," remembers Long.

Nerve-shredding car ride aside, Long would plow headfirst into the script with Wang, and it was clear the latter had a very defined vision for this follow-up.

"Steve really wanted to be more serious than the first," states Long. "Because the first was sort of played for laughs, Steve really wanted to make an epic rubber monster fight movie, with a storyline that took itself seriously, so that's what we did."

Was the epic scale toned down in light of the significantly smaller budget? According to Long, apparently not, as the spaceship in the mountain concept was already in Wang's mind as the core story idea for this more serious follow-up. With the reduced budget, there were still a few elements which had to be scaled down to keep in-line with Wang's initial vision.

"There was definitely a consideration of '*we need to limit this to as few locations as possible*'," remembers Long. "This led to us renting the warehouse out near the Van Nuys airport in L.A. and that's where the Guyver cave set was built."

With the script now molded into something that evolved not only the character of Sean and The Guyver, but also added and expanded its own cinematic mythology to this live-action universe, Wang continued with the last stretch of pre-production ahead of principle photography. "About a month before we started shooting, I left the creature shop full time and let Moto [Hata] take over the remainder of the supervision for the creatures with the effects team," recalls Wang.

"I went off to do the remainder of the pre-production on the film itself - location scouting, casting etc. Basically, getting everything prepped for principal photography."

"We were actually able to shoot for about eight weeks," says Wang. "Which was pretty incredible for the budget we had and because we shot on 16mm. We had a very small crew, we'd end up working very long hours because we were non-union, but everyone was really great and really into the production," reminisces Wang.

Steve Wang's sketch /concept design for the Sten Zoanoid.
Photo courtesy of Steve Wang.

Steve Wang's sketch /concept art for Sten Zoanoid after adding more illustration detail. Photo courtesy of Steve Wang

Steve Wang's sketch /concept art for the Mazzo Zoanoid.
Photo courtesy of Steve Wang

Steve Wang's sketch /concept design for the Marcus Zoanoid.
Photo courtesy of Steve Wang.

Early concept and design art for Crane's Zoanoid look.
Photo courtesy of Steve Wang.

Full body Crane Zoanoid concept sketch done by Wang prior to settling on the final visual look. Photo courtesy of Steve Wang.

Close-up head illustration of the previous Crane Zoanoid sketch, which adds further notes by Wang as the design process continued. Note the details about the Zoanoid's mandibles and the possible use of bladders for part of the head and neck. Photo courtesy of Steve Wang.

The final design that Wang settled on for the Crane Zoanoid
after a two-month process (as noted by the stamp on the illustration).
Photo courtesy of Steve Wang.

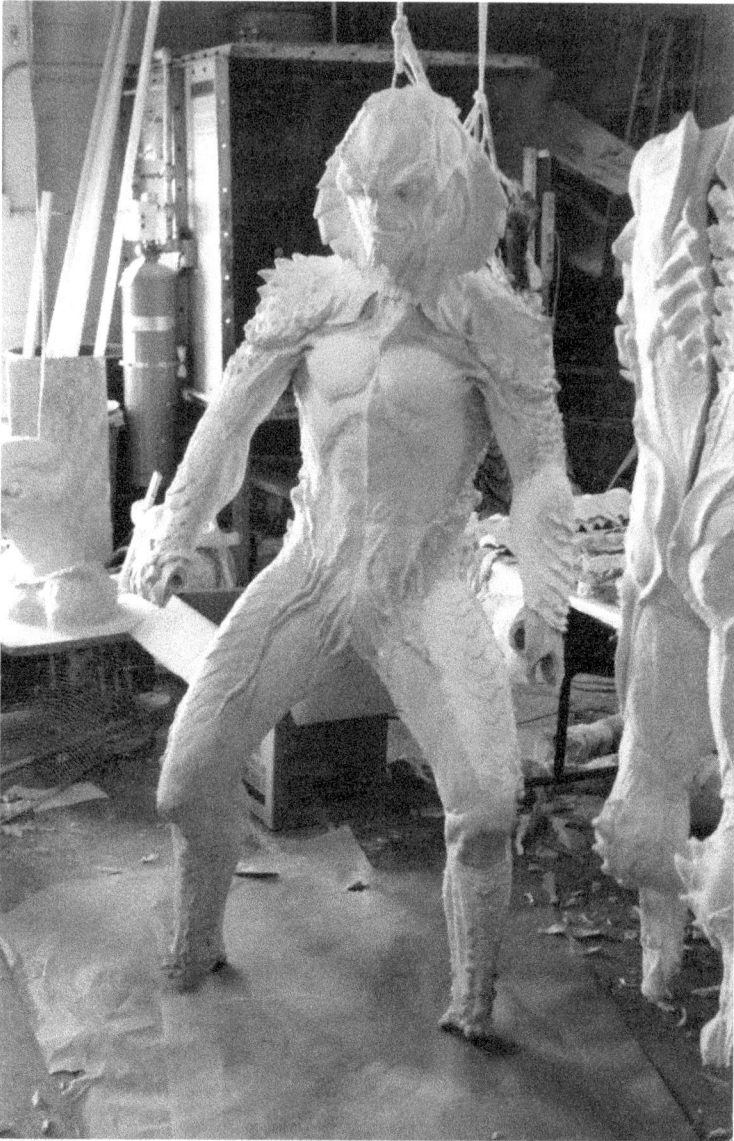

Full body sculpt of the final Crane Zoanoid look. Body moulds for Lisker from *The Guyver* were repurposed and additional sculpting detail was added to create the Crane Zoanoid seen in *Dark Hero* (note the Marcus Zoanoid head sculpt on the left). Photo courtesy of Wyatt Weed.

The starting sketch of Steve Wang's Guyver Zoanoid concept.
Photo courtesy of Steve Wang.

A close-up sketch of the Guyver Zoanoid helmet design
by Steve Wang. Photo courtesy of Steve Wang.

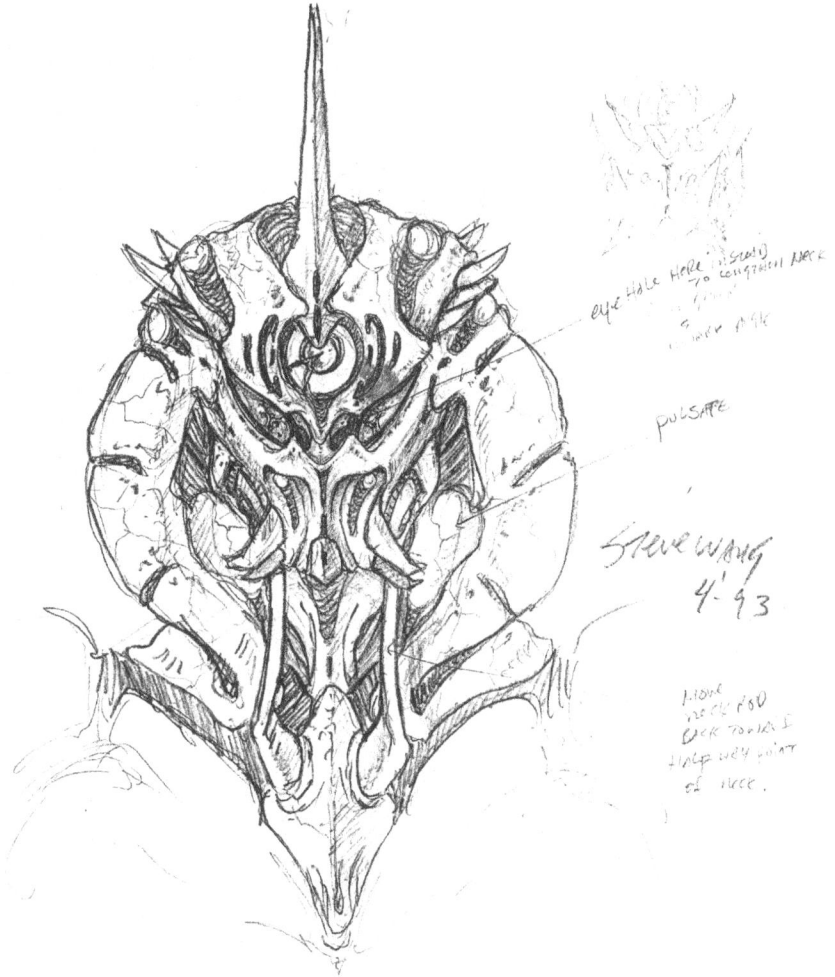

Another profile sketch of the Guyver Zoanoid helmet with
annotations by Wang. Photo courtesy of Steve Wang.

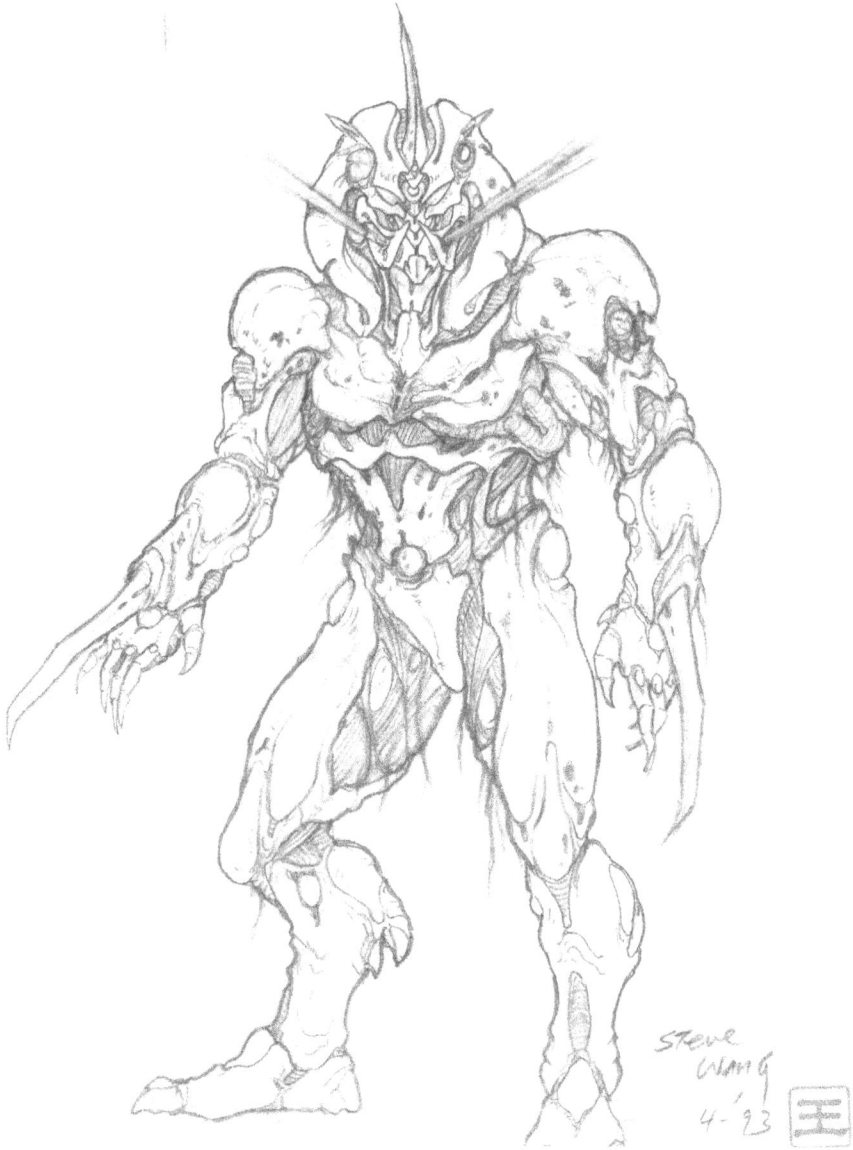

Full frontal suit concept art detail for the Guyver Zoanoid.
Photo courtesy of Steve Wang.

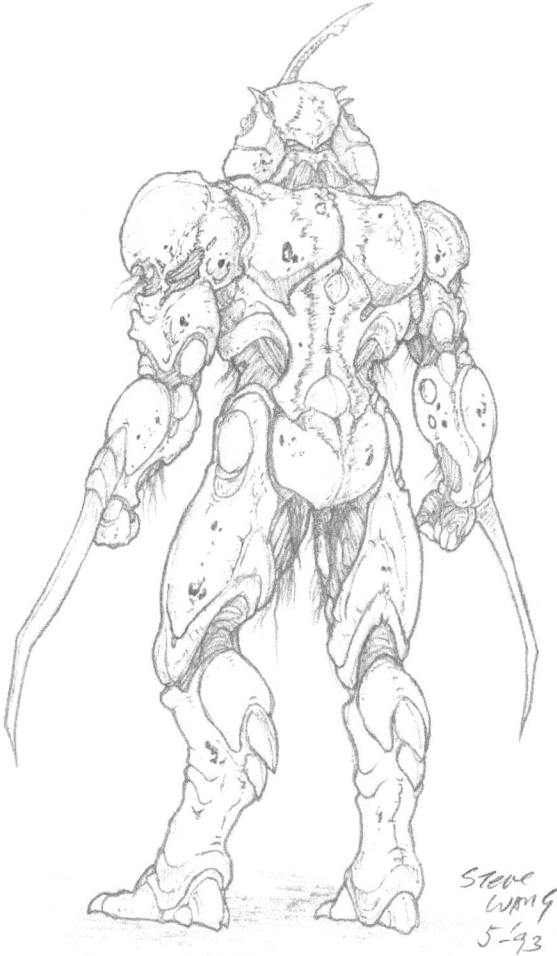

Full body back detail illustration of Guyver Zoanoid.
Photo courtesy of Steve Wang.

The late Moto Hata's full body sculpt of the Guyver Zoanoid for the film's climatic face-off. Wang's concepts were effectively translated to the full-scale suit, with embellished damage details included from Hata. Suit would be maintained by Asao Goto on set. Photo courtesy of Wyatt Weed.

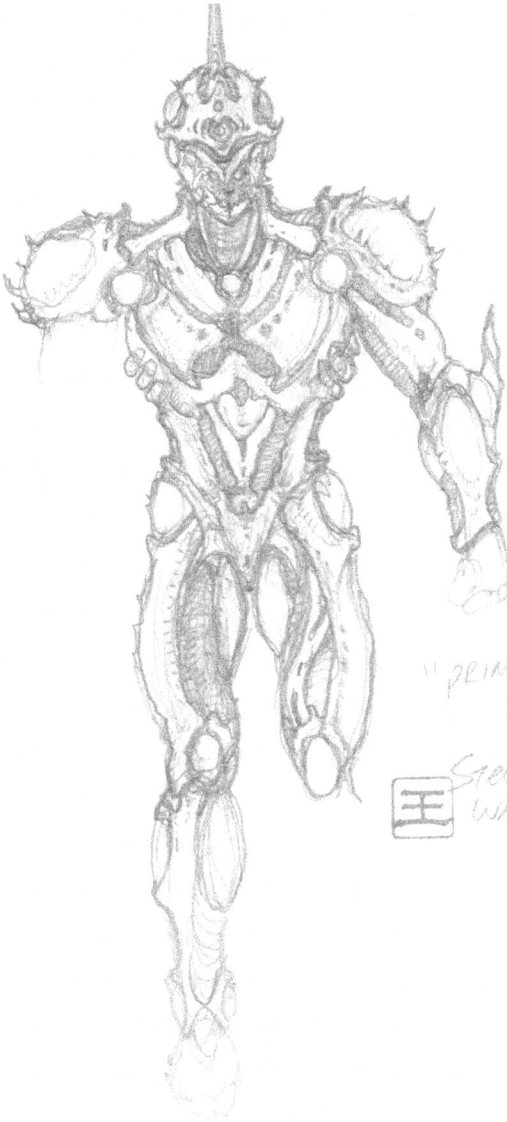

Original design sketch of the Primitive Guyver by Steve Wang. The Primitive Guyver is only seen briefly during the caveman flashback sequence and was portrayed by Kristin Calkins (who also played Lois, one of the student diggers in present day). Photo courtesy of Steve Wang.

With *Guyver: Dark Hero* being both a sequel and a soft reboot of the film series, and it being a second go for Wang to amend for the first entry's faults, this new start naturally required a set of fresh faces in front of the camera.

Much like its predecessor, one of the many highlights from *Guyver: Dark Hero* is the excellent ensemble cast - including beloved voice-actor and scriptwriter David Hayter as Sean Barker; everyone's most recognisable cop character actor, Christopher Michael; and wholesome, but still undeniably badass girl-next-door, Kathy Christopherson (who would later collaborate with Steve Wang on *Kamen Rider: Dragon Knight* (2008-2009)).

It wasn't always Christopherson's intention to be the feisty heroine and love interest of our vigilante protagonist. In fact, it could have been a different film altogether if she had her first choice during the casting process. "I saw a casting ad in *Drama-Logue* for *Guyver: Dark Hero* and decided I would make a great bad guy. I'd been studying martial arts and really wanted to fight in the film, so I submitted myself for the female badass (Sten, one of Crane's henchwomen). It was a small part but required martial arts."

Interestingly, though, it was not to be, and the actor was instead called in for a completely different audition after submitting herself for the sequel. "I was a little disappointed to be called in for the lead female (of Cori) instead. After getting cast it all made sense; I realised my physical stature wasn't nearly as badass as I might have thought when originally submitting for the project. I was, after all, more of a leading lady and thankfully Steve felt the same way."

Christopherson still managed to kick ass by delivering a devastating headshot to the Guyver Zoanoid's cracked control metal. She also appeared front and centre for a feature in the Spring 1994 issue of *Femme Fatales*, where she would showcase her martial arts prowess by executing an impressive high kick over the Volker Zoanoid (played by stuntman extraordinaire Brian Simpson).

The feature includes several comments from the majority of the female cast members, including Marisa Cody (Mary), Ann George (Gail), Kristin Calkins (Lois, and briefly the Primitive Guyver seen in flashbacks) and Veronica Reed (Sten pre-Zoanoid), with the writer going into detail about how each of the women is a force to be reckoned with (and rightly so despite their limited screen time).

Jack Armstrong, who portrayed the young and naïve Sean Barker in the original film, would not return for this reboot. This meant a brand-new actor in the lead role of the *now seasoned* Sean, who was able to bring a dark intensity to a jaded Sean who would have been living with the Guyver for a year now.

While many up-and-coming actors within the Los Angeles area went to audition, the part ultimately became the first starring role for David Hayter.

Despite the boyish good looks often attributed to an actor with a 'leading man' quality, Hayter would become most notable for his prolific voice work within video games (namely that of the gruff Solid Snake from Hideo Kojima's legendary *Metal Gear Solid* series), and as the screenwriter responsible for the most well-received comic book movie adaptations such as: *X-Men* (2000), *Watchmen* (2009), and *X2: X-Men United* (2003) (co-written with Dan Harris and Michael Dougherty).

Unlike his fellow actors featured in both *Guyver* films, Hayter was aware of the manga medium but not overly learned with Takaya-San's particular work, having spent his early years living in Japan. "I went to high school there [in Japan] and also graduated while there. I then lived there on and off for another two years. I didn't know about *The Guyver* specifically, but I was aware of Anime and Manga properties."

This quickly changed once Hayter was gearing up for the audition. "When I got the audition, I went and bought the *Guyver* VHS tapes so I could really know the material and some proper research for the part."

Was Hayter aware of the insanity he was getting himself into, after diving headfirst into the research of the Guyver mythology and character? "I thought it was badass," he continues. "I loved the fact that it was going to be violent and bloody. We didn't have superhero movies like that back then, and I just thought it was gonna be awesome!"

Hayter was determined for his passion to shine through and was going to give it the best shot he had. "Whenever I'm hired for a job, I instantly fall in love with the project and I'm on board 100%. So, when I got the part of Sean Barker, I was like, *I am* Sean Barker. This is my chance to be Batman!"

Hayter clearly wanted to live and breathe Sean, investing more personality into his interpretation of the character, and it's obvious from the finished product that he did. While it could be accused of being melodramatic by the average viewer, Hayter does invoke a raw energy and anger for his version of Sean – an intensity that was sorely lacking from the original film.

With this being his first leading man role, the all-or-nothing approach Hayter took has paid dividends; his performance being one of the key elements which cemented this entry's cult film status, as he flashes his boyish charm at Christopherson's Cori, stares in wide-eyed wonder at the prehistoric Guyver ship, and booms his gravel-voiced vocals at anything related to Chronos (or Kronos as its sometimes seen on home media releases). One thing is abundantly clear, Hayter is giving it his all.

Although he'd been offered the role, there was still a rather strange hurdle to overcome before he could fill Sean's anti-hero shoes. "My manager tried to negotiate a better salary for me and Steve [Wang] was like, '*No, there's only this much money*'. And my manager said, '*Well you know, he could make more than that bartending*', and Steve was like '*Great, let him go bartend*'. Thankfully for Hayter, this minor issue was short-lived.

"The only concession he got me is that my name would be in a box on the credits. I didn't know if that was valuable or not, but that's what we negotiated." With the concession taken care of and Hayter back in the lead role, the cast of character actors was ramping up.

Legendary character actor Christopher Michael, known to many viewers as 'that cop or law enforcement character' would be cast as undercover C.I.A agent Atkins who was keeping tabs on the Guyver dig site and Sean (Hayter).

"I submitted myself for that project as I was between agents at the time," remembers Michael. "They called me in for an audition and I got the part. I knew nothing of the prior movie. And although I'd worked on some big-budget movies, I was very familiar with low budget and how that worked. Honestly, we had so much fun, I never really noticed not having a dressing room or anything like that. We all got along very well; I think we were all on the same page with regard to getting the movie done."

Rounding out the rest of the main cast would be Wes Deitrick as Volker (pre-Zoanoid); theatre actor Bruno Patrick (credited as Bruno Giannotta) would be the film's antagonist as power-hungry Cronos subservient, Arlen Crane; Stuart Weiss would play Marcus (Cori's father and head archaeologist of the Guyver dig site); and Billi Lee would take over (albeit briefly) the role of Mizky from Vivian Wu.

Finally for the opening action sequence, the drug dealer goons were played by Shaun T. Benjamin (as D.C); Koichi Sakamoto (as Sakai); Butch Portillo (as Bo); Ken Goodman (as Dino); Brian Simpson *sans* creature suit (as Benny); and Gary Willis (as Rafe). The rest of Alpha Stunts would round out some of the disposable goons.

A number of the cast would, much like the first film, occasionally pull multiple roles to help with keeping the cost of the budget down. Once again, Ted Smith and Brian Simpson would play a selection of the Zoanoids and background characters, along with both Wyatt Weed and Nathan Long cameoing in the opening scenes (more on that later). To keep costs down further, Wang would reuse a number of older molds to help save on costs.

Eddie Yang's design for Lisker from *The Guyver* was used at least twice in different capacities during the course of the film, first as a fossilised head spotted by Sean on the dig site. The second instance being ahead of the final fight, as the Guyver takes on a familiar looking Zoanoid, making light work of the creature – a wonderful 'hell yeah' moment in a number of ways for hardened Guyver fans or those familiar with the first film.

Finally, for the set-concept design stage, Wang would call on the favour of a fellow designer and Rick Baker alumni, Sandy Collora.

"Steve and I have been friends for a long time," says Collora. "I've worked for him, he's worked for me, he's really an amazing artist and wonderful human being. He really inspired my style quite a bit. But yeah, Steve has been there for me since *Batman: Dead End* (2003) and everything else I've directed, just to help with suits, give advice or give support."

For Collora's concept art and renders for *Dark Hero*, it really leans into the sense of the organic, living organism which the Guyver suit represents. There's a clear aesthetic throughline and carves its own niche within the Guyver mythology. The finished sets, based on the concept art, achieve a lot of the ideas on the very small budget.

"Steve had an idea of what he wanted," remembers Collora. "He described how it [the ship] would look. Based off of that, I did a few sketches and he liked them a lot. From that he picked one and I did a production painting. When I went to set, I was pretty impressed with what the crew had done. Seeing someone else's interpretation of my work was cool."

With the shooting locations confirmed, cast ready, the new more serious script and tone in place, and a production painting done of the cave set, it was onto the set construction.

It seems like a lost art in more recent years, with most sets, particularly for superhero or comic book films, being large green-screen sound stages. The very real and physical tangibility which makes them stand out and ultimately ground the audience in the action, is become more of a rarity in recent filmmaking.

When a feature uses practical sets it grounds the film with a tangible reality, even if there are unreal things taking place on-screen. This is one of the reasons why a low-budget film like *Guyver: Dark Hero* has stood the test of time. On the one hand, the film has a rough, ready, and tangible aesthetic to its action. While on the other, even with the hyper-reality of the on-screen martial arts and violence, the rest of the film (be it dialogue sequences or everyday surroundings) has a grounded sense of reality due to extensive location shooting and minimal set work. Weed explains how they set out to design sets on a minimal budget and the process of getting them made.

"We started around January 1, 1993. I think *Guyver: Dark Hero* might have stretched on a little bit longer. What's interesting is I want to say they were both [*The Guyver* and *Guyver: Dark Hero*] probably about five months of pre-production time each," remembers Weed.

"But then starting in like April/May, when we had our warehouse secure and can start building sets, we relocated over to the warehouse. Around this time the creature shop was winding down and we were starting to move the creatures over to the warehouse. That's when we started ramping up on set construction."

Therein lay the difference with the production of *Dark Hero* when compared to its predecessor. Because the film was non-union, which is unregulated when compared to union work, the time for cast and crew is negotiable, with scheduling, turnaround on work and overtime factored in. For example, because the crew members working on building and constructing the various sets were so dedicated to the production of *Dark Hero, they* were close to burning out from working too hard on the set construction. Because of this, time was allocated for them to recuperate before shooting commenced. Thankfully, Wang knew when to put the crew on a break and during the set construction was one such time. In fact, it wasn't only during the set construction phase, according to Weed.

"We took a couple of breaks, like at one point in time," remembers Weed. "You've got these complex sets under construction, like we had the spaceship interiors, and the cave set under construction, but we had already finished setting up the campsite up in the Angeles Crest Mountains."

"So, while we were continuing on the sets, the campsite was done. That meant shooting could commence on the campsite. So they went to the campsite, and they started shooting that stuff first, while we got the cave, and the spaceship sets done. Then they came back to the stage, they started shooting in the cave."

"And I want to say at one point we were behind. There was a set or two that weren't ready just because they were so ambitious, and I think Steve authorized like a five-day weekend. He said, '*Okay, we were supposed to start shooting here tomorrow, we're not ready. Let's everybody take a five-day weekend. And then the art department crew can push through*'," recalls Weed.

"It was much more loose structure; you were able to roll with the punches easier," says Weed. "That's one of the problems with production, is that people are very scared to say stop. Because once you say stop, they feel like once the production loses momentum, you're going to lose people, you're going to lose financing, you're going to lose the confidence of the production company."

"Nobody wants to stop, but things happen. Things go wrong, things start to crumble, and your instinct is to just push through and on *Dark Hero* there were times when things kind of fell apart and we went '*Whoa, let's stop. Let's take a breath here*', and we ended up getting it fixed."

"We didn't have, you know, a company breathing down our back saying '*No, no, no, you gotta go*', we had the ability to stop and say, '*Okay, we want this to be right, let's fix this*'. And that was the benefit of the less money," says Weed.

"On *Dark Hero*, we were able to sort of wrap the main unit, stay in the stage, stay in the warehouse, and then come back a couple days or a week later and shoot as needed. Because it was a much less controlled environment, we could work on a miniature until it was ready. And then Steve could call the crew back and we'd shoot out that miniature."

"It was very much an indie film," reiterates Weed and based on the budget and how the shooting was structured, it was all the better because of it.

"I say $920,000. And you say, '*Wow, that's so much less money*', but by 1993 standards $920,000 for a bunch of guys who were basically on their third feature film, it was a lot of money to us. I mean, we look back at it now and we roll our eyes. But it felt like we were swimming in money. We were without the ridiculous bureaucratic overhead of a production studio. We were able to do amazing things. I would say we were just 100% more efficient in terms of how we spent the money than the first film was", says Weed.

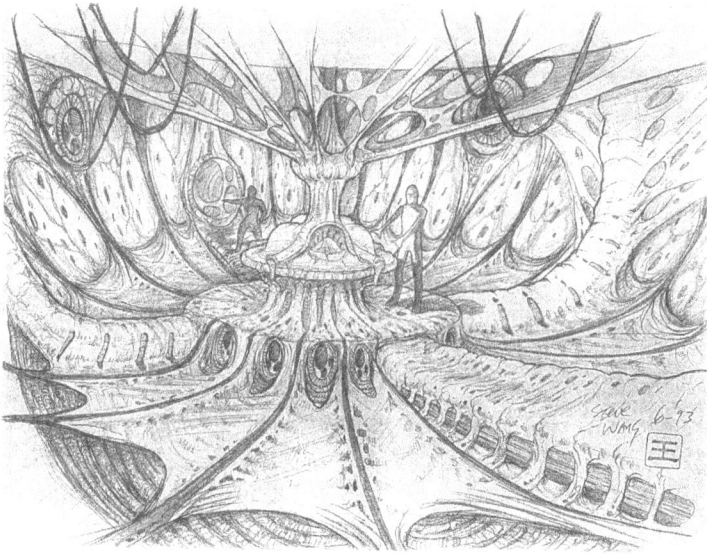

Original design concept for the inside of the Guyver's ship (the location of the Guyver units) drawn by Steve Wang. Photo courtesy of Steve Wang.

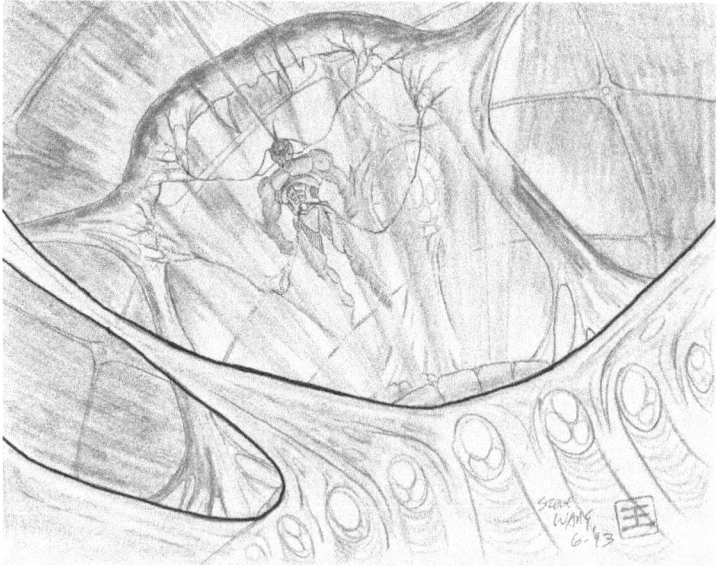

Concept art by Steve Wang for the moment the Guyver connects with the alien ship (leading to the prehistoric flashback). Photo courtesy of Steve Wang.

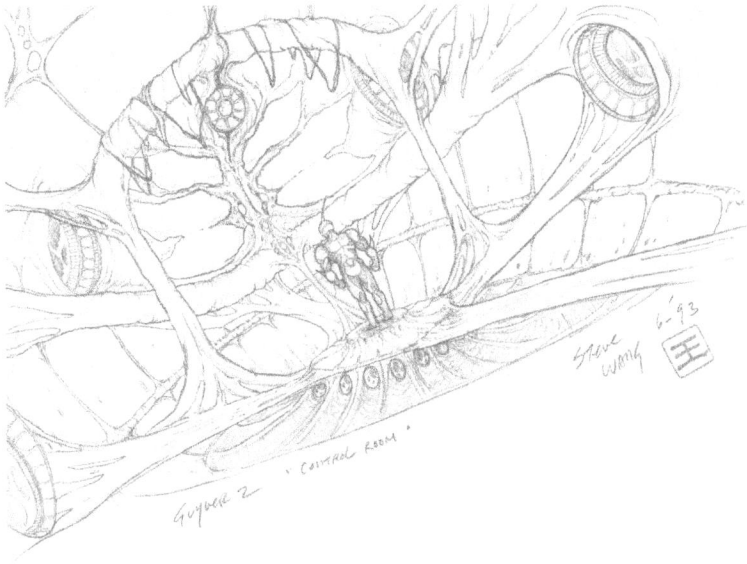

Concept art of the Guyver arriving at the alien ship's control room.
Photo courtesy of Steve Wang.

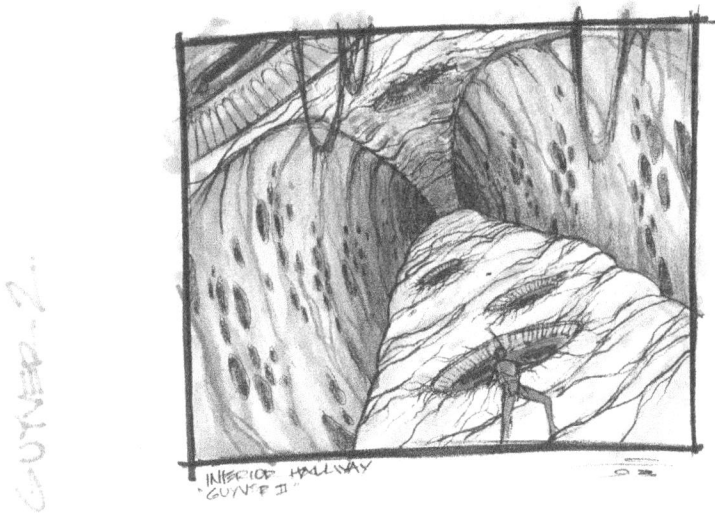

Concept art by Sandy Collora of the interior ship hallway.
Photo courtesy of Steve Wang.

Concept art by Sandy Collora for the entrance to the Spaceship control. Photo courtesy of Steve Wang.

Concept art by Sandy Collora for the communal chamber interior of the Guyver Spaceship. Photo courtesy of Steve Wang.

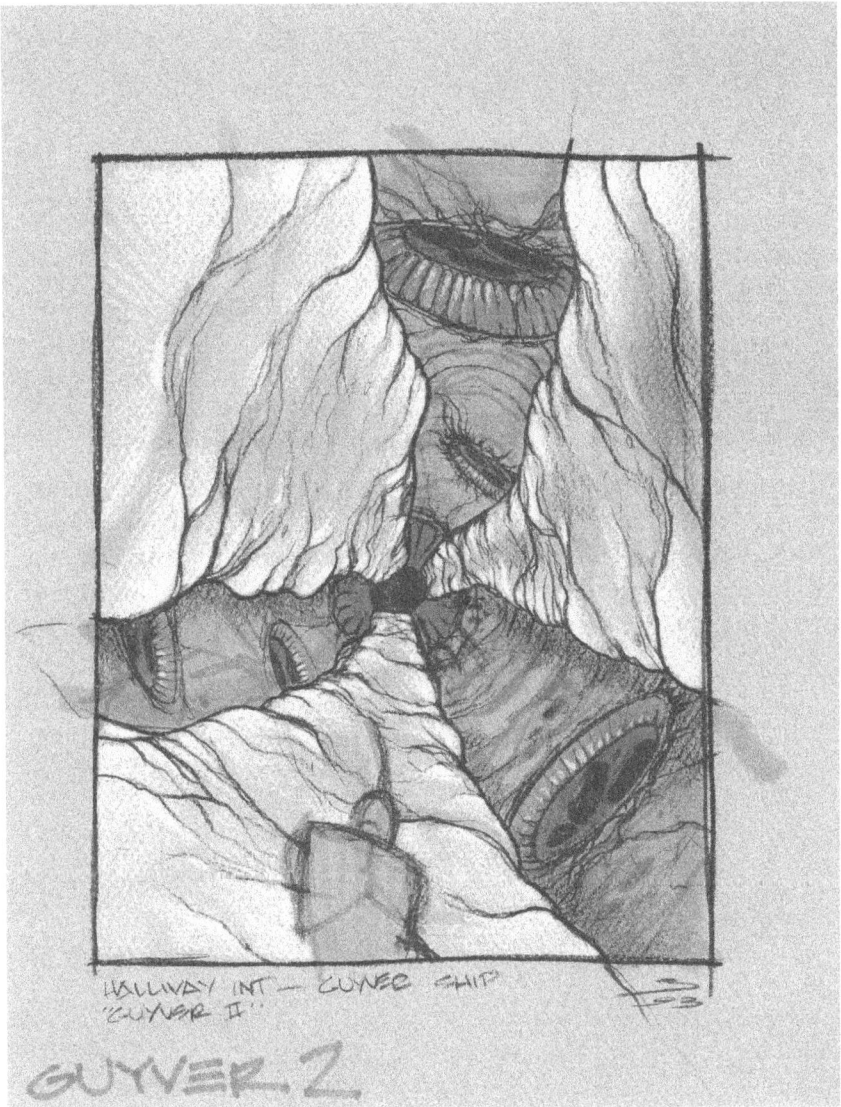

Concept art by Sandy Collora of interior ship hallway.
Photo courtesy of Steve Wang.

The numerous Control Metal pieces (along with a few Gravity Control Orbs and helmet orbs) for *Guyver: Dark Hero*, which had to be prepped in advance of the shoot. This included metalizing them, so they had the right shine and reflection before they were added to the various Guyver suits. Note the various Guyver suits and helmets in a few reflections. Photo courtesy of Wyatt Weed.

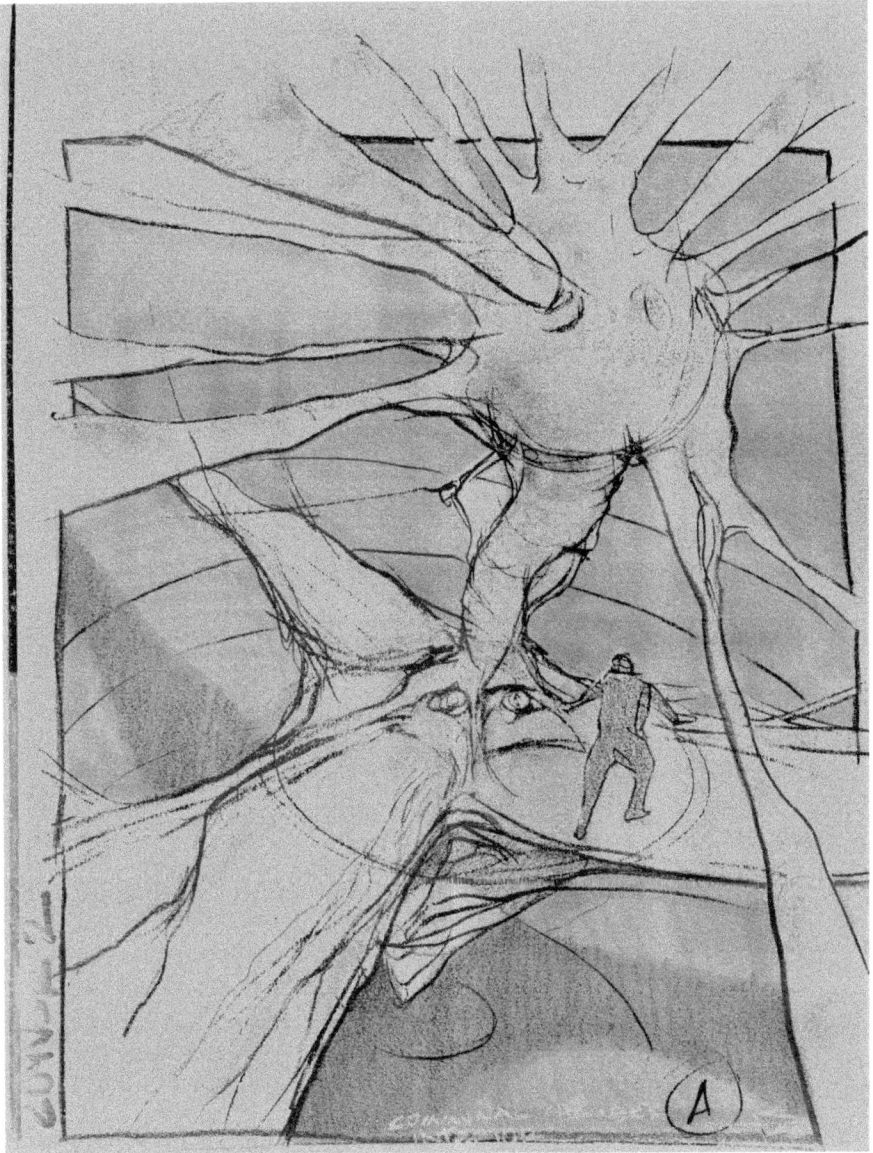

Concept art by Sandy Collora – another angle of the communal chamber with the ship heart. Photo courtesy of Steve Wang.

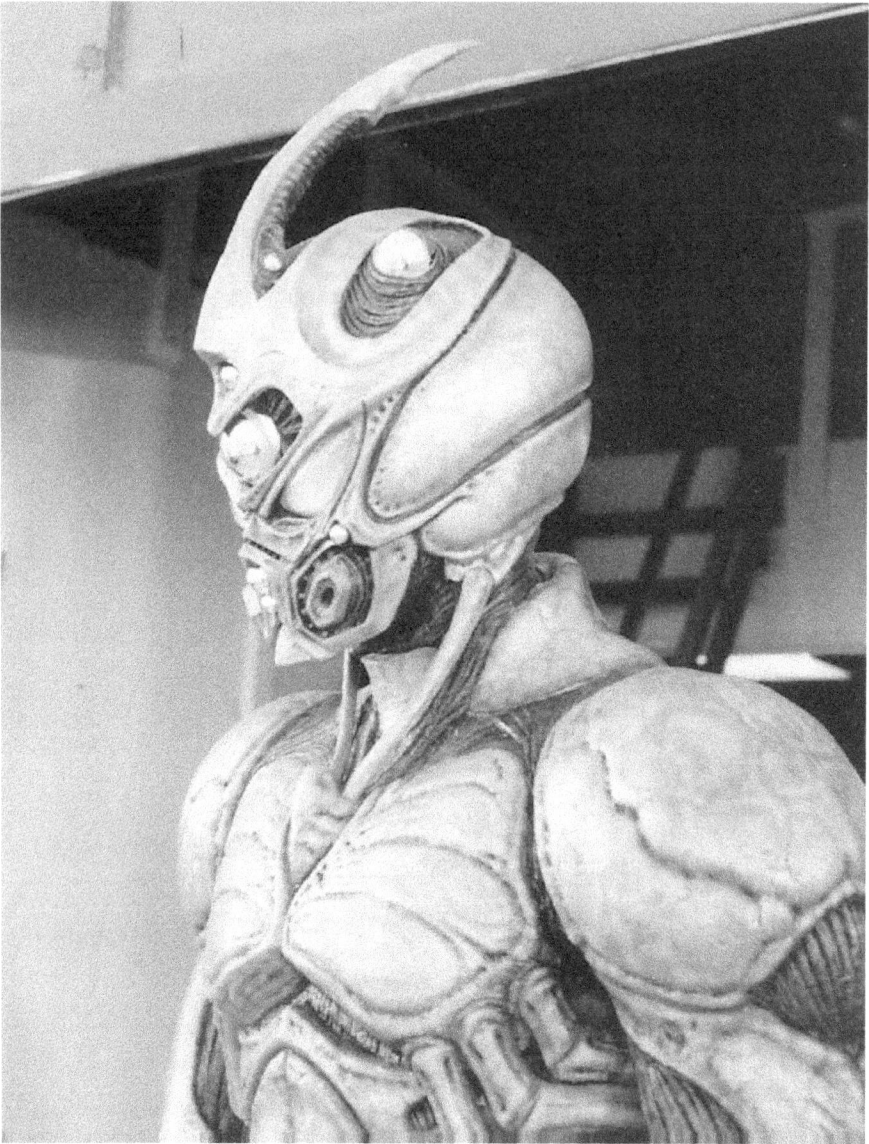

Close-up of the newly designed *Guyver: Dark Hero* suit (worn by main suit actor Anthony Houk), shot outside the effects shop. Although the changes are subtle, they are significantly different from the first Guyver suit. It casts a more stylistic and accurate manga/anime silhouette, has broader shoulders, and has a few aesthetic changes to the helmet, eyes, and body. Overall, a great evolution of an already impressive design. Photo taken by Eric Lasher and courtesy of Steve Wang.

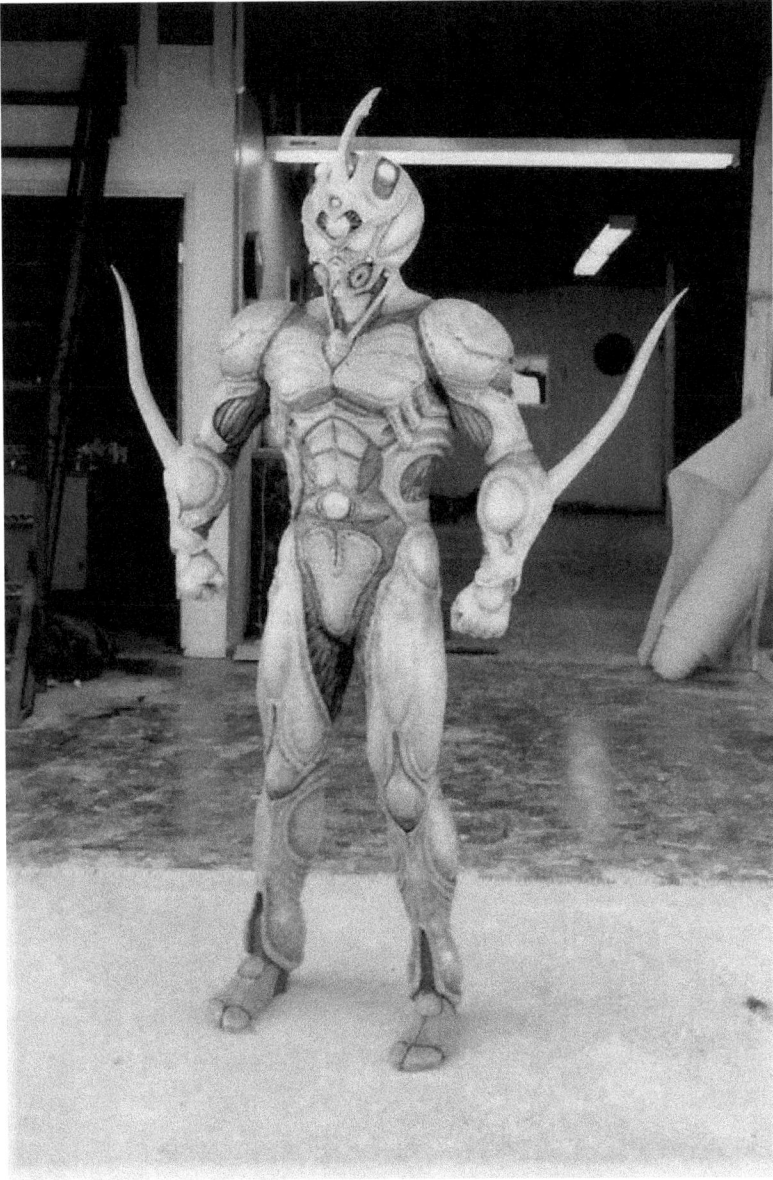

A full-length shot of Anthony Houk in the completed *Guyver: Dark Hero* suit. This would be the second time Houk would appear in a live action adaptation of a manga. The first would be in Clarence Fok's *The Dragon from Russia* (1990), which is a loose adaptation of Kazuo Koike and Ryoichi Ikegami's *Crying Freeman* manga. Houk would play the assassin Heidao. Photo courtesy of Steve Wang.

Another full-length shot of Anthony Houk in the finished
Guyver: Dark Hero suit. Houk would be the main suit performer and the
one to strike all the iconic poses. Photo courtesy of Steve Wang.

Chapter Eight

It Was the Summer of 93'

Part One: Budget Sets, Special Effects and More Miniature Madness!

Before shooting even began, Steve Wang, Wyatt Weed and the rest of the effects team would be working on the Guyver suit designs and creature effects, refining them by modifying what had originally been created and learnt while on *The Guyver* production.

"Before we had everybody hired, and before we started building sets, we had creatures to make. So, I started off again, like I work part of my day with Steve talking about production. And I'd spent part of my day making phone calls and coordinating things. And then I'd sit down and start sculpting. And what was interesting was the carryover, like, I was responsible, again, like everything I'd done on the first film I did on the second film, but to a greater degree," describes Weed.

"Steve was like, *'Hey, you did the blades on the first film. I want you to do the blades again, because you know how to do it, but make it different like this or make it different like that'*. So, because we had that continuity and had guys who did creatures on the first film, that when it came to the second film they were already ahead of the curve because they knew how to mold and do these creatures."

"I also want to focus on better design work," remembers Weed. "I want to focus on better mechanics; I want to focus on a better paint job. So even with less money, we got better results because half the crew had been there for the first film. I wanted the miniature work to be more ambitious and I wanted the sets to be more ambitious."

For the new suits, Wang would design and sketch each of the new Zoanoid designs, before handing them off to the creature crew – such as Moto Hata and Asao Goto – to sculpt and create the live action design. Of the newer Zoanoids designed by Wang, they included Sten; Mazzo; Marcus; Crane; and the Guyver Zoanoid Crane would ultimately metamorphosis into for the film's climax.

With Wang designing a large portion of the new creature designs and Moto Hata in charge of the creature shop, it fell to Asao Goto, Brian Wade, and a young Rob Freitas (who would help supervise on a lot of the Guyver and Zoanoid masks) to keep all the creature suits in tip-top shape during production, particularly as the suits themselves would be put through the wringer with stunts, debris, and environmental conditions (such as water and the blistering summer sun).

Goto would design the look of one Zoanoid in particular – the hulking, charging, rhinoceros looking Volker, which Guyver would have his fair share of run-ins with during the course of the film and had a few visual similarities to the manga (and anime) Zoanoid Gregole

"The design is all in the neck, like a big hunchback," says Goto about his Volker design. It's clear Goto wanted to make this particular Zoanoid an imposing and bizarre creature for the Guyver to fight, essentially a feral rhino. The creature effects team would also reuse one Zoanoid in particular for the majority of the new Zoanoid suits.

"We cast all the body suits for the Zoanoid from the Lisker Zoanoid," continues Goto. This helped for a number of reasons, not least because Brian Simpson returned to don several Zoanoid suits during production.

While there would be some reused molds for the creature effects, Wang decided to completely resculpt the original Guyver suit and create new proportions to make it a more faithful representation of both the manga and anime which had become more widely known since the original film's release.

Gone was the green pearlescent aesthetic, and in its place was a more anime-accurate colour palette with a striking silhouette that felt as though it was ripped from the pages of the original manga. Several decades on, it remains one of the best superhero suits seen in a live-action feature and is possibly the ultimate interpretation of The Guyver in physical form. The shoulders would be more rounded, while the waist would be more defined and slimmer, the eyes of the helmet would lose the insect-like movement from the first film, and the centre antenna (or fin) for the Guyver's helmet would not retract during fights.

"Steve liked the martial artist on the first film, but he was a shorter, stockier guy. On the second film, Steve was like '*I want a taller, skinnier guy, so I could make the actual Guyver proportions*', so we got a taller, skinnier guy, which led to the resculpt of the Guyver suit. The plates of armour that had been stored from the first film, we just kind of cleaned those up and repainted those and used those on the second film," recalls Weed.

"Steve did things within the design like elongated the legs and shorten the torso and made more of a V-shape to the upper body. So, there were all these subtleties that got applied to the second film, all these all-interesting things."

"We also had to make the malfunctioning Guyver Unit, and I would make that by using Ted's molds for the first Guyver Unit. So, I was able to take Ted's mold, Ted's ideas, and Ted's concepts for how he made the first one and adapt that into the next Guyver Unit, but also take it a little farther and add more detail and more functionality," says Weed.

There were also advancements in the suit technology and their inner workings from *The Guyver* to *Dark Hero*. "Steve was starting to come up with the idea of different densities of foam. Those are really something that's very advanced," remembers Weed.

"Steve's thought was, okay, if I could put like soft foam at the joints and firm foam on the parts that, like, if I could put firm foam in the bicep firm, put them in the forearms, but then mix soft foam with the rest of it, then I could have the flexibility where required and then the solid where I needed it. It was a really advanced concept."

"I don't think we ever got to go very far with it on *The Guyver*," continues Weed. "But what I know, he [Steve] was able to do it in the second film as we knew where things were going to rip and tear."

"Like with the Lisker suit, we knew, like the armpits were going to rip out on the various places on him. So going into *Dark Hero* there were reinforcements built, to stop ripping problems under the forearms and recurring ripping problems in the crotch. We went in and began laying in extra pieces of Lycra, we were going in and pre-tearing the suits and then redoing the foam latex in between."

Much like its predecessor, *Dark Hero* would utilize and maximize miniature effects work, inventive set design, and the reusing of molded assets to their advantage and to keep costs low without compromising on the vision Wang had for this grittier sequel. Even with the reuse of assets and tight planning, the budget was still capable of running over, as Weed describes.

"I know one of our early budget overruns was the sets because we really didn't know how the cave set was really quite extensive because it was. It's already Los Angeles in the summer, which in the summer is hot, but then you have the San Fernando Valley, which is even hotter. It's basically a lowland desert and it's very dry. Then we went and built a cave set inside the warehouse in the San Fernando Valley and then temperature-wise you've got hot, hotter, and hottest. By the time you got inside, the cave inside the warehouse in the valley was really freaking hot. Our budget would have gone out the window turning the air conditioning on at that warehouse. So, it was unbelievably hot," recalls Weed.

Despite it being the height of summer and with all the crew working in a hot location, the end result of the cave set, and all its inner corridors and little nooks, were a sight to behold, as Weed recalls. "It was quite the extensive main cave room with the tunnels and corridors going off, could find yourself moving through and wind your way through these corridors."

"It was designed to be a 360-degree set," remembers Weed. "So, when you walked into the cave, and you closed off all the access ways, close off the roof and you turn on the lighting, you could stand in the middle of this set, and you were no longer in the San Fernando Valley, you *were* in a cave."

As previously touched upon, budgetary constraints can lead to bouts of creativity, and this is more than apparent within the film industry. Looking back to sci-fi films of the 1970s, everyday objects were used to create sights never seen before, such as deconstructed model kits for the Death Star trench in *Star Wars: A New Hope* (1977); tubes and piping for parts of the Xenomorph from *Alien* (1979); or a beach ball with glued-on feet in *Dark Star* (1974). They may seem antiquated now, but they are no less creative in a modern filmmaking setting.

This meant building the cave set had to be done within budget and typically the standard way of constructing a film set had to be adapted to said budget.

"Typically, the way this is done is you build a framework and then you bring in people with these big foam guns. With this liquid foam you spray the framework and then the foam expands a little bit. Once it dries it has a kind of a bubbly look to it. So, that's ridiculously expensive and it's also not what we wanted, particularly if we wanted a realistic looking cave," says Weed.

'During the R&D process we literally spent like a week or two just doing different mixes for the walls and coming up with different ideas. We finally decided to mix plaster with tint, like a little bit of black and vermiculite. You'd mix all this with a big power mixer and then people would literally go out to build the framework of the set, which was made with wood and plywood, and we shaped it all with ribbing."

"Then we took this construction paper, which is designed to go on the side of houses, it's a paper with a chicken wire frame, and we took that, and we molded it, shaped it, and pulled it. Think just old-fashioned *Star Trek* underground sets. We basically hand-sculpted, hand-stapled, and hand-nailed all this chicken wire frame to the inside of this thing. And then just a huge Art Department crew of like young cheap labourers went in and just slathered this great plaster vermiculite all over," recalls Weed.

"For the actual stalactites and stalagmites, we'd mix up liquid plaster and we literally get big buckets full of plaster, and start dribbling it on the walls, on the stairs and on the sound. So, the cave was virtually hand-built and hand-painting. We'd be in there with those big hand pump sprayers used for weeding and we'd use them for spraying by putting paint in those things. So, we'd mix it up, pump it up, and then you'd go out there and you can spray entire walls."

This feels almost Roger Corman-esque in its budget philosophy. Use cheap, readily available household items and create bizarre and unique textures, just by experimenting. Because the supplies were cheap, it allows the flexibility to experiment without the fear of it eating into costs. Which in turn means more freedom to be creative. How Wang, Weed, and production designer George Peirson used equally cheap materials, ultimately allowed them to craft a more organic, otherworldly visual aesthetic and stay within budget.

"For the alien spaceship sets, we had ideas on how we were going to do it," says Weed. "But how do you do organic with no money? If you stop and think about organic, weird, bizarre freeform shapes, that stuff is all typically very expensive. Well, we started thinking back to the old 1960s *Fantastic Voyage* film, and we started playing with plastics. So, we got out like thick, 5-by-5 mil sheets, called Visqueen which are polyurethane sheets. We'd suspend the sheets and then we'd go at them with heat guns and blow torches, or we'd take a blowtorch to it and then spritz some water on it and then go tortured against pebbly textures, or we'd stretch pieces of plastic, and then we melt the edges and burn holes in it. So, we got all that weird, amorphous translucent walls and stuff with layers of plastic. And that's all it was," recalls Weed.

It all came down to research and development with Weed and Peirson, who would experiment with the materials to get the desired results. Looking back at the sets from the film over 30 years later, they retain a marvellously schlocky visual that only adds to *Dark Hero*'s charm._

"The alien sets were shockingly cheap at times; we'd literally just invent things as we went and work on things until they looked right. Like we knew Steve would do a sketch and we had an idea, but we didn't exactly know how we were going to do it," recalls Weed.

"Like are we going to cast this or are we gonna make it out of foam, or are we gonna make it out of plastic, we didn't know. So, me, George, and the art director [Coburn Hawk] would go out to the soundstage and in the corner, we had built these wooden frames. I can remember this like it was yesterday, all three of us were standing out there and go, 'Here's a piece of carpet, let's set that on fire, spray and add plastic melt holes in that spread'. Here's this, here's that and we literally messed around with stuff until we came up with that plastic look for the alien membrane."

"Then there's some people doing foam construction and making these weird organic shapes, and we're like, '*Okay, that's gonna be our alien structures*'. So, brought in these guys who were building foam doorways in a H.R. Giger style and then after putting latex on it, we'd paint it," recalls Weed.

"There's this big, long corridor inside the ship. It's just an arched, beautiful alien interior corridor with like these white translucent openings, and we built that out in the parking lot. It was a big wooden abstract frame structure and then we'd make these organic, curved surfaces in it, which was a lot of fun."

"We started going and scrapping all this foam padding from when people pulled up the carpets in their houses. Basically, it was foam padding underneath the foam padding. So, we were dumpster diving all over the San Fernando Valley and bringing back truckloads of old used floor foam. This is another thing that made this film look so amazing for less money, because we would literally build sets sometimes for the cost of the wooden structure."

Putting all of that into perspective and how the production design crew, along with Weed, would reclaim old and unused materials, it makes the inside of the alien ship and its corridor all the more impressive despite its minuscule budget.

"If you stop and think about, making a 30-foot-long, organic alien corridor when you have no money, it's kind of daunting, but we never looked at it like that, and it was never scary. It was always '*We'll figure it out. We'll stay late on Friday night, order a pizza, and get some beer, and just figure it out*', and that's how a lot of the film was," says Weed.

Thankfully the crew knew when to take a step back and enjoy the time on the film, even when no work was being done. "There were often times where production was over, but the party just got started. It would move into the cave set, or into my office, or sometimes the alien set," recalls Weed.

"But there were also nights where people spent the night on the Guyver set, not because they wanted to, but because they had to avoid driving home that night. I remember either the art director, Coburn, or the production designer, George, got so busy and so tired working such long hours. Under the cave set there were these huge recessives that were accessible from the back side. People started building these little apartments under there. Like they put in a sleeping bag and some clothes, and a little light. There were literally people who didn't go home for days and just work, and work, and work, then climb under the set and go to sleep. One of the guys on the crew even set up a solar shower out in the back parking lot, so he could go out and take a shower."

The newly acquired living space became affectionately known by the crew who used it as *Camp Guyver*.

"There was no reason to go home, as a 27-year-old working in Los Angeles on a film, you're like, '*Yeah, I'm living the dream. I'm working 24 hours to do a movie, man, look at the dream*'. We were young and foolish and just had endless amounts of energy."

"It was crazy, really crazy. That's the difference between the first and the second film. Spend the night on the set? Are you insane? It's six o'clock, get the hell out of here. But on *Dark Hero* we had none of those limitations. If somebody wanted to stay all night and work, well, we're not getting paid for it, but I don't care as they want to finish this thing, so as long as they were safe, they could stay to get this one wall finished."

"I'm like, '*Okay, I'll pay for the pizza. You just keep working*'. And that was the difference right there. The first *Guyver* was a labour, whereas the second *Guyver* was a labour of love. It was a party, an incredibly difficult, hot, and sweaty party, and sometimes it was horrible, but it was still a party. And that's like the whole difference between the two films; the first one was business, the second one was passion," enthuses Weed.

The cave set was constructed as an optical illusion of sorts to maximise both space and budget, clearly to trick the audience into thinking it was bigger than what had been constructed. Essentially, movie magic at its finest. "The entrance to the spacecraft went back about 10 or 12 feet down. It was sort of forced perspective, but then it just kind of stopped," remembers Weed.

"There was enough room for three or four people to move into it. You'd then cut to a different part which was the interior spacecraft corridor and that was a separate set out in the parking lot. The interior corridor was kind of neat because it was sort of a big, long arc, where if you stood in the middle, you could see either end. But if you stood at either end, all you could see was the curve. So, depending on how you shot it, you could avoid giving away its length."

"Then I think we had like two off shoots that again would go like five-feet off in separate directions. So, you could walk up and turn a corner, and then if you flipped the angles, it would look like a different part. Essentially it looks like infinite amounts of quarters, kind of the *Star Trek* effect, where you could make it look like you were going anywhere."

Wyatt Weed with Production Designer George Pierson as they test out various plastics to create the alien textures for the inside of the Guyver Ship. Although not seen in these photos, Coburn Hawk would be the art director for *Guyver: Dark Hero*. Photo courtesy of Wyatt Weed.

Wyatt Weed, Steve Wang, and George Pierson discussing production design. Photo courtesy of Wyatt Weed.

A shot of the full-size alien ship face (in the cave set), before it was covered over with a fake rock surface that the actors would uncover during the digging montage. Photo courtesy of Wyatt Weed.

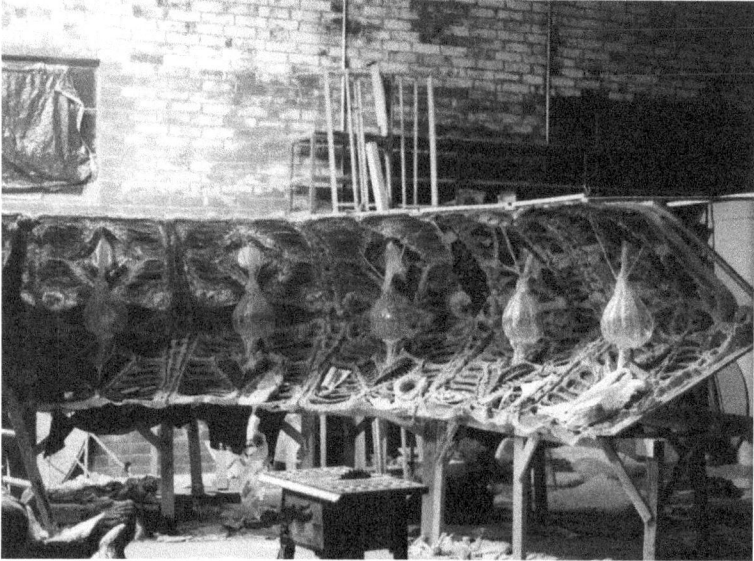

Set construction of the prehistoric growth chamber (seen during the
caveman flashback sequence). Photo courtesy of Wyatt Weed.

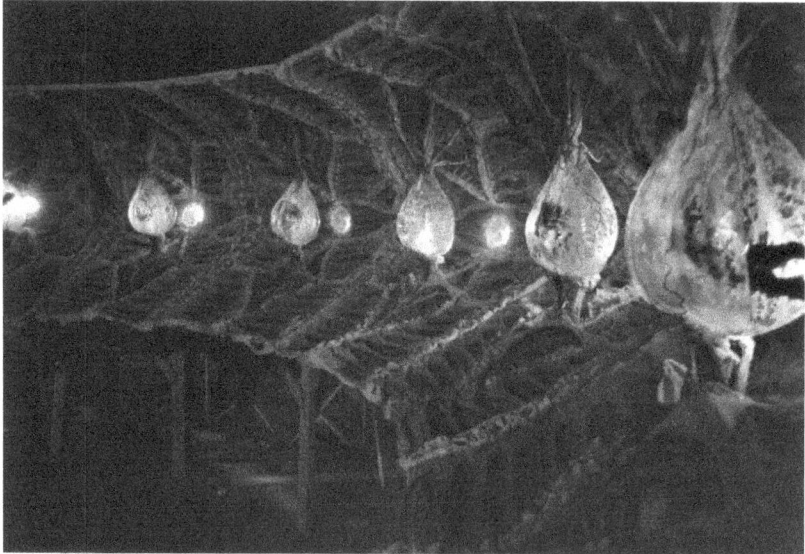

The prehistoric growth chamber, fully lit for use in the
flashback sequence. Photo courtesy of Wyatt Weed.

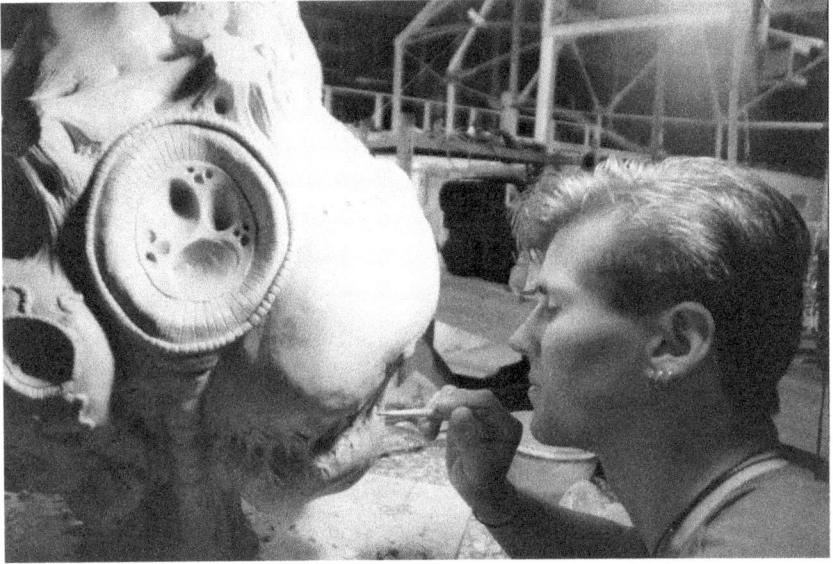

Dean Satkowski sculpting the Guyver ship heart, which was done as a foreground miniature. Photo courtesy of Wyatt Weed.

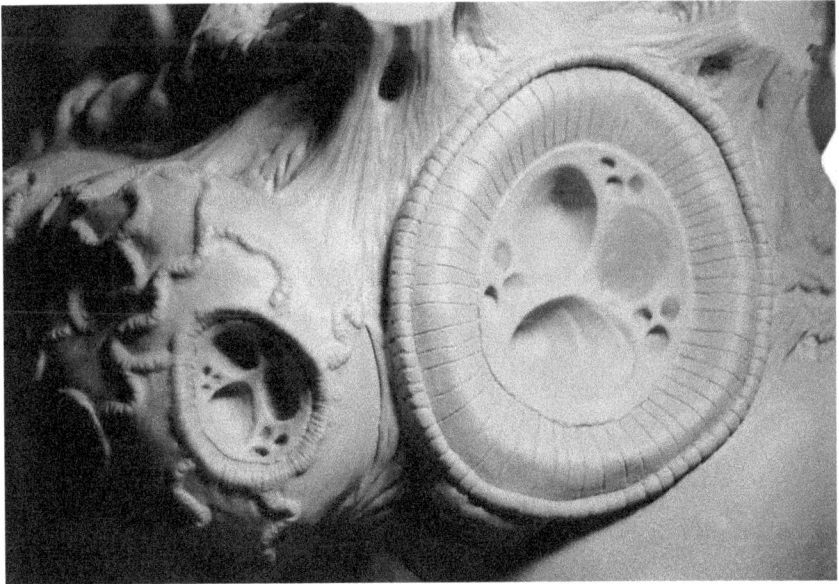

Close-up of Satkowski's ship heart sculpt. Photo courtesy of Wyatt Weed.

Another shot of the sculpted ship heart. Photo courtesy of Wyatt Weed.

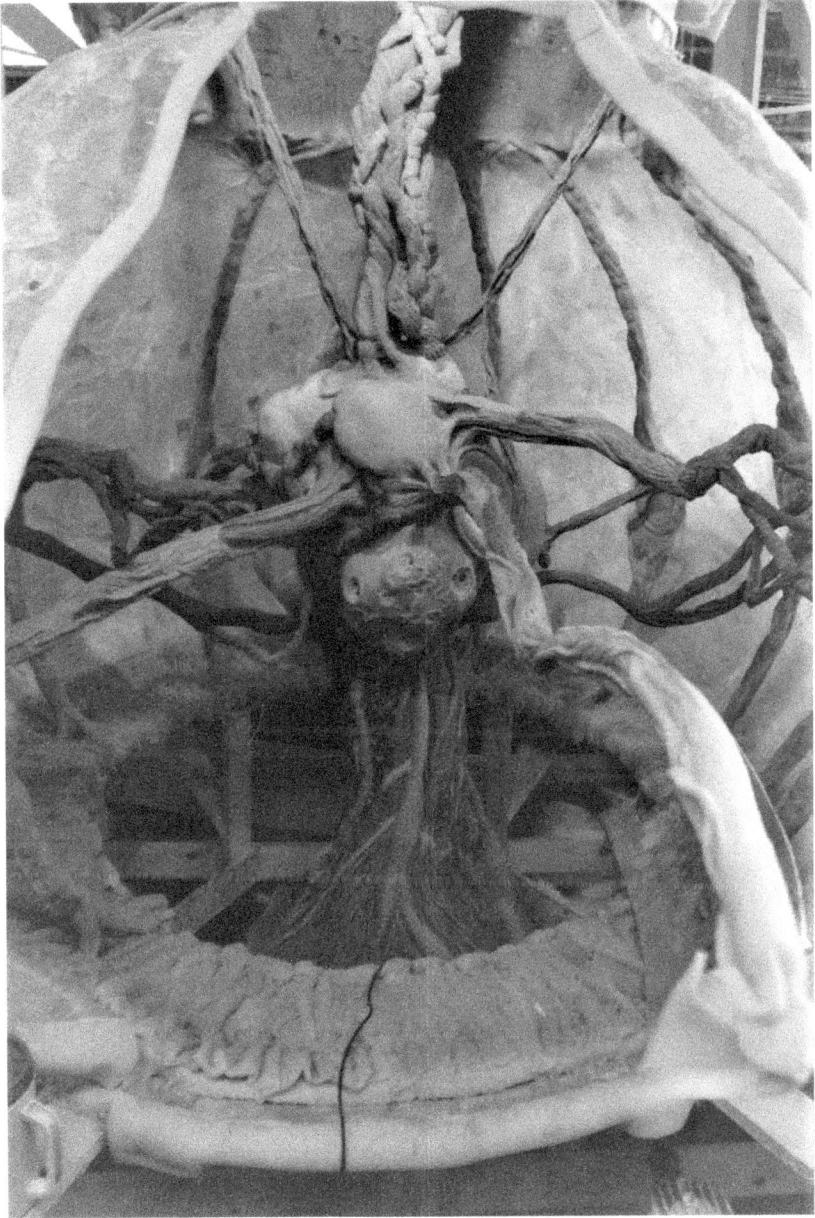

The finished and painted sculpt of the heart. The aesthetic
continues to expand on the bio-organic nature of Guyver's
origins. Photo courtesy of Wyatt Weed.

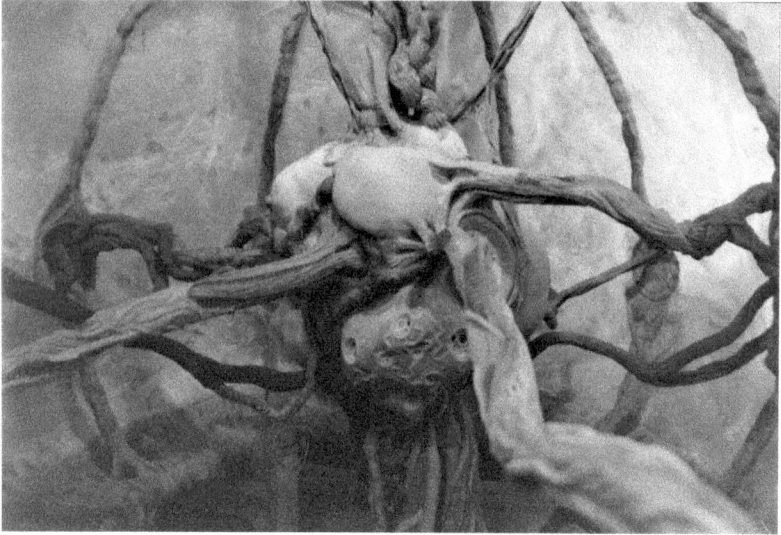

Close-up of the painted heart sculpt within the surrounding
ship chamber. Photo courtesy of Wyatt Weed.

Once again, painstakingly crafted miniatures would be implemented similarly to their use in *The Guyver,* but to a much greater extent to capture a grander sense of scale and scope. Wang would again enlist the expertise of Weed, Asao Goto, and miniature effects cinematographer Ted Rae to capture the detailed models and miniatures.

Specific moments that would have otherwise been impossible with the limited budget include several action sequences. In particular, the instance where a jeep falls off a cliff; a land mass of prehistoric Los Angeles covered in Guyver ships; the lower part of the cave towards the end of the film as the Guyver ship takes off; and the exploding mountain top following that.

The miniature jeep would be used in several shots during the Zoanoid attack sequence and would be exceptionally detailed, much like the previous miniatures from *The Guyver.* The sheer level of minutiae for its additions, such as the sticks of dynamite, dirt in the tire grooves, and full canister on the back of the vehicle, showed a level of detail not seen in low-budget features like this. While the real jeep would be used for the pre-cliff fall sequence and part of the flip, the miniature was so detailed and pretty much identical to its full-scale counterpart that unless you were looking, it would be doubtful a viewer would notice which was the full-scale vehicle and which was miniature.

The sequence would combine several elements to achieve its action-packed moments. For the first part of the sequence, the real jeep would be lifted with superhuman-like strength. The technique used would be familiar to anyone who grew up with classic 1970s sci-fi television, for instance *The Six Million Dollar Man* (1974-1978) or *The Incredible Hulk* (1978-1982), as Weed describes.

"For the vehicle being raised by the Marcus Zoanoid, we used these hydraulically powered scissor-like devices. You had to sort of dig a rut in the road and bury one end of the scissor device. And then the other part of the scissor device would like clamp to the frame on the bottom of the vehicle. And when you apply the hydraulic, or the pneumatic pressure, those big clamps would spread. And because of the leverage, and the point you were at, it would literally pick up the part of the car. You either block the back tires, or you block the front tires, and you put these lifts under there and create a teeter totter effect."

"For the shot inside, where you see the driver and the background is tumbling, we took a large piece of foam core, and put crinkle paper and dirt and roots and grass and stuff on it and made a fake cliff wall. We were actually out in the parking lot of the studio shooting that. So, we'd start rotating that background piece and the guys in the car acted out like it was falling. That quick brief cutaway is the vehicle sitting on the ground and the background outside is rotating," says Weed.

Following those shots, the miniature was used as an insert of it falling towards the camera, and again this was done in the parking lot ahead of the miniature cliff fall. Weed would be the one pulling the jeep away from camera, staying out of shot as he lifted it up exposing its undercarriage. This, mixed with occasional insert shots of the jeep rocking, created by Weed literally shaking the miniature that was laying on a table outside, all add to a delightfully low-tech approach in several shots.

As previously mentioned, the jeep miniature was only used for part of the flip but, as Weed describes, they did actually flip the real jeep onto its roof to get several shots which appear in the film. All of which led to its own issues. "We had to actually take the full-sized Jeep and flip it," recalls Weed.

"What ended up happening was, because we were running out of light and things were getting a little crazy, Steve got the entire crew to surround the jeep, which was like 15 of us, and we lifted the Jeep up, pull the jacks out, then lifted and flipped this Jeep up ourselves. Flipping it sounds easy enough, but the tires start to rock, and things start to shift and when you get a car high enough up at an angle, it tends to want to roll away from you."

"It got very dangerous as the car almost got away from us a couple of times, so imagine like 15 guys trying to flip something that probably weighs a ton and a half. At a certain point everybody just kind of had to let go and walk away as the thing fell back on its own. It was probably, maybe, our dumbest and most foolish moment," says Weed.

"Thankfully, it worked out well and nobody got hurt, but we left the Jeep up there for a couple of days because we broke it and let it crash on its roof. And of course, the oil drained out of the engine and all the fluid spilled out, and this is in a national park. So, we leave a flipped-over vehicle on a road in a national park in California, with oil and motor fluids flowing onto the pathway. So, we get our butts chewed a little bit by the Park Service. We sent some guys up there and I think the tow truck was able to flip it back over and then one of our art department people went up there and had some buckets and a shovel and scooped up all the oil and scooped out the motor fluid," recalls Weed.

When it came to the jeep falling off the cliff and towards its explosive finale, a scale miniature of the cliff was constructed in the parking lot of the studio, with the jeep miniature placed at the top and then shot at a low angle as it teetered on the edge, replete with small rocks that simulated the cliff debris, to complete the effect.

The jeep miniature was then pushed from behind the cliff miniature by a hidden Weed, to simulate the Zoanoids being thrown against it. Following the fall, a separate shot was set up for the wrecked jeep, leading to the explosive climax for this impressive sequence and miniature.

Behind-the-scenes shot of the miniature jeep and cliff set piece
being ready to shoot. Photo courtesy of Wyatt Weed

Low angle shot of the miniature jeep and cliff prior to
shooting the sequence. Photo courtesy of Wyatt Weed

Miniature jeep being prepped for its cliff tumble.
Photo courtesy of Wyatt Weed

Miniature shooting crew outside the L.A. studio, post-jeep fall, on a
sweltering August day. Photo courtesy of Wyatt Weed

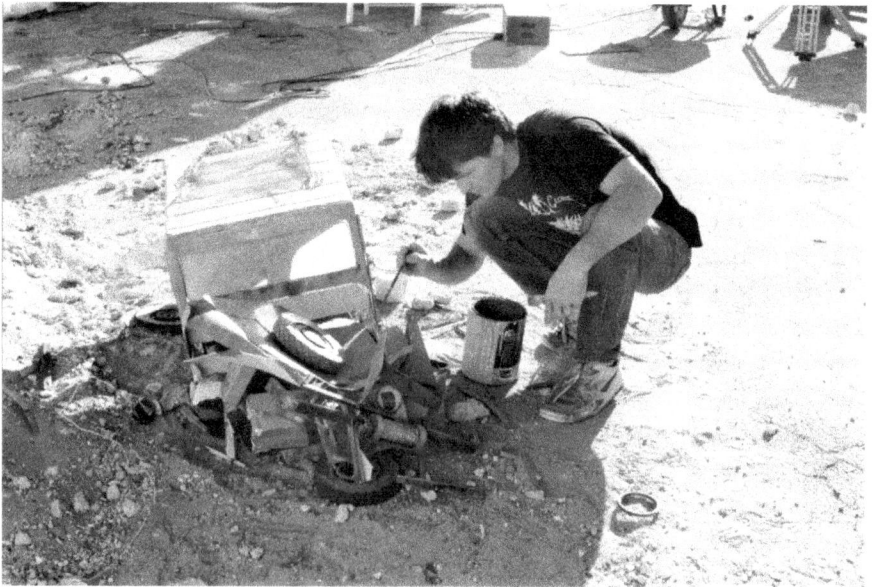

Weed touches up some paint detail on the wrecked jeep miniature
(made to 1/4 scale). Photo courtesy of Wyatt Weed

Steve Wang behind the camera and in amongst the fiery action for the miniature jeep's explosive send-off. Photo courtesy of Wyatt Weed

Wang films the final smouldering embers as they burn on the miniature jeep. Photo courtesy of Wyatt Weed

Where the miniature effects were most extensively used was for the prehistoric Guyver ship sequences. For this, a scale model of a prehistoric California was created, with miniature Guyver ships created by Weed and Goto (who also created the larger scale ships in the shot), and hand-painted backgrounds detailing different environments or periods of time were used to help create depth and a sense of scale.

The final few insert shots during the climax of the film are also miniature shots; in this case the bottom portion of the Guyver ship in the dig-site before it explodes and takes off into the atmosphere. Again, this was shot by Ted Rae and his miniature effects crew, with a few lights, clever camera-shaking, and miniature set destruction used to simulate the ship's moment.

Whether watching it unfold in real-time or just looking at still images, the detailed use of miniatures, for a variety of instances, invokes the spirit of effects work found in countless Tokusatsu properties during the 1970s and 1980s. The Tokusatsu filmmaking sensibility emanates off the screen despite *Dark Hero* being a Western feature. It's possibly one of the many reasons why it continues to have such a lasting impression on viewers, particularly those interested in more tangible, low-tech aspects of filmmaking.

Outside of the extensive miniature use, there were also several other low-tech effects called upon during certain sequences. For Asao Goto, if he wasn't working on effects shots with the miniature effects team, he would be found supervising the creature suits and maintaining them with Rob Freitas. Goto would also do a handful of incidental, low-tech effects for a couple of shots that ranged from Volker's snapped fingers during the fight with Guyver; Sean's pulsating neck-ports, which was a simple bladder effect; and the wonderfully entertaining exploding eyes of Volker during the aforementioned fight.

Clearly, Goto was bringing to *Dark Hero* all of his crafty expertise from working on Tokusatsu shows in Japan, which in turn helps to give *Dark Hero* that unmistakable heightened, cartoonishly violent reality found in Tokusatsu shows like *Kamen Rider*.

Low-budget creativity was also used during the final moments of the intense Guyver and Volker fight, where the audience is treated to snapped fingers pumping out blood, culminating in some exploding eyeballs for the physically battered Volker.

"The fingers had wire and tubing inside the hand. They were moveable, so when they were bent or snapped, blood started pumping out of them. The suit hands had a cut in them to allow it to pump out," remembers Goto.

According to Goto, the popping eyes was done by one of the special effects team, where they used small amounts of gunpowder and fake blood to create the explosions of the Volker's eyes from Guyver's laser. Two of the gnarliest effects in the film were also some of the most simplistic.

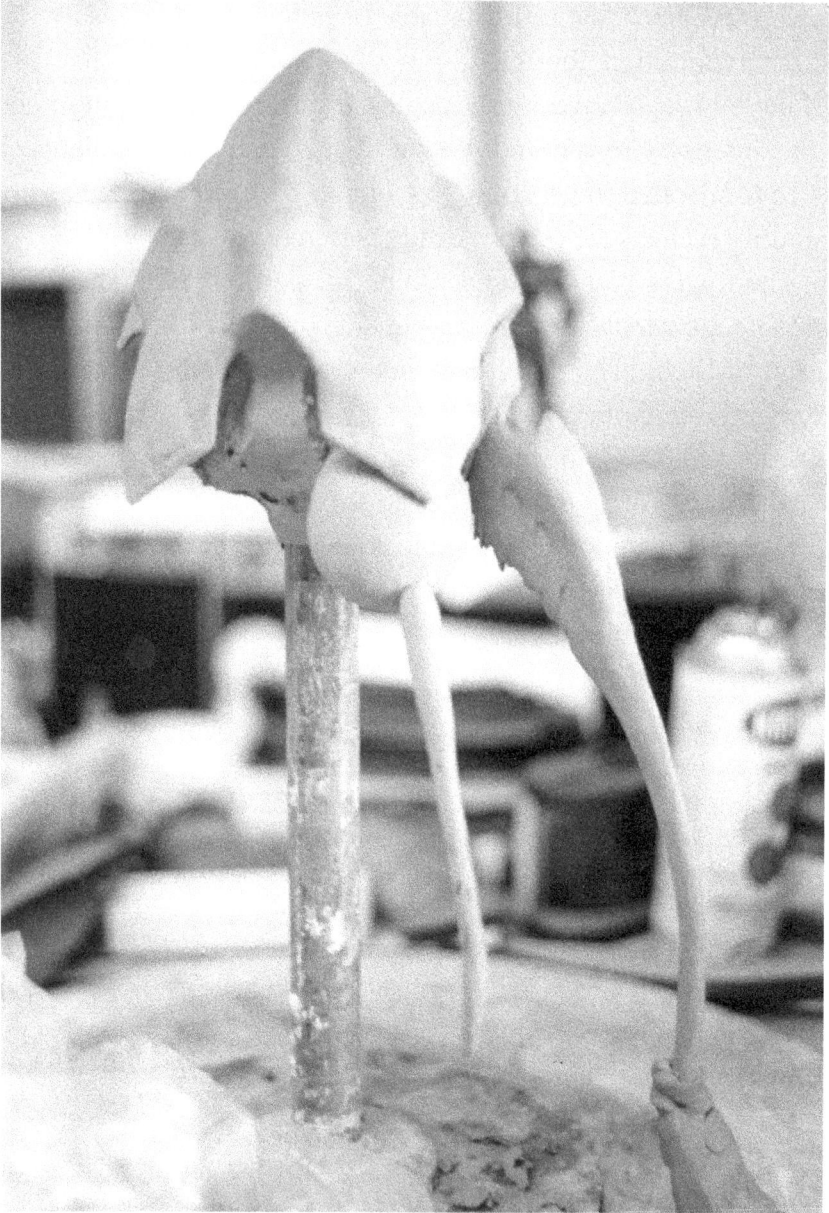

Weed's prototype miniature sculpts for one of the Prehistoric Guyver ships, that was ultimately not used. Photo courtesy of Wyatt Weed

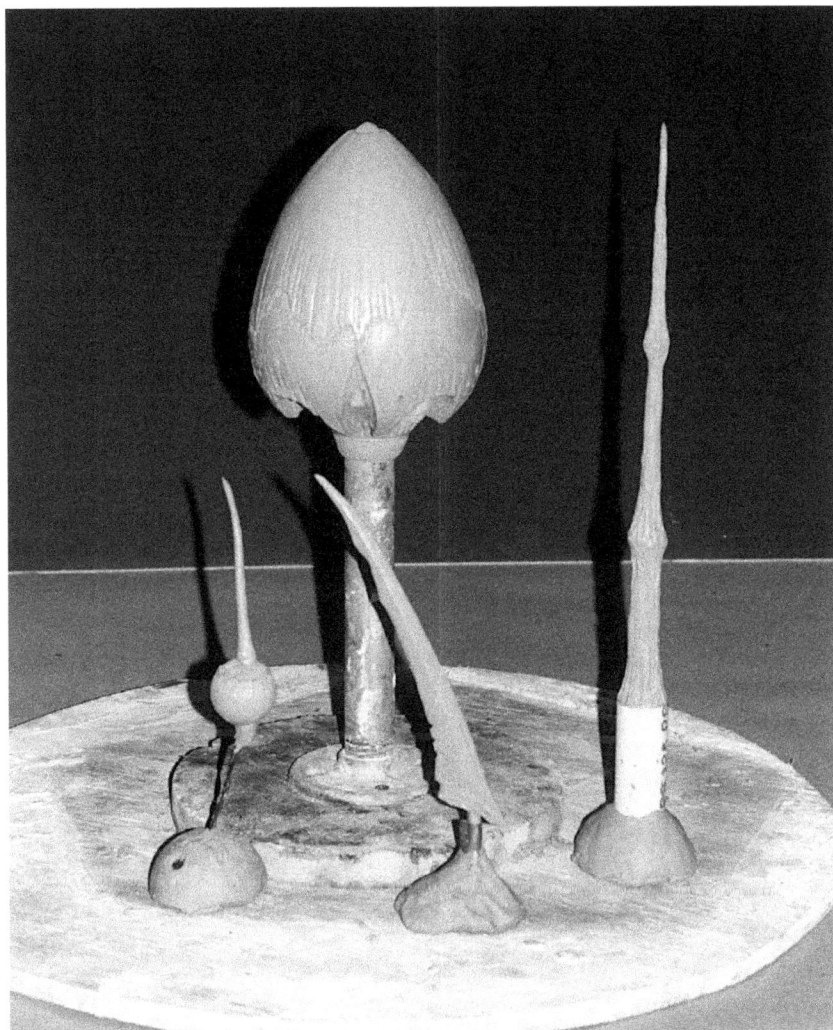

The miniature Prehistoric Guyver Ship sculpt that was used.
This was again sculpted by Weed. Photo courtesy of Wyatt Weed

Additional sculpting detail of the miniature Guyver ship
in the mold. Photo courtesy of Wyatt Weed

Asao Goto adds further sculpting detail to several miniature
Guyver ships. Photo courtesy of Wyatt Weed

A fully completed model for Weed's miniature Guyver Ship
(before it is painted). Photo courtesy of Wyatt Weed

Asao Goto begins work on assembling his Guyver ship, stopping
for a brief moment to model the latest in high Guyver fashion
accessories. Photo courtesy of Wyatt Weed

Asao Goto adds detail to his large-scale model of the Guyver ship.
Photo courtesy of Wyatt Weed

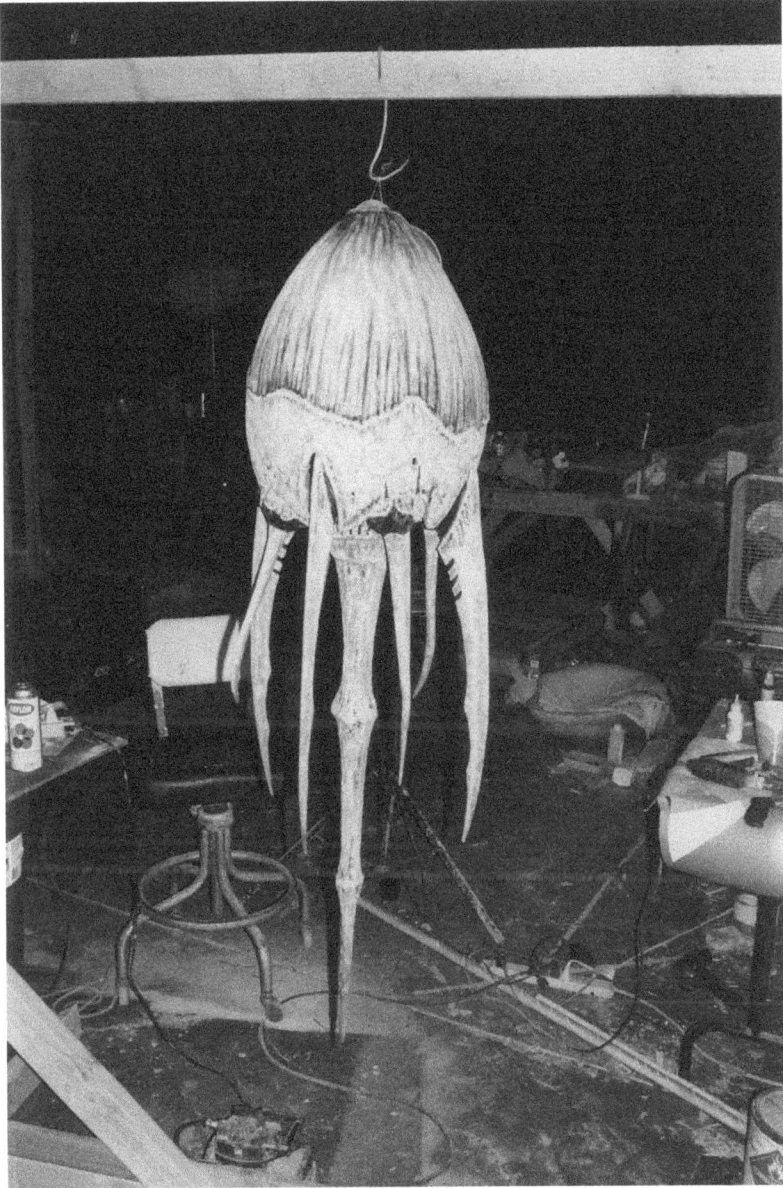

The finished large-scale Guyver ship model (with all ship parts such as the tail and leg struts attached plus added coats of paint) hanging in the effects studio ready for the explosive mountain climax. According to Weed, the model was around 1/72 scale. Photo courtesy of Wyatt Weed

Early prehistoric landscape with a friendly warning (in French) from the crew not to use this as a table. Photo courtesy of Wyatt Weed

The background for the prehistoric Guyver ship flashback during the early stages of creation. Photo courtesy of Wyatt Weed

The completed prehistoric landscape set, being prepped for a shot with assorted sizes of scale Guyver ships. The lava flow was bottom lit, with a flame bar placed in front of the camera to help create ripples of heat for the shot. Photo courtesy of Wyatt Weed

Close-up of the prehistoric landscape prior to shooting.
Photo courtesy of Wyatt Weed

Close-up of the prehistoric landscape and Guyver ships with
Steve Wang setting up the correct angle for the upcoming shot.
Photo courtesy of Wyatt Weed

Behind-the-scenes shot of the miniature effects crew ready to shoot the
prehistoric landscape sequence. Photo courtesy of Wyatt Weed

Weed preps the background of the landscape for a different and less prehistoric, time period. Photo courtesy of Wyatt Weed

Close-up shot of several Guyver ships during one of the flashback sequences. Photo courtesy of Wyatt Weed

A Guyver ship lays in smouldering disarray for a scene. Taken from the flashback where the destroyed Guyver ships litter the land before the remaining ships decide to escape. Photo courtesy of Wyatt Weed

Asao Goto tends to one of the miniature Guyver ships
in-between shots. Photo courtesy of Wyatt Weed

A behind-the-scenes shot of the aged Guyver ship.
Photo courtesy of Wyatt Weed

Asao Goto rigs a number of wires to pull the smaller Guyver ships out of the ground, giving the illusion of self-guided flight. The ships were mounted on bungee wires so they could be moved upward. Photo courtesy of Wyatt Weed

Asao Goto and another effects crew member survey the Guyver ship miniatures mid-flight. Photo courtesy of Wyatt Weed

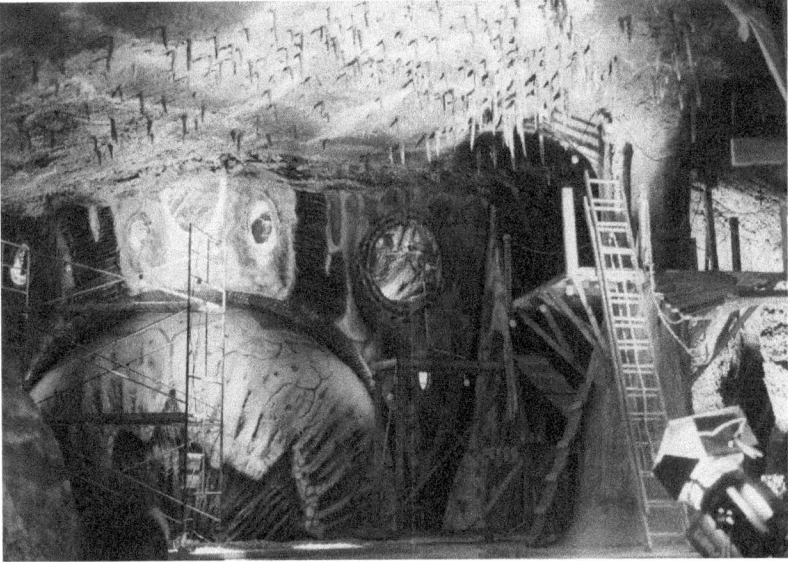

A close-up shot of the miniature underground cave set which showcases part of the dig site and lower half of the Guyver ship. Photo courtesy of Wyatt Weed

Lighting and a few additional corrections are made to the miniature set ahead of shooting this sequence from the film's climax. Photo courtesy of Wyatt Weed

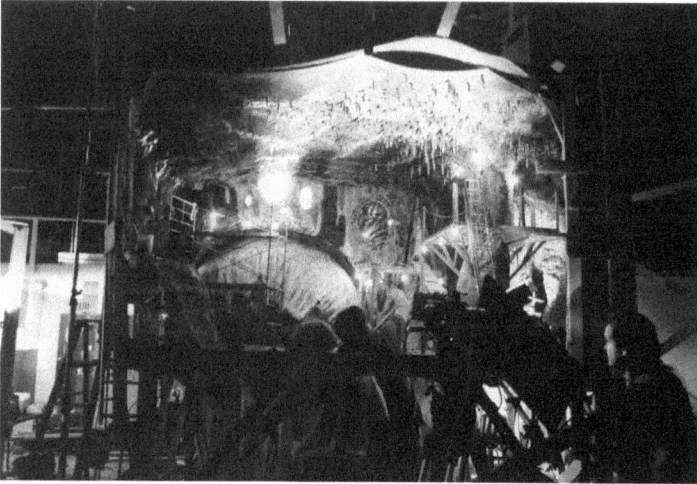

Shooting the first part of the Guyver ship's exit out of the lower part of the mountain. This 1/6th scale ship (created by Wyatt Weed, Dean Satkowski, and Asao Goto) would move during the shot and a fire extinguisher was be used to simulate the smoke/exhaust from under the ship. Photo courtesy of Wyatt Weed

Clever lighting, camera wobble, miniature light bulb explosions, and breakable pieces of set were combined to give the impression of the Guyver ship waking up and working its way out of the mountain. When edited together with the live-action footage of the actors, it's hard to tell this was miniature work (again due to the exceptional detail put into the set by the effects crew). Photo courtesy of Wyatt Weed

Wyatt Weed preps the large-scale miniature mountain set for shooting the film's climax. "This was a wood frame with a fiber carpet backing, covered in plaster and then the fiber was teased back up like grass. The top was open, and an air cannon was placed below it. Rocks and debris were placed in the cannon and then fired into the air," recalls Weed. Photo courtesy of Wyatt Weed

Lisa Hannan preps part of the mountain set ready for shooting. Photo courtesy of Wyatt Weed

Asao Goto keeps watch over his large scale Guyver ship miniature, with executive producer Ken Iyadomi (the legendary producer of *Ghost in the Shell* (1995), *Ninja Scroll* (1993), and *Macross Plus* (1994)) and director Steve Wang (from behind). Photo courtesy of Wyatt Weed

A number of crew members, including director Steve Wang and Wyatt Weed, discuss the upcoming shot in the parking lot where the miniature climax is shot. Photo courtesy of Wyatt Weed

Wyatt Weed preps some additional debris on top of the mountain miniature ahead of the Guyver ship flying out of it for the climax. Photo courtesy of Wyatt Weed

Smoke and debris erupts from the miniature mountain set for the film's climax. Photo courtesy of Wyatt Weed

Another shot of the Guyver ship exiting the miniature mountain set with a hefty dose of smoke and debris. The crew would shoot the sequence at 250 fps (frames-per-second) to get the dramatic shot and would use a white bridal veil to help to create a sort of atmospheric haze as the Guyver ship exited the mountain. The Guyver ship would be pulled on a wire from an overhead stand (out of shot). Photo courtesy of Wyatt Weed

Chapter Nine

It Was the Summer of 93'

Part Two: Location, Location, Location

Following pre-production, principal photography would take place during the height of summer 1993; on location in and around California from the Van Nuys warehouse location for the cave set; a brief stint at the City of Industry; to all the way to Angeles National Forest or Angeles Crest as it's known (located in the San Gabriel and Sierra Pelona Mountains in Los Angeles County).

"I believe we started shooting in June/July 1993. I'm not aware of the exact number of days, but I want to say we shot off and on over the course of probably eight to 10 weeks. And we took a bit of a break as well," recalls Weed.

Unlike the first Guyver film, *Dark Hero* would utilize more location shooting, in much the same way Wang & Co. had done previously for *Kung Fu Rascals*. Historically, shows such as the various Showa era *Kamen Rider* series' *(1971-1975)*; *Kikaider* (1972-1974); *and Himitsu Sentai Gorenger* (1975-1977) would be shot predominantly in the Japanese countryside due to budget constraints, and *Dark Hero* would be no different. The use of more extensive location shooting not only kept costs down but also ensured that *Dark Hero* would follow the Tokusatsu tradition and aesthetic which helped capture the imagination of the Tokusatsu-loving crew during their younger years.

Due to the limited budget, interior locations were kept to a minimum and included Sean's apartment, the hand-built interiors of the inside and outside of the alien ship, the excavation and dig site and the impressive industrial steel plant used during the opening sequence.

The steel plant factory used for this sequence and subsequent fight between Guyver and the drug dealer's goons, was a sight to behold and an impressive get for the production, as Weed recalls.

"It was an old factory in the City of Industry, and I don't believe it was operational. It wasn't condemned or shut down; they just weren't working at the time. It was one of these things of like, '*We're done making the orders that we need to make, so we're going to shut this down for a few weeks*', so it was available, we still had power, we could still turn on the lights, and we could still operate the overhead crane. But it was unbelievably godawful dirty, like they were processing and manufacturing and grinding and drilling. So, every surface was covered with black grit and metal, fibre, and dust."

Guyver suit actor Anthony Houk stands on his marker ready for the upcoming shot. Photo courtesy of Steve Wang and taken by on set photographer Eric Lasher

Anthony Houk (in Guyver costume) in a fearsome pose as the new improved Guyver makes his entrance. Photo courtesy of Steve Wang and taken by on set photographer Eric Lasher

Anthony Houk (in Guyver costume minus helmet) strikes a pose for photographer Eric Lasher as Asao Goto makes some paint adjustments to the Guyver suit in-between shots at the steel plant. A young Rob Freitas hangs onto the Guyver helmet. Photo courtesy of Steve Wang and taken by on set photographer Eric Lasher

Weed ended up wearing a lot of different work hats during *Dark Hero*'s production, with each role bringing different levels of responsibility.

"So, I was the associate producer and also the second unit director, those were my primary duties. But I also worked a lot on the miniatures. Now I don't mean to take away from him, but there was a guy called Dean Satkowski and he was the official miniatures supervisor, and I was sort of overseeing him and the miniature crew. So, I was kind of manager/supervisor again, and I've worked on a lot of the miniatures, but because I had second unit and associate producer duties, he [Dean] was officially the day-to-day supervisor," recalls Weed.

"And then, as the associate producer my main responsibility was being there on set every day, working with the production designer, and making sure those sets got finished once we dove into set construction in like May and June."

"And this was another case of, you know, I had two titles, but I was out there helping make the cave, I was out there figuring out how to make realistic looking stalactites and stalagmites. I was there on the spaceship sets trying to figure out how to make the spaceship sets look cool," remembers Weed.

The camp set was also built from scratch in Angeles Crest.

"The set for the campsite was up in the mountains and what's interesting there is we literally had a campsite with real tents and real fire and real pathways and everything. And then up above the camp set there was the entrance to the cave, which we built out on the mountain side. We created it in wood and wire construction and plastered it all in. And it would go about five or 10 feet back."

"So up in the mountains, you could literally film the actors walking into the cave in the Angeles Crest Forest and then cut to them entering the cave set in the San Fernando Valley. They'd enter the cave set, walk around the cave set, go into the spaceship, which then was the corridor out in the back parking lot, and then depending on where you went next to the cave, we had the control metal area, we had the main huge alien control centre. And that was where the main sets were," says Weed. Editing would then seamlessly blend the locations together.

"We didn't have to be up in the Angeles Crest to shoot interiors. We literally brought the tent back to the valley and set up the tents out in the parking lot. We'd then shoot conversation scenes using sunlight from outside the tents in the parking lot of the sound-stage."

The brief location of Sean's apartment at the start of the film was an equally close location for the shoot. "For Sean's apartment, we had a bunch of offices and corridor in the front of the warehouse. So, we took over one of these offices and just decorated it like Sean's apartment. So, his apartment was literally part of our warehouse stage," remembers Weed.

Despite the creative freedom the *Dark Hero* crew would have, it was not without its physical challenges while shooting on location. "The shoot was fairly intense for a low-budget film," recalls Christopherson.

"Shooting on location meant long, early, and daily morning shuttles into the national forest when it was still quite cold. By noon it was blazing hot. Long hours, little sleep, sudden temperature, and elevation changes, working with the elements - all of these realities made the days more challenging."

Even with these obstacles from Mother Nature, nothing would deter the cast and crew from achieving their goal - not even the occasional medical issue - as Christopherson recalls: "I remember getting a bad stomach-ache one day on location and it seemed kind of funny because Steve had one too. We were all in the same rocky filmmaking boat, going on a fun trip together."

And what about working with the intricately built set of the cave and ship interiors? They were a work of art and physical craftsman-ship from some of the most talented individuals in the film industry.

272 • Dom O'Brien

"The set for the cave was local and didn't seem low-budget to me at all. We were so lucky to have Steve and his crew because their expertise and skills gave this film the look and feel of a much higher budget project," says Christopherson. "The cave was pretty cool inside, which made it a lot more fun to explore as an actor. Every day it was like being a kid in the candy shop."

"I did have some 'firsts' on this shoot," recalls Christopherson. "Getting all wired up so a Zoanoid (Crane) could transform with me in his clutches. Getting to act with these creatures was great fun. The suit performers were incredibly committed, and the suits were as creepy as you might imagine."

Although Christopherson would be up close and personal with the imposing creature effects during key scenes (usually being terrorised by the hulking monstrosities), it didn't stop her from watching the crew hard at work on the creature creations, in-between setups.

"I didn't get to experience the creature effects as much as some of the others, but I'd get to peek in on the effects room from time to time. Steve and his team were tiptop, so it was a rare treat getting to see the effects team working."

The real terror and screams weren't hard to portray either, especially during the river action sequence, as Christopherson recalls. "I remember being genuinely afraid when I was being attacked in the river. I was already on edge because the water was cold and surrounded by little frogs, so adding in a relentless Zoanoid attack was a 'no acting required' situation," reminisces Christopherson.

It wasn't all bad though, particularly when it came to the professional skill of Koichi Sakamoto's Alpha Stunts team, as the actor recalls. "Alpha Stunts were incredible. I was constantly mesmerised by their expertise and commitment to the fight scenes."

"Not only were they fearlessly executing full-scale stunts but were doing it in heavy creature suits. They were top-notch martial artists, one of the most courageous stunt teams I've witnessed to date, and they never complained. Super sweet guys and I loved working with them."

While shooting a feature (regardless of budget), creativity can sometimes butt heads, especially in demanding environments. It was certainly the case with Christopherson and Wang during a particular scene within the cave set.

"Steve and I once got into a heated debate over my line: *'That one's alive!'*. I didn't want to say it because I was referring to a human being and it seemed callous. Steve ultimately won, so as you may recall, I do in fact say that line or something callous like that. I'm still sore about it," chuckles Christopherson.

Thankfully this was the only time she and Steve disagreed on how something should be performed, and there were still a few hijinks that took place during the shoot, which Christopherson fondly recalls.

"I often tell the story of one of the night shoots. I was sleeping in the green room and suddenly woke up, finding myself being escorted to set by two PAs. Moments later I was shooting the scene in the cave where I'm excitedly sharing the discovery of the alien ship with Sean [David Hayter]. It's hard to imagine that I had been sound asleep about two minutes earlier."

"There was also the time David, and I had a kissing scene in the car, which Steve was not impressed by. *You can do better than that!*, he said, at which point I blamed it all on David, naturally. So, when we had a pickup scene, which involved another make out session, I showed up with a six-pack of Mickey Big Mouths and demanded we all relax. As it turned out, that kiss went quite well."

It wasn't always awkward during scenes with David, as off-screen they were just two actors looking to hit the big time. Much like her lasting friendship with Wang, Hayter also keeps in regular contact with Christopherson, due to the friendship they forged all those years ago.

"David and I were pretty young and new-ish, so we were enjoying the moment of making a feature film together. I remember us bundling up in blankets in the early morning, freezing to death in the middle of nowhere, talking about how the movie was going to be a big success."

Like any good low-budget feature, every crew member is maximized to their fullest effect and will (as mentioned in a previous chapter) be asked to cover more than one role within a small team. For *Dark Hero*, several of the crew members would turn up in brief character roles or cameos, thus in turn saving on production costs for the film.

After his expansive behind-the-scenes work for *The Guyver*, and now as a producer for *Dark Hero*, Wyatt Weed would join other crew members Lisa Hannan, Kristin Calkins (who would briefly play the Primitive Guyver during the flashback sequence), Nathan Long, and even set medic Mark Ritchie, with a small role in front of the camera.

For Weed's role, he would play security guard Donnie who meets a violent end at the hands of drug dealer D.C. It was also painful for several reasons, chiefly the sheer number of squibs Weed had to endure during Donnie's death sequence. "Yeah, that was the cameo that Steve gave me," says Weed. "Honestly don't know how many times I was squibbed, but all I remember was the sound of them going off like: *boop, boop, boop, boop, boop.*"

Wyatt Weed as hapless night security guard Donnie, being held
at gun point by head of Alpha Stunts Koichi Sakamoto (as Sakai).
Photo courtesy of Wyatt Weed

Steve Wang directs Wyatt Weed ahead of his climatic
death scene. Photo courtesy of Wyatt Weed

Wyatt Weed's Donnie, is gunned down by D.C. in the opening scene's last
moments (the Guyver unable to save him). Weed was rigged with several
squibs (small explosive charges filled with fake blood) which simulate
the bullet hits. They are quite painful to experience but look impressive
on-screen. Photo courtesy of Wyatt Weed

In the same opening sequence both Nathan Long and Lisa Hannan would cameo as the two officers investigating the warehouse disturbance and, much like Weed, it would be one of a number of roles each would do during *Dark Hero*'s production.

"Yeah, I worked on the crew, mainly as a gopher just because I wanted to be around when it was made," remembers Long.

"I helped build the cave, I'd do endless runs to various electrical companies and lighting companies, all that sort of stuff. I think I drove a half ton truck. Like, just all the usual shit jobs that have to be done on a movie set. I remember one of the guys saying, '*Who the fuck is this guy? Oh, that's the writer*'. I had never been on a movie set before, so I wanted to soak up as much of it as I possibly could."

With so many crew members working multiple jobs, it ultimately lent the production a sort of guerrilla filmmaking mentality. It wasn't just Wang who wanted to make the best film possible, but also every single crew member, who would muck in and help where they could with the expertise they had or were willing to learn.

"It was guerrilla with a tremendous amount of quality, you know? Like still making sure that the focus, the lighting, the color, the execution, the safety, and the choreography was there. So, it was guerrilla filmmaking with a very artful edge to it," says Weed.

"There was much more of a willingness to let people play in different areas, but everybody still wanted their department to look good. And being right. They weren't stopping each other. It was more along the lines of everybody was gathered around like, '*Wait a little, let me fix my creature makeup*' and then '*Oh, wait, let me make sure the focus is set*'. So, it was more of an artistic collaboration to go farther because everybody was willing to work hard."

"I don't know if on *The Guyver* we ever broke 20 setups a day. But I think on *Dark Hero*, we regularly smashed through 20 setups a day. We were probably closer to 30 setups on a lot of days. I don't think we ever made 40 setups, but there were probably days where we were doing between 30 and 35 setups," recalls Weed.

"There was never a time where somebody said, '*Steve, what do you want here?*', because Steve could go and say, '*I want this*'. There were even times where Steve and I would literally communicate through pieces of paper. He'd doodle something and go '*Like this*', and I'd go, '*Sure, okay. Based on what's happening, can we do this?*' He'd then follow-up with, '*Yeah, but do this and do this*'. So, it was literally like cartooning back and forth," remembers Weed.

Because Wang had brought on a trusted creative team, he could execute his vision to the fullest extent possible (within budgetary limitations). It also helped that he knew what every second of *Dark Hero* would look like, and director of photography Michael G. Wojciechowski was receptive to Wang's ideas.

"I think there were times when the director of photography wouldn't understand. So, Steve could literally take the camera, put it where he wanted it and go, '*Okay, this isn't right. Give me a 55*'. We'd put the lens on there and Steve would be '*Like this?*' and the DP would look through and go, '*Oh, okay*'," explains Weed.

"Sometimes Steve was operating a camera, sometimes we had cameras going. Sometimes there was a night shift, sometimes the regular director of photography would get tired and go home, and they'd bring in a second guy to shoot in the evening or on the weekends. So, we were just able to eliminate a lot of bureaucracy, a lot of fumbling around and really streamline the process," recalls Weed.

When Wang wasn't behind the camera, he would occasionally call the shots from his director's chair. In lieu of the moments when the director did sit down, he would use a megaphone jokingly labelled with the title 'Mr Mouth'. Despite the hard work on display and the long hours all the crew would pull, sometimes with multiple roles, everyone still knew when to inject some levity into a shooting day.

One moment that David Hayter now looks on humorously, was during the redone flashback of Sean bonding with the Guyver Unit for the first time. "There's the nightmare scene where I'm tied up with my arm stretched out as the Guyver attaches itself to my body," remembers Hayter.

"This was in the middle of the night, I was in my underwear, and they covered me with methocel, which is the goo that comes out of the *Aliens* mouth. It's disgusting and it saps your body heat. So, they covered me in all of that and I was freezing because I was tied up for like two hours. It was like an S&M video or something," jokes Hayter.

"And then Steve, you know, put the helmet on me and glued various pieces of the armour to my body and then pulled them off and then shot it in reverse, so it looked like they were all attaching on to me. And that was just a miserable, miserable night. And that was the only time I really wore any of the suit."

In the grand scheme of things, this was a minor misery compared to the rest of the enjoyable shoot, as Hayter describes. "When we went up to Angeles Crest to shoot up there for a couple months, it was awesome. It felt just like a summer camp for beautiful actors. What a crazy summer that was."

Despite not getting to wear the full Guyver suit due to height differences between himself and the stunt crew, or do any martial arts, Hayter did get one moment to shine with a little bit of fisticuff action, as he recalls.

"Oh, I did get a fight. There's one moment where I've been drugged and Atkins is like '*You know kid, you can't go after them*' and so on. So, I elbowed him in the face and like backhanded them or something. That was my one bit of action I got to do."

Although Hayter's fight work was minimal, he was still part of the Guyver transformation shots and one in particular stands out early in the film. The sequence in question is during the forest fight confrontation between Guyver and Volker. As Sean runs to the aid of the hunter and reporter (sadly not in time to save said reporter), he shouts the iconic 'GUYVER', causing a transformation during a run. What starts out as a brief composite shot – the suit plates shooting out of his neck – quickly becomes another exercise in creative, low-tech filmmaking. As was the case for a lot of *Dark Hero*'s effects.

"This is as low-tech and cheesy as you can imagine. We built a big turntable, I want to say maybe six feet in diameter, and I think we may have gotten just some regular caster wheels, and we built a big turntable. Then we put tree branches and leaves and stuff up all the way around it and then put black curtain behind it," recalls Weed.

"David [Hayter] is in front of camera, moving his arms like he's running, and then we're rotating things behind him, so it looks like stuff is passing behind him. Then we would have, like, a piece of the armour on him. And as he's going like this, so then we're rotating the piece backwards. So that when we run it forward, the back to the pieces moving forward, it looks like he's running. And those pieces are flying on to him. Yeah. So yeah, it was reverse action of him moving in front of a turntable, and reverse footage."

The oldest tricks in the book are the best for a reason, and in an age when CGI was still a relatively expensive tool during the early 1990s, knowing how to combine various tricks and cheats to achieve an effects sequence or shot really showed skill and creativity.

One such sequence which used several different filmmaking elements, would be the cliff jump sequence towards the tail end of *Dark Hero,* which sees Sean leaping off a cliff and transforming mid-air into the Guyver to heroically come to the aid of Cori. Despite potentially influencing many a young viewer to jump from countless sofas and scream 'Guyver' at the top of their lungs, it's often cited by fans as one of the key moments in the whole film. Which makes its creation even more impressive, given the film's budget.

While the impressive stunt work by Alpha Stunts triggers the start of this sequence (more on that in the next chapter), it's the wide shot fall and subsequent mix of elements that'll be looked at first.

For the shot of Sean in the air and falling towards the camera, Hayter was strapped into a harness and suspended in the air against a green screen background, all while several stuntmen hoisted him above the alleyway in which they shot the plate. Hayter would then strike the required pose as Wang shot from a low angle.

The green screen of Hayter posing was then composited onto another plate of the live action shot of a cliff. The camera was then tilted down as a Guyver-suited actor landed in frame, who would have AB smoke – a liquid compound used to create smoke or steam on-screen - on their feet, so when they landed and ran off, it gives the impression the Guyver's feet were smoldering from hitting the ground so hard. "So, there was AB Smoke on the ground and AB Smoke on his feet, so that when he hit the ground (from the jump) the smoke happened. I want to say that Guyver leaving the frame, to the whip pan of him already way down the road, were different shots," says Weed.

"So, you had a cliff plate, a second landing plate, and then a whip pan to him in the distance. So that was like three different shots stitched together. Then we had David hung on wires in front of the small green screen, which then Ted Rae I believe took some miniature Guyver plates from the first film and animated them against some kind of a composite screen and lined them up, so they looked like they were going on to David's body," recalls Weed.

David Hayter and the stunt crew film the green-screen section of the Guyver cliff jump. Hayter, suspended in a stunt harness, strikes the pose before the armour attaches to Sean mid-jump. Images taken from Stan Giesea's behind-the-scenes footage and used with permission

One area where the budget was stretched particularly thin, was in the costume department. For the management of those (mostly) human clothing items, the job fell to Jennifer McManus to keep tabs on, organize, and maintain continuity for the actors clothing.

"When I first started in the industry, I kind of ended up being thrown into effects work," recalls McManus.

With her background in puppetry, McManus would find herself working with the likes of the late John Carl Buechler and do effects work on films like *Ghost Town* (1988) and *The Garbage Pail Kids Movie* (1987). McManus would ultimately step more into her love of costume design following *Dark Hero* and with her husband Rob Burman, would design and create the detailed Power Rangers suits for the *Mighty Morphin Power Rangers: The Movie* (1995). She would later reteam with Wang on *Drive* (1997), and it was by working with Wang on his various projects, that McManus was able to dive further into her love of costume design.

"I really wanted to be able to drive myself more toward costume design and working that way. By working with Steve Wang, who's an amazing designer in his own right, I was able to express my costume design abilities. I've also worked with a lot of other amazing designers as well, and it's just very humbling," says McManus.

Even with the small budget, McManus was able to create a narrative with the choice of clothing for each of the characters, even if its subliminal to the average viewer.

"I would use very subliminal colors or a specific print to say something about their personality. A lot of the time I will use certain pieces to cover up that somebody is a bad guy. Like, I won't use black or dark colors, or ominous colors, because I want you to think, '*Oh, this is a really nice guy*', when they're not," says McManus.

For the design look of Sean, whose gone from clean-cut teenager to jaded hero during his time as the Guyver, McManus injected a bit of rough and readiness into his wardrobe and this came from getting to know the character more during the costume fitting period.

"I like to work with the actors in terms of their characters. So, we'll start out by asking them questions about how they're perceiving their character. Would your character wear orange, would you know? What do you think? Etc. I'm basically asking their character these questions. I wanted Sean's clothing to look layered because he's traveling. But I also wanted there to be some kind of contrast with a bit of color to throw you off a little as well," says McManus.

It's in the minutiae where this comes out, as Sean's undershirt was a light grey, and this played into his dual personality of light and dark sides battling for control. As McManus has said, it's incredibly subtle, but it's still present for those wanting to read into the character's psyche a little more.

Working within a small budget for costumes also means that, much like other facets of production, creativity and ingenuity is frequently called upon.

"The actors agreed to utilize thrift store clothing, but you have to be very careful, for sanitary reasons. So, when I use thrift store clothing, I always make sure that I have them absolutely clean before giving them to the actors," recalls McManus.

Despite the extensive cleaning process for the budget clothing, due to the location shooting and with it being the height of summer, each item worn by the actors had to be clean before the next day's shoot. This led to long days for the costume department.

"Some of the challenges that we had were early mornings and very late nights because you still have to wash it and have it back there in time for the next shooting day," says McManus.

One particular instance led to a few problems for the department, especially due to the on-location shooting.

"I will say that one day I was warning everybody on set, 'Watch out for poison oak' and they're like 'Oh, right'. They took a bunch of my wardrobe to go do some second unit shooting and when they came back and threw it in my arms, I was instantly like 'They've *been in poison oak'*. Oh boy, did I give them grief about that," chuckles McManus.

Even with the hardships and the minimal budget, McManus still looks back at the experience fondly.

"Usually, it was getting up early to drive to set, which was usually way up in the Angeles Crest Mountains for a lot of it. Then having a long day and driving home late at night and having to do the laundry, ready for the next day. Yes, the job was a bit tough, you know, and long, and we all did our best to stretch our imaginations and wrap it all around Steve's ideas to make it. But I will say there are some lifelong friends that have been made."

"You start to feel like family when you spend so many hours together and you're collaborating. And it's a lot of work too, to get things so it's copacetic for both of you, so that each other's ideas are coming across and you're not squashing anyone else's."

"I will never stop teasing Steve about Kathy's hat, which he absolutely refused for her to wear. I'd often give it to Kathy so she could continually tease him with it," recalls McManus.

With the minimal budget, Ted Smith would also have a few additional, if brief, roles in the film after both his Zoanoids (Mazzo and Sten) met their violent, untimely ends. The first instance would be as one of Atkins' hapless rescue commandos, who'd meet a rather grizzly death (throat ripped out) after encountering Crane's Zoanoid underling Corbin (a reused Lisker suit from *The Guyver*).

Finally, during the climatic showdown (before Guyver uses his Mega-Smasher ability to finish off his opponent), Smith briefly plays the melting Guyver Zoanoid and provides some rather magnificent overacting as viscous gloop slops to the floor. Smith's recognizable, larger-than-life suit performance again emanates through the latex and gloop.

The suit performer did encounter one small mishap while performing as the defeated Guyver Zoanoid though.

"We're in this cave in August, within the valley, and the heat was so friggin hot during the day. So, we are doing the last dialogue scenes at the end of the day and there's a scene where the Guyver hits the Guyver Zoanoid, and he staggers - all that stuff is me. Steve's like '*Okay, now you drop to your knees and when you come back up and he punches you in the head*', and I'm like '*All right*', and he was like '*No, he has to actually punch you in the head. We're shooting it in high speed, so we have to get it slow motion so we can see the impact to your head*'. And I'm like '*What are you paying me?*'", chuckles Smith.

"Steve screams action and sure enough, you watch it, and although it goes by fast, the martial artist was able to hit me, but not punch so hard that it went all the way through my skull. He was able to pull back a little bit, but you get that inertia of when he makes that initial impact and hits me in the head. I stagger back and they call cut."

"So, where the control metal was inside the helmet they had some LEDs and wires. Those were pressed in my forehead for, like, at least a minute after the helmet was taken off and you could see in my head," laughs Smith.

Suit performer extraordinaire Ted Smith gets some suit touch-ups done by a crew member (possibly Rob Freitas) before he continues to act as the Mazzo Zoanoid during the water fight. Note the spare Guyver suits drying in the sun between shots. Photo courtesy of Ted Smith

Wyatt Weed makes some repairs to the Marcus Zoanoid suit
(performed by David McDonald) in-between shots during the
river fight. Photo courtesy of Wyatt Weed

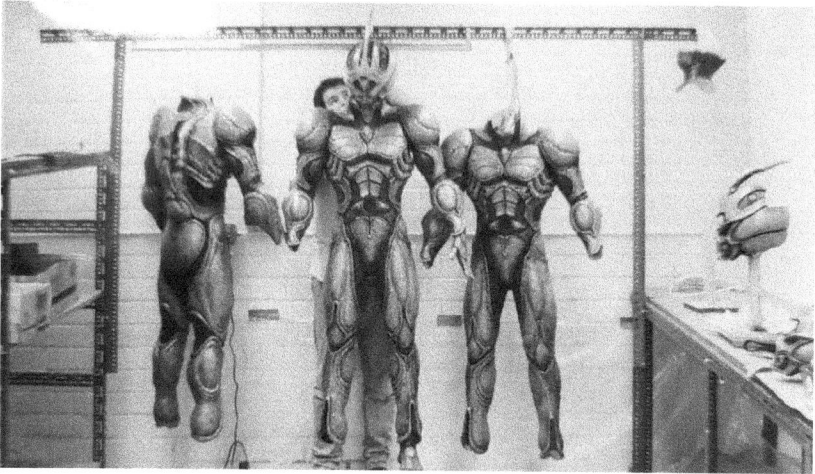

Rob Freitas makes some adjustments to a few of the Guyver suits
while in the effects shop. Photo courtesy of Steve Wang

Wyatt with art department lead Sara Tune in the completed
alien ship corridor. Photo courtesy of Wyatt Weed

Kristin Calkins (who played Lois and the Primitive Guyver
during a flashback) helps out with construction of the Guyver
Unit room (where Cori ends up finding the damaged Guyver Unit).
Photo courtesy of Steve Wang

Behind-the-scenes shot of Cori (Kathy Christopherson) finding the
damaged Guyver Unit inside part of the ship. Photo courtesy of Wyatt Weed

Director of Photography (DP) Michael G. Wojciechowski, Kathy Christopherson and Wyatt Weed, shoot a close-up shot of Cori finding the damaged Guyver Unit. Photo courtesy of Wyatt Weed

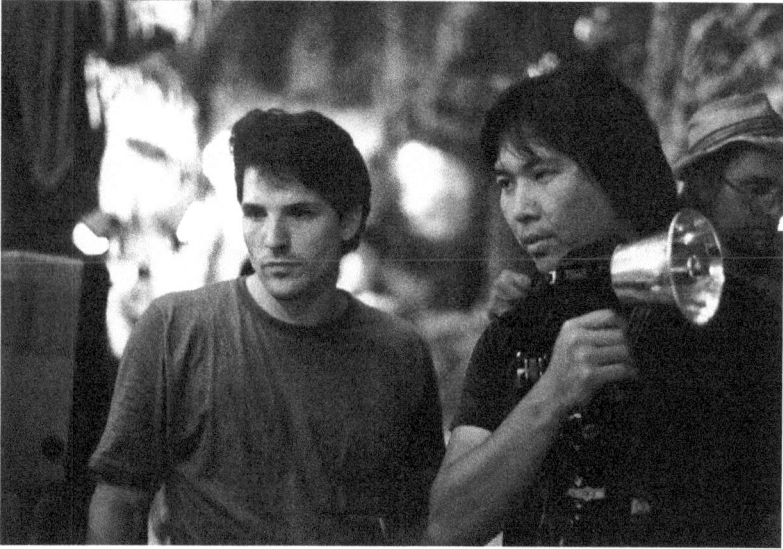

Steve Wang and Wyatt Weed on the set looking at a recent shot on the monitors. Photo courtesy of Wyatt Weed

Asao Goto assists in adding some gloop to part of the Guyver Zoanoid's disintegration. Ted Smith would slip into the slimy suit for part of this sequence. Photo courtesy of Steve Wang

Asao Goto puppeteers the final stage of the Guyver Zoanoid melt sequence, which shows a more advanced stage of the disintegration following his defeat at the climax of the film and would be used for a few insert shots. Photo courtesy of Steve Wang

Behind-the-scenes shot of the melted Guyver Zoanoid before Guyver uses his Mega-Smasher chest cannon to blast the gooey mess into oblivion. Photo courtesy of Steve Wang

Chapter Ten

A Whole Lot of Kung Fu Kicks and Backflips

As previously touched upon, *The Guyver* suffered from several underdeveloped areas once the final product was released. Despite the use of aikido as Guyver's martial arts of choice for this first entry, it unfortunately lacked anything gratifying – due in part to looking anything but cinematic.

A more practical martial art doesn't always transition well to the screen, often lacking the excitement found within movie fight sequences and being wholly unentertaining. For the follow-up, this was one of the most important areas for Wang and Co. to concentrate on; to create adrenaline-pumping and creditable action sequences more akin to the chorography Wang had grown up on as a child.

In that respect, *Guyver: Dark Hero* is both visually and aesthetically closer to *Kung Fu Rascals* than its predecessor; with more location work along with action cues from Hong Kong cinema.

This new action approach to *Dark Hero* would make up for the lack of visceral and bloody fight chorography absent from *The Guyver*; ultimately bring the characters back to their violent manga roots. Wang would start *Dark Hero* off with a violent bang, setting the tone for the remainder of the action set-pieces. To say the pre-opening credit warehouse sequence would be the least exciting fight in the whole film, yet still more exceptionally crafted than anything from the prior installment, is a testament to *Dark Hero*'s stunt team and clear vision Wang had for the action.

With the film opening on a more seasoned Sean narrating how the Guyver Unit calls him to fight (and kill), it makes sense that his physical attributes and overall fight capabilities would further develop in the year since the Guyver Unit first bonded with him. Thematically, through Sean's fighting prowess, we see how he is losing control with the power of the Guyver (as evidenced by the slitting of drug dealer D.C.'s throat).

After the Guyver's stunning entrance – which feels as though its ripped straight out of the pages of the manga, silhouette in steam and heroically showcasing a new streamlined and leaner suit design (again more manga and anime accurate) – as viewers we are teased with a faster and more brutal depiction of the Guyver's abilities.

Ankles are snapped like twigs, thugs are thrown as though they weigh nothing, bullets are ricocheted back to their owner, and throats are slit. And it only escalates further throughout the remainder of *Dark Hero*'s runtime. Gone was the slow-moving aikido; in its place was action-packed brutality, orchestrated by one of the most inventive stunt teams; Alpha Stunts.

Now working predominately within Japanese Tokusatsu shows such as *Kamen Rider* and the various *Power Rangers* series, in-between their own theatrical features, Alpha Stunts have gained a reputation as one of the best stunt teams within the action genre.

With *Dark Hero*, Alpha was only a fledgling team consisting of three key martial artists and stunt performers – namely Koichi Sakamoto, Akihiro Noguchi, and Tatsuro Koike (with Ken Goodman credited as doing some minor stunt work with the team during this time). It has since grown exponentially from its humble 1990s roots.

This original trio of exceptional athletes would go on to create some of the best low-budget action committed to direct-to-video filmmaking, before and after 1994, further showcasing their skill with a larger stunt team in *Drive* (1997). It was on *Dark Hero*, though, where they are their most organic, taking influence from their native Japan and Tokusatsu shows, along with the fluidity of Hong Kong action cinema (the wirework of the Wuxia subgenre for instance), bring a unique fighting style to the west ahead of films like *Rush Hour* (1998) and *The Matrix* (1999).

Who were these new wonderkids and where did they hone their fighting craft? "Tatsuro and Koichi were former members of the Kurata Action Club," says Akihiro 'Yuji' Noguchi. "They left the club a few years after I joined. The teacher, Yasuaki Kurata, had long been an action star who is extremely popular in Hong Kong and other Asian countries."

Outside of his native Japan, Kurata would be most familiar to Hong Kong film fans after starring in a slew of possibly some of the best representations of Hong Kong's action film industry throughout the decades. His most recognisable role being in Jet Li's *Fist of Legend* (1994), where the Japanese martial artist goes toe-to-toe with the Wu-Shu champion in a blindfolded fight. In a film full of standout fight sequences, this might well be the most impressive of the bunch.

"I started my stuntman career in 1985, shortly after graduating from high school," continues Noguchi. "Strictly speaking, I started by joining a stuntman training school and learning the knowledge and skills necessary for stunts, and in the process, I often appeared in TV and movies as a bit part. I then joined Kurata Action Club." Despite working at the same stunt school, Yuji, Koichi, and Tatsuro wouldn't begin to form Alpha Stunts – or at the very least what would be the beginning states of Alpha Stunts – until Yuji himself would depart from Kurata Action Club.

"Tatsuro decides to visit the United States after receiving a report from Koichi, who was working as a stuntman alongside a student in the United States," remembers Noguchi. "Tatsuro contacted me to go with him. I think it was the very moment when we founded Alpha Stunts. Of course, at this time, we hadn't established a team yet, and we didn't have a team name. Tatsuro and I joined Koichi, and we went to the shooting site where Koichi was involved as a stuntman and saw the shooting site in the United States. Koichi wasn't working all the time, so we focused on stunt training every day while we were free."

"Training in the United States was a very meaningful time for us to use the facilities and equipment efficiently. In the trampoline training, you can wear a safety belt, and a professional trainer will prevent dangerous falls when it is dangerous with a tied rope, and the trainer will teach us various techniques. At the gym, there are safe spring mats and pits with lots of small sponge cubes that won't hurt you if you fall off your head, so you can safely try out new tricks." It wasn't just physical training which this small stunt team would endure; on the contrary it was important to educate themselves by viewing and studying countless martial arts films, particularly how stunt coordinators and stuntmen would create the vibrant and engaging action.

"After we arrived in the United States, there was a movie theatre nearby where we could watch Hong Kong movies cheaply, so we used to go there frequently. Among them, we must have been influenced by the action of Tsui Hark's *Once Upon a Time in China* which featured Jet Li." This appears to be where Yuji was most influenced, with his fast-flowing style.

"I mostly referred to Hong Kong movies, especially Jet Li's movements and tricks, whereas Koichi grew up watching a lot of anime and manga since he was a child, and there is no doubt that *Dark Hero* reflects that taste within his action coordination," suggests Noguchi.

It wasn't long after arriving in the States that Sakamoto, Koike, and Noguchi would first learn about *Guyver: Dark Hero* going into production. With their extensive training behind them, the newly formed Alpha Stunts set out to create a show reel in the hopes of getting involved with the stunt work on Wang's sequel.

"Upon hearing that *Guyver: Dark Hero* was scheduled to be filmed, we put a demo tape of the stunt techniques we had gained from previous training, and we visited Steve's home," says Noguchi. "The show reel itself incorporated the various stunt techniques we learnt in the United States, along with our unique skills. Steve saw the show reel and immediately told us to do it together."

With the newly christened Alpha Stunts team now hired by Wang for *Dark Hero*, the small crew (with Koichi Sakamoto taking the lead) set out to develop and choreograph the extensive action set pieces for this sequel, quickly rectifying the sorely lacking action from *The Guyver*. Despite its impressive creature effects work, use of miniatures and false perspective, and puppetry, there was no denying the action (or lack thereof) was one of the predecessor's biggest flaws. This was all about to change with Alpha Stunts onboard, ready to prove themselves within the stunt field, particularly at a time when stunt teams weren't a known quantity outside of Asia like they are now.

"As a stunt coordinator, Koichi summarized the stunts we wanted to do and created an action scene. We incorporated a lot of physical reactions and action with wirework," remembers Noguchi. "At that time, it was still commonplace in the United States to lay down a safety mat when reacting, so I think we, who are good at reacting without a safety mat, were differentiated from other stuntmen. Also at that time, American stuntmen were mainly engaged in individual activities, so there were only a few groups that were active in the form of so-called stunt teams, and we weren't conscious of what was different from other stuntmen when constructing actions. We were 120% focused on what we wanted to do, what we wanted to challenge and change."

Martial artist and actor Anthony Houk was credited as the suit performer for the Guyver, despite David Hayter really wanting to perform in the suit. Houk would perform the whole of the opening warehouse fight and often be the main Guyver they used for acting portions (bringing the Guyver's iconic poses to life), with the more gymnastic or wire-assisted feats in the later fight sequences performed by Sakamoto and Noguchi, depending on what the action sequence called for.

Wang explains it the following way, "Anthony did almost if not all (around 90%) of the acting with the dialogue. He did all of the warehouse fight in the beginning and then he did some of the shots in the forest with Volker. It was a combination of him and Koichi, it would go back and forth. All the water stuff was Anthony [during the fight between Volker and Mazzo]."

"We used Anthony in the whole film, but it was a matter of, like, who would be best to do certain things, and then we put the appropriate person in the suit to do it. Because Koichi and his team did all the choreography, he was able to perform it very quickly, because we're always on a tight schedule, so he [Koichi] would do a lot of the fighting, so he was in quite a bit of the film as well."

This is also something Yuji corroborates. The Hong Kong action sensibility clearly carrying over to Alpha Stunts by using the right person for a specific action sequence or move, as individual stunt performers all have their own strengths and weaknesses.

"Koichi was the main Guyver stunt double and was responsible for the hand-to-hand fight coordination, but also as the lead stunt coordinator who put together the whole action. Tatsuro oversaw stunts such as gymnastics and high falls as the actor's stunt double and Guyver double."

"He [Koichi] was also doing the overall wire coordination at the same time as all the actions of Guyver Zoanoid. My responsibility when doubling Guyver's action scenes was mainly wire stunts, special kicks, and no-mat reactions. The three of us were in charge of our own parts for all the action scenes and all three of us wore Guyver suits and other creature suits and played the actions in turn," recalls Noguchi.

Watching the numerous fight sequences, it ultimately becomes a seamless blend of the three performers (all varying in height) to achieve the best possible action seen on-screen within their limited budget.

It's old school, think-on-your-feet filmmaking using false perspective, camera angles and clever editing to make the performers become one character – in this case Guyver – without giving the illusion away to the viewer. Much like the classic Hong Kong films Alpha Stunts had watched and learned from.

"We called Anthony the 'Hero Guyver' as he looked the best in the suit, particularly as the suit was made for him to begin with," says Wang. "Koichi was much shorter but did more of the fighting, whereas Yuji would perform a lot of the gnarly falls or any of the wirework, because you couldn't have a larger Guyver on wires, it didn't work on-screen, so we called him [Yuji] our Snack Size Guyver," chuckles Wang.

Where *Dark Hero* once again excels in the areas that *The Guyver* failed is in the sheer number of action set-pieces on display. Gone were the stilted and brief fights of the first entry and instead Alpha Stunts would consistently raise the bar for the subsequent sequences; each one outshining its predecessor without regurgitating previous moves or action beats.

The end product is high-octane action on a budget, which puts most modern fight chorography to shame. A unique feat for a low-budget action feature and newly-formed stunt team.

With the first fight in the warehouse, Guyver effectively uses the location to his advantage; whereas in the second fight (Guyver against Volker) Guyver again uses his terrain – this time a specific tree – to help counteract the Zoanoid assault.

It would be echoed again with Guyver's rematch against Volker and Mazzo for the river fight and during the final third of the film against Crane and the remaining Zoanoids in the cave showdown. While it might seem inconsequential to the average viewer, Alpha Stunts used the mundane exterior and interior locations to their advantage to create dynamic action. This keen attention to detail would be further cemented in Alpha Stunts' work post-*Dark Hero*.

There is also an interesting thematic resonance to this slew of action insanity. Whether it was intended or not, each fight invokes some form of environmental element – metal, earth, water, etc. – which again plays into the bio-organic nature origins of both the Guyver and the Zoanoids. With that in mind, how did Alpha Stunts create these impressive action sequences, and what was the genesis behind each of the individual fights? For starters, it's about being invested as a viewer.

Like all good set-pieces, it's no good if the audience doesn't care about the characters, as there is nothing to hook them into the action. As Wang says, "I've had the same fight many times, it's always '*cut to the action*' and I'm like, '*people won't care about the action, if they don't give a shit about the characters*.'"

Unlike the prior film, *Dark Hero* does make the viewer actually care about Sean's ongoing struggle and it's thanks to Hayter's boyish charm and screen chemistry with Kathy Christopherson's Cori. It also helps that the fights are visually impressive as well.

Any action film which is filled to the brim with fights and martial arts sequences often involves extensive planning, rehearsing, and testing. Sometimes that isn't always possible due to either limited time or budget. This was exactly the case with Alpha Stunts while working on *Dark Hero*, due to the minimal time and budget; pre-vis or rehearsed fights done before principal photography wasn't doable and as Noguchi explains, much of the action was rehearsed only on the set or just before shooting.

"As far as I can remember, we didn't make any pre-vis. Koichi shared ideas at a meeting with Steve, made choreography and rehearsed at the set. We then showed it to Steve and shot it then and there."

"So, almost all the choreography of hand fight is improvisation. For wire stunts and big stunts, decide what to do the day before the shooting or when there is no scene we play, set the wire, have rehearsals, and then have Steve check it, and shoot on the actual day. We and Steve trusted each other, so I don't think there was any disagreement about the action scenes," remembers Noguchi.

With the lack of time and money leading to pre-vis and extensive planning being ruled out, how long did it actually take Alpha Stunts to choreograph all the fights? And were there any sequences they had to cut for time which they planned to shoot?

"As mentioned earlier, there wasn't a way to build a choreography by devoting a lot of time to rehearsals," says Noguchi. "So, I don't know how long it took to build the overall action. Koichi took the time to roughly put together the action scenes onto a storyboard, and then we created the action based on that. In *Dark Hero*, there are no cut action scenes. Steve used all the actions we put into the action sequences. Just as we have respect for Steve, we also know he has respect for us."

The Alpha Stunts team were also in front of the camera, *sans* Guyver and creature suits, during the impressively violent opening warehouse fight. Noguchi, along with Sakamoto (as the metal pole-wielding Sakai) and Koike, make up the reminder of the goons who meet painful (sometimes bone-shattering) outcomes, following their encounter with this more vicious Guyver.

The remainder of DC's (Shaun T. Benjamin) gang would comprise of Butch Portillo, Gary Willis, Ken Goodman, and Brian Simpson (who is the first to meet physical punishment from Guyver with a specatular highfall).

"Yes, I played one of the villains in the opening fight at the warehouse," remembers Noguchi. "I was in charge of the stunts where people were thrown by Guyver and then fall to the ground, usually with a gainer." For those curious to know what a gainer is, it's an acrobatic trick where the performer or stunt person will do a backward somersault while still moving forward. Essentially, this is a reverse rotation of the whole body, which looks both painful and impressive.

Steve Wang and crew on set during one of the nights shooting at the steel mill. This particular moment is taken from the opening of *Guyver: Dark Hero* as D. C's goons unload a barrage of bullets into the distance, leading to Guyver's dramatic reveal. The goons include Butch Portillo (as Bo), stuntman Akihiro 'Yuji' Noguchi, Gary Willis (as Rafe), and stuntman Ken Goodman (as Dino). Photo courtesy of Steve Wang and taken by on set photographer Eric Lasher

"I also did the stunt where I'm kicked by Guyver landing on my back onto a wooden box, breaking it," continues Noguchi. "The wooden box stunt didn't hurt because I had a protector on my back. It does shock you and is unlike anything you've experienced before, a bit like the shock of being in a car crash. I think I did it twice. Tatsuro is also doing a stunt in the scene where he is thrown by Guyver and hits the wall and falls into the gap between the car and the wooden box."

Even with a large portion of the wirework in Yuji's nimble hands, there were still challenges while filming the complex stunts, regardless of the time and budget they had. During the climatic fight between Guyver and the newly transformed Guyver Zoanoid, the wirework is amped up to 11, pushing what had been previously seen in a Western action film at the time, whether theatrically or direct-to-video. With each successive action sequence outdoing the last, the fight choreography truly hits new heights prior to its third act. Ahead of the climatic showdown, we get to see Guyver take on multiple Zoanoids in a quest to save love interest Cori, in one of the penultimate action sequences.

The sequence starts off with a bang, as Sean heroically leaps from a cliff face, transforming into the Guyver before hitting the ground. In a filmmaking age where CGI is used as overabundance in action, this sequence with a combination of practical location shooting, stunt doubles, wire-rigging, minor CGI effects work, sound design, and old-fashioned hidden cuts with multiple people in the same costume, is the very epitome of budget filmmaking.

It's a sequence that was no doubt emulated by many a pre-teen viewer by jumping from their living room couch onto cushions that were carefully positioned on the floor, much to their parents' probable confusion.

"I remember when we were shooting that," remembers Wyatt Weed. "I did contribute something for second unit where Sean goes up to the edge of the cliff and he looks down, you see his vertigo view and there's rocks tumbling down. That was second unit. And it was another case of Steve going, '*Hey, come back here someday and get rocks tumbling down the cliff*. It just was like a checklist on any day and sometimes Steve would turn around to the script supervisor and he'd be like, '*Oh, tell second unit we need this*'."

"So, the script girl would come to me at the end of the day and go '*Steve needs this. Okay, so he runs up to the edge of the cliff and he looks down into the valley and he realizes he has to jump*'. We originally were going to go down into that valley. Like we were literally going to go to the bottom of that valley and do the shot up of him standing way up there. We had such heavy reports of rattlesnake activity that summer, that valley he was looking down into had been nicknamed something like Rattlesnake Valley. The park rangers were like, '*Don't go in that valley, seriously do not go into that valley*'."

"We just decided, okay, we're not going to go in that valley," remembers Weed. "So, whatever the cliff was that we looked up at when he jumped off, it was a different cliff. We went and found a different cliff where he runs up to the edge of the cliff and looks down. So, if you can imagine the location was such that there was an upper level and a lower level. To look over his shoulder and see the valley before him, you'd go to the lower level. To look up at him, as he's looking down at the valley, you'd put him back up on the upper level, and you'd get on the lower level," explains Weed.

"Whenever he was seeing him, he was on the upper level, and we were on the lower level, whenever we were seeing what he was looking at, he'd go to the lower level, we'd go to the upper level. The behind shot where he runs, and he jumps off into nothing. We went back to the upper level, put all the stunt pads on the lower level. And so, the stunt man dove off the upper level and landed on the crash pads. It gave you the impression there's one cliff edge, but we're either in front of it or behind it. There were two cliff edges right near each other and we were always on one of those cliff edges."

While Hayter wasn't the one to complete the swan dive off the cliff, he is shown heroically running towards the edge prior to a cut and then the jump taking place. Although he would only do the beginning part of the run, there was still a brief moment of unease for Hayter.

One shot that makes it into the final film has Sean (Hayter) looking over the edge towards a precipice of death; the camera following his view in all its handheld glory. It's a minor moment, but one which had its own set of fears and, rather strangely, hilarity. Hayter explains it as an interesting challenge, particularly for his first starring role.

"It was non-union, so there weren't any rules about how many hours we could work, and so on and so forth. The shot where I'm standing on the giant rock, and I'm sort of like, thinking about life and kind of walking out to the edge of the rock. Well, that was probably a 30-foot drop to the road below. So, as I'm walking, you can actually see it, I'm sort of talking to myself. Steve whined, '*Go on David, walk out to the edge walk out to the edge*', but there was no edge. It just dropped down, just a sheer drop to my death."

"So, I'm walking up, but I'm, like, sort of inching along and trying to make it look like Sean is in thought, but I'm trying to not die. And he's [Steve] like, 'No, go out to the edge, go out to the edge!' and I'm like, '*I'm on the edge*', and he goes '*You look afraid*' and I just say, '*I am afraid*'. So that was kind of fun."

"We did another day where I had been working 24 hours straight. And you know, I was game, I was like 'great, it's a movie, let's get it done'. I think it was my last shot of the day after being up 24 hours straight and it was when Sean is ready to run off the cliff; it's a big moment."

"There's the cliff wall that I'm against," continues Hayter, "And there's a road, like a one lane dirt road, and then a drop of 400 feet. I mean, like just death straight down. So, Steve is on the edge of the cliff with the camera. And he's like, '*Just run at the camera as fast as you can and run past it*', and I'm like, '*Yeah, except if I'm running as fast as I can straight past the camera, it's a sheer drop*', and he's like, '*No, no, you'll be fine. You'll be fine*'. I was like, '*Steve, I've been working for 24 hours straight. It's a dirt road, I'm gonna slip and slide right off the cliff*'."

"Steve's like, '*Oh, geez*' and calls over Brian [Simpson] one of stunt guys. He had been one of the *Predator* stunt people; he was enormous, something like six-foot-six, this huge blonde guy. Steve goes '*Brian, get on the edge of the cliff and catch David if he falls over*'. And so, Brian goes and stands on this lip of stone with one foot behind him and his other foot on the road, and I'm like, '*Dude, I'm nearly 200 pounds, I'm going to take him off there*'. Then suddenly Steve was like, '*Okay, ready and action!*'"

"So, that moment where it's shot in slow motion and I have my game face on and start running, it was terrifying. I mean, standing on the rock was one thing but I wanted to be committed and knew this was gonna be this amazing shot in the movie, so I did it. I just hammered as fast as I could pass the camera, then, you know, stopped as soon as I could, trying not to kill us both and we got the shot."

Following Hayter's butt-clenching shot passed the camera and into the arms of Brian Simpson, it was then ultimately up to Alpha Stunts to coordinate the impressive swan dive off the cliff, as Hayter was doubled for this majestic, heart-pounding leap of faith. The higher ledge above was used for the leap, leading to the stunt double landing on a mat where Hayter's running scene had taken place. The camera is cleverly positioned as to avoid revealing the different locations to the viewer, but despite the relative safe distance to fall, it was no less dangerous.

"That stunt was done by Tatsuro, doubling David [Hayter]," remembers Noguchi. "Ken Goodman was a very versatile and excellent stuntman, but I think Tatsuro did it because the schedule didn't fit."

"The cliff high fall had two stages," details Noguchi. "The height to the second cliff was less than eight meters. We didn't own an air bag at the time, so we did it with a lot of cardboard and crush mats. Compared to an air bag, the surface area of the mat is quite small, and it is quite difficult to jump out from the run because you cannot see the mat until you jump out. Moreover, in the scene it has to look dramatic, so the attitude in the air must be impressive because it is what leads into the transformation."

"It's a stunt that will lead to death if the calculation goes wrong even a little. You have to be aware of all the various factors to complete the shot. Thankfully, Tatsuro did more than just do it perfectly," remembers Noguchi.

"He was thinking of his own gag to ease the nerves of the crew. Tatsuro was discussing the situation with the crew who were on the second stage. Tatsuro jumped, landed on the mat, and then proceeded to crawl on the ground like a frog. It was very impressive because up until then the atmosphere on the site had been tense and as such the crew were seriously worried. Thankfully, after the take, the atmosphere changed completely, and the crew began to laugh loudly. We were surrounded by laughter," remembers Noguchi fondly.

When Guyver does finally arrive at his fighting destination, viewers are treated to some unique aquatic-based martial arts, before making his way back to land. Ted Smith was in the Mazzo-Zoanoid suit, frolicking in the waist-high water in an attempt to terrorize Kathy Christopherson's Cori. One undeniably heroic moment – as though it was taken straight out of a manga panel – has the Guyver jetting out of the water and proceeding to sever Mazzo's bug-head from his body. What sounds simple in theory and on-screen, was ultimately one of the more challenging aspects for Yuji and this wire-gag.

"Yes, in River Fight, Koichi and I played Guyver's stunt double," says Noguchi. "The shot of Guyver jumping out of the water was carried out by setting a wire on a camera crane. The suit got water in it and would double in weight. It must have been quite heavy when pulling me up."

"The River Fight is definitely one of the memorable fight scenes. It was shot in a desert area during a hot summer, and we would get easily dehydrated if we didn't remember to stay constantly hydrated. The Guyver suit was pasted with glue, so you couldn't take it off immediately. We [Koichi and I] tried not to waste energy by avoiding unnecessary movement and sitting still as soon as one shot was over. The staff around us also took care of the stunt performers, such as always bringing water," remembers Noguchi.

Another standout moment of physical dexterity takes place during the final fight and entails a complex wire-gag, which Noguchi was again due to execute. This brief sequence of moves was probably the most complex of the entire shoot for the stunt performer.

"The most difficult stunt for me was to run up the body of the Guyver Zoanoid and kick it in the head after performing a backflip," remembers Noguchi. "The position of the pick point [a point where the wires connect at the stunt performer's harness] was too high and I couldn't backflip well. I think it took about eight takes to succeed. Wire action can be performed smoothly, but only after understanding the inertia of the object," details Noguchi. "And sometimes we called the American stuntmen for help and asked them to do the stunts, but we were worried if they could safely do the dangerous stunts we wanted. But they often did the stunts incredibly well," says Noguchi.

And how was it to act and perform in the Guyver suit? Were there any physical problems Noguchi encountered, especially with the use of extensive wirework? "When I first wore the Guyver suit, I felt it was much lighter and more elastic than I had imagined," remembers Noguchi. "There is no doubt that Steve has devised a way to reduce physical stress and make the performers wearing these suits feel easier to move around."

"We had hard stunts to do, so the suits get sweaty and very heavy. When I took off my boots and turned it upside down, sweat would often flow out like a waterfall," continues Noguchi.

"The eye position of the Guyver mask and the eye position of the performer who wears it are not in the same position. The reason is that by adjusting the position of facial parts such as eyes and mouth and arranging them in a balance peculiar to the hero, the design becomes sharper and the hero feeling increases."

"Performers wearing masks will see through the round holes above the mask's eyes. A silver sphere is placed in the centre of the round hole, further narrowing the field of view. At first, the object was out of focus, and it was difficult to get a sense of perspective. So, to some extent, we performed by moving with our own senses," describes Noguchi.

"After the adjustment, for stunts where ensuring visibility is the highest priority, and stunts that move quickly and the details of the mask cannot be recognized, we were able to safely carry out the stunts by having the details of the hole part removed. In the wire stunt, I was a little cramped because I wore a Guyver suit with the harness attached, but I was focused on the performance, so I didn't mind."

"However, since the suit is covered with glue it was difficult to easily change the pick point that connects the wires. So, I predicted the position suitable for the stunt and decided the pick point. However, I thought that it would be quicker to adjust the technique sensuously than go through the process of peeling off the glue, adjusting the pick point, fixing it with glue again, and drying it, so I continued as it was. As a result, it took eight takes, so considering it now, it may have been faster to change the pick point. Either way, I'm happy with the result," says Noguchi.

Where there any other physical restrictions for Noguchi and the Alpha Stunt team while performing in the Guyver suits?

"Performance in the Guyver suits had various restrictions, such as weight and poor visibility. It's clearly different from doing stunt work without wearing a suit. Performers must act on that limitation without the viewer knowing it. The modelling part that can be physically corrected can be corrected by a professional, but it is the minimum range. The reason is that if the design collapses significantly due to stunts, it will also reduce the quality of the entire work. I believe that performing stunts while coping with limits will challenge your skills and, at the same time, lead to a further evolution of yourself. Stunts in suits are also difficult in that regard, and that's the real thrill," says Noguchi.

"In a nutshell, I think it was a fight with myself. From the moment you put on the Guyver costume, you are cut off from the surroundings. So, focus on the logical calculations to complete the stunt and try to moderately suppress the rise in adrenaline. The reason why you need to moderate the rise in adrenaline is that the more dangerous the stunts are, the more excited you are, so you need to calm yourself down to be able to perform the dangerous stunts safely."

Clearly a pragmatist, Noguchi looks at being a stuntman as thus: "What can be dealt with as a stuntman is dealt with as a stuntman."

One fight sequence that often gets left out of discussions of *Dark Hero's* impressive wirework is the brief, but no less effective, nighttime confrontation between Guyver and the first Zoanoid seen in this feature – Volker. The sequence wouldn't feel out of place in a Hong Kong Wuxia fantasy with its eerie forest atmosphere and abundance of fog. Outside of the climatic fight at the end of the film, this is possibly the only other fight sequence to use a lot of wirework gags (whereas the opening warehouse fight and the later river fight sequence would only use brief wire gags).

Noguchi remembers shooting the fight in the forest. "I think this was the first wire stunt sequence done in the Guyver suit," says Noguchi. "In fact, there were many wire stunts in this scene. I also remember Koichi having a stomach-ache. So, I was in charge of the acting part that he was supposed to do."

Akihiro 'Yuji' Noguchi in one of the Guyver stunt suits between shots during the night forest fight sequence that he helped Koichi Sakamoto with. Photo courtesy of Akihiro 'Yuji' Noguchi

"I did all the wire stunts in this scene and the trampoline stunts. I had so much fun and wasn't worrying about any limitations inherent in new suits. I was very tired the next day," recalls Noguchi. "The shooting time for this scene was very full on, sunset to dawn. Not only the action but also the first reveal of the Zoanoid was being filmed, and we were doing wire setting and rehearsal during that time, before it was filmed."

"Nowadays, most of the wire setting teams and performers will operate as separate teams, but back then we did everything with almost only three of us. It was super busy," recalls Noguchi. And did Wang use different frame speeds to help extenuate the action, much like in Hong Kong cinema? "Yes, the frame speed was decided by Steve's feeling, such as making it high speed to add slow-motion or dropping frames to add a sense of speed. Of course, Koichi's opinion as a coordinator was also respected by Steve," says Noguchi.

During the whole end fight sequence, there was a lot to contend with for the stunt performers and crew. It was now the height of summer (August 93'), the cave set was often boiling, the suits (both Guyver and Zoanoid alike) would become uncomfortable to wear despite the changes made to their flexibility (suit performers would only wear the headpieces when shooting), coupled with the exhausting physical feats from Alpha Stunts; it was still an enjoyable production for all involved.

Alpha had one or two mishaps while filming the action over a number of days, such as Noguchi landing awkwardly after a backflip onto a higher level; Koike would backflip off a small trampoline (which was then pulled out of shot once the jump was started) and was supposed to land on a padded mat, but possibly due to the weight of the helmet of the Guyver Zoanoid suit, Koike would miss the crash mat while landing and slip on the gravel floor. Thankfully, he would avoid any injury during the stunt and like any good stuntman, would brush it off and perform the move again.

Koichi Sakamoto and Akihiro 'Yuji' Noguchi quickly choreograph
a few moves in the cave set, in-between shooting the final third of the
Dark Hero's action sequences. Images courtesy of Stan Giesea
(taken from his behind-the-scenes footage)

A collection of stills which detail the behind-the-scenes shooting of the start of the action-packed final third, which includes Koichi Sakamoto (in the Guyver suit) facing off against several Zoanoids, Steve Wang overseeing the action on the playback monitors, and Asao Goto fixing some makeup on Ted Smith's Zoanoid of Sten. Images courtesy of Stan Giesea (taken from his behind-the-scenes footage)

Another collection of stills which details Koichi Sakamoto and Akihiro 'Yuji' Noguchi briefly rehearsing a complex backflip which takes place during the exhilarating final fight, between Guyver and Guyver Zoanoid. While Sakamoto and Noguchi would both double the Guyver, it would be the latter who pulled off the backflip on the trampoline due to his more compact height, which allowed him to clear the tight arc for the jump. Images courtesy of Stan Giesea (taken from his behind-the-scenes footage)

Stuntman Brian Simpson (as the Zoanoid version of Crane) rehearses a confrontation with Kathy Christopherson's Cori, as the actor walks through the Zoanoid punching her and the subsequent fall (onto a stunt mat) which takes place during the third act of *Dark Hero*. Images courtesy of Stan Giesea (taken from his behind-the-scenes footage)

Interlude II

A Brief History and Evolution of the 'Guyver Kick'

Due to Alpha Stunts' love of all things from Hong Kong action cinema and Japanese, Tokusatsu, Noguchi, Sakamoto, and Koike would not only wear those influences proudly on their sleeves but also innovate what came before in new and exciting ways. These influences (to those *au fait* with the minutiae of Hong Kong action cinema movement) are visible during a handful of moments in the latter half of *Dark Hero*.

For instance, during the final confrontation between the Guyver and the Guyver Zoanoid, the team pays homage to Sammo Hung's western-themed extravaganza, *Millionaire's Express* (1986). More specifically, they reference a few movements seen during the Yuen Biao and Dick Wai confrontation (the film would also feature Alpha Stunts' old mentor Yasuaki Kurata facing off against Richard Norton at one point).

Aside from the tense climactic face-off, one of the standout moments from *Dark Hero* which garnered a lot of respect from martial arts fans revolves around one particular kick. A kick that, despite evolving in the years since, has continued to garner adoration from all who witness it - whether the viewer is a fan of the film or not. The move in question is the eponymous Guyver Kick.

This gravity-defying move - executed by Noguchi in the film due to his stature and flexibility - elevates the already brilliant extended final fight extravaganza to new heights. Both figuratively and literally. Director Steve Wang and cinematographer Michael G. Wojciechowski effectively frame Noguchi's kick in a wide shot and at a higher frame rate to fully capture the remarkable display of action in all its glory.

With it gaining in popularity among Guyver fans and the action film community, post the release of *Dark Hero*, it stands to reason that audiences would see different iterations and interpretations as the years have rolled on.

Interestingly, while *Dark Hero* would not be the first film to showcase a version of this unique kick, Alpha Stunts and Noguchi would be the first to truly innovate and expand on what had come before to create an iconic martial arts kick.

"In the process of creating the flow for the action scene, you may instinctively feel that something special is required. I tried several patterns of special kicks with Tatsuro and Koichi, and the Guyver Kick was chosen as ultimately the most impressive, logical, and best-looking move. The special kick itself was modelled after several action moves and techniques that our predecessors had demonstrated," remembers Noguchi.

The first instance of a similar kick, or at least a form of it, would crop up in David Lai Dai-Wai's stylistic 1992 martial arts actioner *Operation Scorpio* (羯子戰); the move appears during a fight between South Korean martial artist Won Jin (Kim Won-jin) and the legendary Lau Kar-Leung, where the former executes the impossible looking gymnastic move in a blink-or-you'll-miss-it moment; apropos given for Won Jin's gymnastics background. In the same year, Alexander Lo Rei performed a variation of the kick, albeit less polished, for the low-budget Taiwanese action film *Life is a Bet* (dir. Liu Sung-Pai).

Yet it would be in the summer of 1993 when Alpha Stunts would reinvent what could be done with low-budget action, by crafting their spin on Tokusatsu-tinged action with a fusion of dynamic wirework and (the previously mentioned) Hong Kong action cinema influences.

This new, higher, and more elaborate kick quickly became a focal talking point for many martial arts enthusiasts, practitioners, and action fans who saw *Dark Hero*. Thus, the Guyver Kick was born.

A few years later, in 1996, the kick would appear in Isaac Florentine's short-lived TV series *WMAC Masters* (1995-1996) during the episode "Fired Up" (Episode 4, Season 2), where martial arts competitor Tsunami (Hien Nguyen) would perform it during his match with Great Wolf (Jamie Webster). Noguchi was also part of the cast (starring as Cyclone in Season 2) and would work with Nguyen on *The Mighty Morphin Power Rangers* during the same year, so no doubt the latter picked up a few tricks from his colleague.

Following the short-lived show, Wang and Alpha Stunts would reteam in 1997 for Steve Wang's cult action hit *Drive*, where martial arts star and actor Mark Dacascos (along with stuntman Tatsuro Koike briefly doubling the martial artist) would perform a variation of the kick during one of the high-octane fight sequences. For the sequence in question, a small motel room would play host to an evolution of the kick, as both performers used the space to dynamically kick off the wall (using the bed as a springboard) to cause untold pain to the goon on the receiving end of the foot.

It would be several years before the kick would appear again. When it did remerge, it would more than make up for the lost time by appearing in not one but two equally impressive low-budget martial arts films in the same year.

The first would be in Prachya Pinkaew's acclaimed Thai fight-fest, *Ong Bak* (2003), with star Tony Jaa performing the kick during a one-on-one fight with a goon as part of the painful final fight sequence.

A few months later (the still relatively unknown) Scott Adkins would be taught the kick by Noguchi during his time as stunt coordinator on Isaac Florentine's martial arts military thriller *Special Forces* (2003).

Adkins would later state in various interviews that Noguchi passed the kick down to him during this film, with the British martial artist using it again in Florentine's *Undisputed II: Last Man Standing* (2006), during his first stint as the prison fighter, Yuri Boyka.

His performance as Boyka would cement Adkins as one of the best martial artists in modern action cinema and lead to the signature kick becoming synonymous with the star (occasionally being dubbed the Boyka Kick by fans of the series).

Adkins would continue to use the kick in several of his future films, allowing a new generation of action fans to marvel at the martial arts skills and overall prowess required to pull off this particular kick. An impressive feat when factoring in the sheer height Adkins achieves with this kick. For reference, Noguchi is just over five feet, whereas Adkins has several more inches to factor in, making the height he can reach even more awe-inspiring.

It feels disappointing when the kick is absent from one of his films, as it's now so ingrained into his signature move set.

The Guyver Kick would also return to Asian action cinema before the start of the 2020s. During the climax of *Commando 2: The Black Money Trail (2017)* Bollywood superstar Vidyut Jammwal would briefly perform the kick during the film's climax. Although less visually spectacular due to the angle of the shot and the distinct lack of height on the kick, it's still an impressive feat when factoring in Jammwal's muscular stature into this complex manoeuvre.

A few years prior the kick would appear in another Bollywood feature titled *Boss* (2013). Actor Akshay Kumar would be the one to perform this move, albeit in a wire-assisted form that sadly reduces the impressive gymnastic feat into a dull moment during the fight sequence.

Most recently, it has appeared in Steven Kostanski's *PG: Psycho Goreman* (2020), a love letter to the 1980s and 1990s creature features which the director grew up with. Kostanski would also state it as a direct homage to *Guyver: Dark Hero*, one of his favourite films growing up. It appears to be only the second time a stunt performer has done the kick in full prosthetics or some form of creature suit (with the first being *Dark Hero*). For this kick, fight choreographer Alex Chung would perform the stylistic move.

Finally, German stuntman and martial artist Mike Möeller has begun incorporating it within his own martial arts skill set and has been seen demonstrating an even faster version on his many stunt reels. It's safe to say, the kick (whether you know it as the Guyver or Boyka kick) continues to be a badge of honour for any martial artist due to its technical complexity.

Even now, over 30 years on, Noguchi and Alpha Stunts' work with this kick remains incredibly influential within the action film community. It's exciting to think how the move might evolve several years from now, with its limit only being the athleticism and physicality of the human body.

Regarding the legacy of the kick, Noguchi sums it up best. "I didn't expect the Guyver Kick to be so famous, but I am very proud there are so many people in the action industry still talking about it, and I am grateful for being involved in the work," says Noguchi.

Decades on and Alpha Stunts' legacy continues to grow following their jaw-dropping work on *Dark Hero*. Whether Sakamoto, Noguchi, and Koike are working together on projects or separately on different properties, the initially small team set a new standard within low-budget action cinema that inspires and impresses countless new fans, much in the same way the dedicated work from Hong Kong cinema and Tokusatsu shows previously inspired Alpha Stunts.

Chapter Eleven

Papa's Got a Brand-New Bag!

If *Guyver: Dark Hero* was the opposite of *The Guyver* with its relatively easy-going production and even more independent with its budget and creativity, it would still encounter the occasional hiccup during its post-production process, particularly during the scoring and sound effects mixing.

Although *The Guyver* composer Mat Morse wouldn't return for this sequel, Steve Wang would reach out to a long-time friend and collaborator from *Kung Fu Rascals*: one Les Claypool. For *Dark Hero*, Claypool, and his very small team, would create the score and (now iconic) sound effects that would become another key component in the energetic lifeblood of this sequel. These key sonic elements helped to create a more unique flavour for *Dark Hero* and would help further separate it from the prior comedic entry.

Despite not being part of the original Guyver film, Claypool's background in film and having worked with Wang and Co. before, meant he'd always had an affinity and passion for filmmaking. All of this started with he and a friend's mutual love of Kung Fu movies.

"I used to have a friend of mine who lived across the street from me, a guy by the name of Yancy Calzada, who's worked on a ton of big visual effects in movies. Well, he and I wanted to make a film because we were studying martial arts at the time. We love Kung Fu movies, we love Bruce Lee, so let's make a Super 8 movie," recalls Claypool.

"So, we starred in it, and we wrote it together. I have my old Sensei and his Karate school dojo helping out because, you know, when it's a Super 8 movie, getting people to work for free is the key element. You don't have to act. You don't need to know anything. '*Are you free? Yes. Good. You're in it*,'" chuckles Claypool.

"So, we're making this movie and doing all this crazy stuff, all these big fights, and then one day, Yancy and I are sitting there watching dailies of it. We look at each other and go, '*Oh my God, we're making a Kung Fu movie that doesn't have a single Asian person in it. How did we get this far with no Asian people in a martial arts movie?*'

"Yancy knew a guy that was Filipino, and he worked at Rick Baker's creature shop. And he's like, '*Well, he's a martial artist, so there you go*'. Then we found out he has this other friend, guy by the name of Steve Wang who also makes Super-8 movies, and he also knows how to fight."

"We're both like, '*Oh, yeah! We need to talk to him*'. So, we got Steve into our movie. I can't remember what we did, although I think he did some fights, got beat up, whatever it was. And that just slowly morphed into, you know, me eventually becoming his son's godfather," recalls Claypool.

"I would also help him out and do the sound and music for an early Super 8 film he did called *Code Nine*, which he made in order to try to get financing to make a real feature length film. It was like a little demo going '*Look, we can make movies*'; sadly, that didn't really work out, but it did eventually lead to another project."

It wasn't long before Claypool's expertise was again called upon by Wang for *Kung Fu Rascals*, and like all collaborations with the director, it would involve more than one role for the composer and martial arts practitioner.

"Steve calls me up and is like '*Okay, you can fight. You're the main bad guy. And you can compose so you're going to be the composer and you've got a garage studio, so doing all the sound effects*', '*And how much am I getting paid for this?*' I ask. '*Taco Bell and McDonald's*'? '*I'm not sure I could live on that*'. Anyway, we got through *Rascals* and that eventually led to my dubbing career."

With *Kung Fu Rascals* being a springboard for Claypool's career in the industry, leading to him working on an eye-watering number of anime dubs and films, he would still collaborate with Wang on several other projects over a number of years. Much like Ted Smith, Wyatt Weed, Moto Hata, Asao Goto, and countless others, Wang would hire people who he knew he could trust and who understood his working patterns.

The kung fu enthusiast-cum-composer would become another part of the Wang repertory due to being multitalented and highly capable. "Every time Steve would get a project, he'd call me up. I actually auditioned for the first Guyver," remembers Claypool.

"I went into the office and played a little piece of music for him. What's ridiculous about that, it was roughly the main title theme which ended up in *Dark Hero*, but I had put this little Asian fla-voured comedic break in it – kind of *Kung Fu Rascal*-esque – in the centre of that cue, because I wasn't quite sure what direction they were going to go with the first movie."

"Afterwards, Steve pulls me aside and goes, '*Why did you put that thing in the middle? That has nothing to do with the movie we're making*' and then it ended up being what it was. I think I might have been ahead of my time. I wasn't really known or tapped for sound effects at that point, particularly when they did the first *Guyver*. I'd only really done *Kung Fu Rascals* and that's not exactly a calling card to score a multimillion-dollar movie. I was just a knucklehead in a garage doing sound and music," chuckles Claypool.

It wouldn't be long before Claypool did ultimately make a name for himself within the industry pre- and post-*Dark Hero*, specifically for anime dubbed into English. He, along with his wife Mary Claypool (after *Dark Hero*), would be responsible for English-language conversions of some legendary features such as: violent samurai feature *Ninja Scroll* (1993); *Armitage III* (1995); Mamoru Oshii's cyberpunk classic *Ghost in the Shell* (1995); *Street Fighter II: The Animated Movie* (1994); the 2000 release of *Lupin III: The Castle of Cagliostro* (1979); *Perfect Blue* (1997); the English dubbed version of *Guyver: Bio Booster Armor* in the early 1990s (1989-1992); and countless games in the 2000s including *Devil May Cry 3* (2005) and *Binary Domain* (2012).

When Wang started to assemble his team for *Dark Hero*'s production, Claypool was called on by Wang, having missed out on doing the music for the original film. "I was working on a number of anime titles at the time," recalls Claypool. "I had a one- room studio with a prefab voiceover booth, that's all I had."

"When I got tapped to do *Dark Hero*, I didn't even have any other employees. I was just dubbing, mixing, and doing sound effects work on all this anime. When Steve got me on to do the *Dark Hero* music, I didn't even have a legit music rig to do it. So, then I had to start researching that and trying to figure out what I needed to actually score a real damn movie," chuckles Claypool. He would be part of the project for roughly eight months, working as both the composer and supervising sound editor (along with his team), and it would be manic to say the least.

"It involved me finally buying my very first computer which was an Atari 1040 ST, which was really more for games, because it held a cartridge plug in the side for the games. If you spent the crazy money, you could max the computer out at 4 MGs, but it had no hard drive, so it was basically a cartridge and 4 MGs of RAM."

"I'm doing all this research and at the same time, I'm trying to figure out where I'm going to physically score *Dark Hero* because if I have one little studio with a voiceover booth, which is for anime, then I need a place where I can sit and compose a score on a new rig, especially as it wouldn't fit in that room anyway. So, I ended up taking over a little section of my landlord's office to try and convert that into a place where I could compose music for a feature film."

"Right next to me are telephones ringing and his office personnel, one of whom eventually became my wife. So, I'm doing that insanity, I'm trying to design, build and hire contractors to build a new studio because my landlord's let me take over a little bit more room because we're getting too busy for one little studio," recalls Claypool.

"In the midst of it all, I have to find somebody to help on *Dark Hero* because even though I did the music and helped with the sound effects on *Rascals,* it's not really going to work with all this other stuff going on. So now I have to hire somebody, hire facilities, figure out who's gonna do all the sound mixing and everything else while I'm scoring. I ran into Mark Allen, who I'd known previously, and then eventually I had to finally hire my first engineering employee because I can't score a film and dub countless anime simultaneously," recalls Claypool.

The score for *Dark Hero* would ultimately take on a new, darker life, to echo the change in the tonal shift. Gone were the whimsical heroics of the original music and instead a melodic, straightforward, and repetitive motif was woven into the film. Getting to these new sounds wasn't without its fair share of teething problems, though; in fact, based on Claypool's recollections, it's amazing the final film even exists.

With this being Wang's passion project, did he have any a specific idea of where the new score should go tonally? According to Claypool, Wang had an idea of how big he wanted to go with the sound, using various other cues as a jumping off point.

"You know, I honestly can't remember if he [Steve] gave me any actual directives, but what he did do, if I'm not mistaken, was put together a bunch of cues he liked 'cause he's a big soundtrack freak, like me, and he'd listen to soundtracks all the time. So, he has a whole bunch of cues that he thought would go with those scenes and I could listen to it."

"I'm like, '*Well, that's great if you know if our scoring budget's two and a half million dollars and a world-famous Academy Award-winning scoring conductor, but it's just gonna be read a couple samplers on a synthesizer sitting in an office cubby. I don't think I can replicate*'. The general feeling was that it was a combination of something mechanical, but since it's a bio armour, it doesn't have a human element to the mechanics of it all."

"So, I was basically looking for something that would kind of push the action forward with some sympathetic minor key tones, and I added an extremely loud frickin anvil sound," chuckles Claypool. "That was to try to give it that mechanical edge, along with, you know, more minor, sympathetic string section stuff. So that was kind of the general thinking."

"I didn't even have a rig at the time, and it took me a few months to build the rig. I think it was like September (1993) that I bought my first little significant purchase for the music, was some RAM for my sampler that I already actually had. I'm borrowing money left and right, including from Steve, so I could go out and buy all of this music gear."

"I ended up spending, over the course of a couple months, something like $9,900- odd dollars just to get this music rig up. And then I have to buy these office panels to have a little bit of privacy from his office; that was another 1,000 bucks almost. So now I'm paying to work on *Dark Hero*," remembers Claypool.

"I had a custom rig that I designed because only having the one little studio, there was no way for me to actually record the score when anime was being dubbed. So, to record the score, I'd have to take all that gear into my little room when they weren't using it. When I was ready to record, I'd take it in that room, record a few cues, drag it all back out and then start composing again," recalls Claypool.

This wouldn't be the only technical challenge Claypool would encounter while trying to record the score for *Dark Hero*. It would be a massive learning experience for the musician as he'd have to understand new (at the time) technological advances; in particular how to properly operate the computer that would be used to help compose the score.

It never rains but it pours, so the saying goes, and this was about to be the case for Claypool as Mother Nature had other plans on January 17, 1994, as The Northridge Earthquake hit at 4:30am.

"When the Northridge earthquake hit, it completely destroyed our home. I was living with my then girlfriend and soon-to-be-wife, Mary, in her third-storey condo. It completely destroyed and buckled the whole building. Elevator is out, stairs are a mess. So, I'm dealing with that as well. I was actually in the studio taking a nap on a couch and woke up after I was thrown onto the hard studio floor," recalls Claypool.

"I didn't find out until later that day that the condo had been so heavily damaged it became red-tagged. We had to evacuate, and because we were on the third floor and the elevator was unusable, everything had to be removed either by taking it down the stairs or lowering it with ropes over the balcony."

"1st of February 1994, I hired this guy, a consultant Peter Bruner, and he hung out with me for one night at my little station to basically teach me how to turn the computer on. *'This is how you launch the program, assign all this to that, that way they'll talk to your sequencers, these are your modules, your noisemakers, your sampler and then when you hit record'*. So, he's trying to give me the basics. I've never done any of this before. I had to deliver the opening credit thing and get it okayed less than a week after my time with Peter."

It's easy to see why most musicians could take composing on modern rigs and software for granted. The now antiquated Atari system is positively prehistoric compared to what can be achieved at the touch of a button in more recent years. It's hard to imagine a modern gaming console being used to create a full film score, but Claypool did so with the versatile Atari 1040 ST.

"That little game port on the side of the Atari is how the Cubase program works for sequencing MIDI instruments. It came on that cartridge because they knew everybody liked that Atari computer to do that stuff with it. There was no program to download or anything, you know, it's just a cartridge you plug in. Then I was like '*Okay, now we have a scoring program*', and that's how that whole thing started."

Claypool was clearly in awe of how the Atari worked for composing the score, particularly as this was his first time using something so complex to create the desired soundscape for *Dark Hero*.

"Here's the real deal on that. As I'm doing this composing, you know, it's not like I really had been doing this for years on end and could phone it in in my sleep, every single thing was like, '*Oh my God, I can't believe it, that's almost a cue. Oh, thank you Lord*'. Some of the same cues are used over and over, so it was a little repetitive, but I didn't have time to score every scene. Steve would often go '*Let's see what needs music*', then it we'd see if we could reuse certain cues," remembers Claypool.

When Claypool wasn't working out the score for *Dark Hero*, he would check in on the team he'd assembled to create the sound design for the film. This included working with the sound editor – in this case Mark Setrakian – who oversees the different foley work (every day or otherworldly sound effects reproduced within a sound studio for the film) for the Guyver and Zoanoids. This also includes all the kicks and punches and everything else that is heard in-between (such as footsteps, doors opening, gun sounds etc).

"I was the supervising sound editor and normally there will be the custom sound designer, who's in charge of anything you hear," recalls Claypool.

"They'll oversee the foley of the sound effects and backgrounds. Basically, they're involved in everything you hear no matter how minute. Well, there was no way in hell that I could do that and compose, so I ended up being more in charge of trying to find the right people. I knew Mark Setrakian, who would be the lead sound designer and he'd came up with a lot of cool custom sounds for *Dark Hero*."

"Mark is actually an amazingly brilliant animatronic artist," recalls Steve Wang. "He's one of the best in the business in creating animatronics and has created robots for industries like search and rescue, he's just a brilliant guy. For a while he was dabbling in music and sound effects, which led to him working on *Dark Hero*. We had a lot of creative discussions about how I wanted the suit to be organic."

"I wanted to feel like its living and so whenever he [Guyver] is moving you could feel the energy of it, feel it crackle," describes Wang. "You know, the whole undulating sound with the Guyver Unit and remind people that it's a living organism. So, Mark actually created all those sounds based on our conversation. He just did a brilliant job."

Claypool would also bring on a handful of other guys within the sound department in order to help where he might have been spread too thin during the composing stages. Whether it was foley artist Jeff Floro; Mark Setrakian; Mark Allen; or Stephen Tibbo who'd help mix the sound, Claypool was in good, supported company. With this crew, it allowed Claypool to focus on creating the distinct score, and distinct it was.

"I knew Mark Allen had an involvement with this place called Cubic Post that was still under construction at the time," recalls Claypool. "They would use Pro Tools and digital editing, and that was all fairly new back then. So, I basically just had Mark run with it like '*Okay, you guys are going to be in charge of all that, and Mark Setrakian will be our main sound designer, because he's, he's great at these crazy sounds*', he's like the mad scientist guy."

"Mark and I both knew that Guyver's foley would be really important and we needed somebody that was good and knew how to do this stuff. I honestly don't know who found Vincent Guisetti, but it may very well have been Mark. When I saw his [Vincent's] credits and some of the stuff he had done, along with having his own full rig that came with all his foley props, I'm like 'Okay, this is the guy'. I still have $1,000 deposit check stub for him from Valentine's Day 1994."

"I'd stop by occasionally and see what they're up to. Mark Allen would play me some sounds and I'd go 'That's great'!" and then I'd go back to composing. Then I'd go over to Mark Setrakian's house and be like, 'Well, that's excellent. Okay, back to composing'. So that that was kind of my involvement."

The sound design is another area that feels synonymous with *Dark Hero*'s distinctive quality, which in turn helps to differentiate it from other low-budget action fare. So good was the sound design, that Claypool and Wang would sneak in a little audio Easter egg towards the latter half of Wang's cult classic action-comedy *Drive*. During the final fight between Toby Wong (Mark Dacascos) and the Advanced Model (Masaya Katô), the organic Guyver suit sound can be heard when Toby's artificial heart starts malfunctioning. A nice little audio nod for fans of *Dark Hero*.

One sequence that required heavy foley work from the whole sound team was the water fight between Guyver and Zoanoids Mazzo and Volker (with Marcus thrown into the mix). As Claypool describes, it was an interesting experience for all involved.

"Cubic Post was definitely not ready or equipped for all the water foley taking place in their mix room," says Claypool.

"I'm sure you've noticed, there's a bit of fighting going on in the water. In *Guyver*. Well, there's no way to fake the sound of water, you have to fully use water, it's the only way to do it. That's why foley places have water pits and can allow for everything in a 15- or 20-feet area to get wet. That's why they're there."

"Well, Cubic Post, in their slightly infinite wisdom of construction, decided that in the mix room, since there's always a big, long area in front of a mixing board, before you get to the screen and the speaker, put like ping pong tables in there and couches and places to eat and all that because it's essentially dead space."

"Well, Cubic decided that'll be where we'll do all our foley, in that big empty space, since they were space limited. I don't think they counted on their very first show, which I believe was us, having all these water fights and splashing around in a kid's wading pool as water went all over the place, on their gear, their carpet, everything else," chuckles Claypool.

"I remember going in there and seeing this wet mess and seeing Vincent happy as a clam because he's doing great work, whereas the owners and everybody else had a look on their face like what did they say yes to." Water antics aside, Claypool would encounter another issue while the mixing of the score into scenes was taking place.

Due to the overall hectic nature of the sound production time and budget constraints, Wang and Setrakian would start to physically mix the movie in the same room. Although this was done with the best intentions due to time limitations, as Claypool would describe it ultimately led to losing some time due to him not being present during the mix.

"At one point Steve, and I think it was Mark Setrakian, started to physically mix the movie in that room and were getting really happy with the way it was coming out," remembers Claypool.

"Before this all got laid back to video, I ended up getting the tapes and hearing it and I'm like, '*Guys, this is all wrong. I listened to it, but I don't think you're hearing what's being printed to tape*'. This is just my memories of dealing with it, but what they were hearing and what they were mixing is not what was making it to tape – they had to figure that whole thing out."

"I don't know if to this day, for me at least, if *Dark Hero* sounds incorrectly mixed. There are things that are too loud, there are things that are too low there. There are times when there's not a consistent balance between sounds, so there are those types of issues, I think because of money, lack of time, and then some sort of technical issues you know."

Claypool would encounter another audio issue during the climatic fight sequence between Guyver and the Guyver Zoanoid. Initially, the scene wasn't due to have any musical accompaniment, as Wang wanting just the sound effects to be the main dominant fixture.

"That was one of those things where I wasn't even supposed to score the scene," says Claypool. "Steve didn't want music, and the sound effects guys, Mark Allen and his crew, Mark Setrakian and all those guys, they were getting kind of tired of my big bombastic music, covering all of their sound effects. When they heard I wasn't putting any of the music over the whole end fight, they were probably like '*Excellent*'," chuckles Claypool.

"We were so rushed as the delivery date was in, like, three days or something to have this movie finished. I'm like, '*Okay, I'll just start working on the end credit score*'. I mean, I'm exhausted, burned out, I don't even know what a bed looks like at this point. So, as I'm just gearing up to start that process to do the end cue and then the end credits cue, Steve calls me. '*We're mixing the end fight, but it's not exciting enough*', and I'm like '*The one that you said you want the sound effects to carry the fight?*' '*Yeah, that's not working. We need a music cue*'. I was like, '*I don't even know who the president is, or the last time I was in bed, dude, I'm exhausted*'. They were mixing that scene then and needed a music cue. So, I run into my catering area in the studios and suck down a load of caffeine beverages."

Extremely caffeinated and mentally fried, Claypool would meet with Wang and the rest of the sound team to get the impromptu final music cue done at short notice.

"I'm completely fried. I have to compose a music cue while they're waiting for it in the little mix room. So, I go back in, and I get on with composing. Because I'm caffeinated through the roof you can hear how fast that cue is if you listen closely," chuckles Claypool. "There are plenty of wrong notes that made it into the movie, but there was just no time to do anything about it."

"So, I do all of this, I feel like I'm about to die and then I'm like *'Oh my God, that's just the sequencer'*. Now I got to record it to tape, and they've got to come pick the tape up and take it over and transfer it for the mix guys."

"After all that, I give it to them, and I just collapsed. They mix it into the movie. Steve calls and goes, *'Oh my God. Now the incredible fight is too exciting. It's so fast and cranked up'* and I'm like, *'Yeah, so would you be if you sucked down those caffeinated drinks.'* That's the ridiculous story of the end fight," says Claypool.

"I do know that both the Marks and everybody else in the sound crew were not happy, as Steve ended cranking up that music and put that new cue over their beautiful fight scene."

A highly caffeinated Claypool ultimately worked in the film's favour, as the frenetic energy underpins the entire final fight. Along with the sound design and score, it raises the stakes during the final confrontation. It's hard not to get goosebumps while watching the scene play out and proves last minute, stressful creativity can work for certain scenes.

"Another crazy thing which happened during all of this, is that I had hired a supposed film music mix engineer who came from the mix place they were going to use to actually mix the film itself," remembers Claypool.

"He came into my studio and was in my little room mixing the cues I had finished while I was still composing in my little office, because that's how crazy the deadline was. Plus, every once in a while, I would have to pack up and go listen to something they were doing to make sure it's all okay."

"This is why Mark Allen, if you want to get into semantics, was really the supervising sound editor, even though I was hired to do it. He ended up doing most of what I was supposed to be doing, because I was just overwhelmed with the score."

"Anyway, this guy comes in and he's mixing in my room and I'm composing. I go in and listen to what he's done, and everything is either in the left speaker or the right speaker. I'm like, *'That's the freakiest thing I've ever heard in my life. What is that?'* Basically, there's nothing up the middle in the whole movie."

"The kettle drum is to the left and the anvil is to the right, nothing made sense. So, I said *'No, that sounds horrible'.* And he says, *'Well, that's what the Dolby box wants to hear'.* Wasn't sure what Dolby box was, but I bought enough soundtracks in my life, and I said, *'No, you got to have stuff up the middle, they can always dip it, you know, or re-equalize it, that's what mixers can do'.* He grumbled about it, and I just said, he needed to remix these cues."

"I go back in, it may have been the next day, I'm listening to the new version and it's essentially the same mess with maybe a little bit of difference. I just looked at him and go, *'I'm sorry dude, I gotta let you go'.* I essentially had to remix the majority of the film score in a day, so I could get it to the guys so they could, you know, mix it in, I then go back to composing in the madness," remembers Claypool.

On March 19, 1994, the audio layback (the process of putting the audio back into the final version of the film) was added to the first half of the final mix. These next two days would be a particularly bizarre and hectic time for Claypool.

"Basically, the videotapes they're going to use for this premiere, they didn't have sound added yet, and this was the morning before," recalls the composer.

"So, at 4am I'm sitting there, laying back the audio to the video for the first half of the movie. We have an aftershock from January's earthquake and the whole damn place just shuts down. There are power failures and everything else, and we're like, *'Our master tape is in that machine!'* We get through the aftershocks and the power comes back on, we check the tapes, and they are fine. We finished that layback, you know, whatever stupid hour of the morning it was. Keep in mind, the next day is a screening, and so now Steve has half a movie."

March 20, 1994, *Guyver: Dark Hero* would receive a premiere fan screening at the L.A. Comic Con (in the Shrine Auditorium). Finally, the hard work for all involved on *Dark Hero* was about to be screened for the first time. Except there were a number of problems.

"At the screening, what ended up happening was they're filing into the comic convention for *Dark Hero* and there is no second half of the movie in Steve's hands for the premiere. I was actually writing the end credit music while people were waiting to see the movie," recalls Claypool of the final stressful period.

"Producer Ken Iyadomi was sitting behind me saying, '*Fine, moving on*', every time I stopped playing because he's panicking. I had to tell him that I was simply playing the music into the computer, and nothing had been recorded yet."

"I finished the end credit cues, which ended up being kind of a cut-and-paste thing. If you listen to it, you're like, '*Oh, I remember that part from that*'. It's not pasting music cue stuff, it's pasting data. So, I grabbed this data, throw it there, '*Oh, look, there's a string section playing the Guyver theme, lets add that*'. I finish it and then I have to lay it to tape. To do that, we have to run it over to the same video lay back house that shut down from the aftershock."

"We lay it back to tape and Ken drives it back out to the Shrine Auditorium. The people in the screening have been waiting roughly three hours for the second half of *Guyver: Dark Hero*," recalls Claypool.

Clearly the film had struck a chord with a number of attendees if they waited around to see the second half of the film. "Steve [Wang] told me this recently, he said roughly 80-ish percent of the people stayed. Even though the convention itself was closed, the booths were shutting, and people were packing up, there are still people in the audience."

"I was working as fast as I can, so after roughly three hours, everybody got to see the rest of the movie. I just thought to myself, *'The movie industry really can't work like this all the time?'* Then, of course, years later, I find out it's not all that rare and there's craziness out there on a daily basis," chuckles Claypool.

How does Claypool feel about this film, especially considering how difficult the post-production process was to finish it?

"Obviously, look at what was going on with Steve. He had no money and some of the hours he worked were inhuman, spending months sleeping on a floor with an hour to sleep a day. You know, 'Welcome to the low-budget movie industry'. So technically, the movie shouldn't even exist. I think it's a miracle that it exists for the budget."

"For *Guyver: Dark Hero*, it's one of those things where I'm not sure how to even phrase it," contemplates Claypool.

"I'm incredibly proud of what everybody did within the circumstances and what it was done under. I look at it and go, *'Damn, that's a great shot'* or *'Damn, that's an amazing stunt and, wow, those costumes are so cool'*, you know? I'm relatively happy with the overall arc of my score. Maybe not the minutiae of the mix, such as the notes and all that. But I don't really get to look at it in any other way than that," says Claypool.

With its repetitive beat and sinister undertones, the score for *Dark Hero* very much lingers with the viewer, even after a first screening. It's direct, to the point, and personifies the new tone of this soft reboot/sequel. Claypool's score is the final piece of the *Dark Hero* puzzle; without it the film would, without a doubt, lose some of its unique identity.

Despite the composer's humbling opinion of his own work, the score continues to resonate with fans and audiences' decades on. Much like John Williams' iconic theme for *Jaws* (1974) or even Fred

Myrow's score for Don Coscarelli's cult classic *Phantasm* (1978), it proves that regardless of budget, the best and most long-lasting themes are sometimes the ones which are the most simplistic or repetitive.

If Mat Morse's score for *The Guyver* taps into the whimsy and gonzo nature of the first film's erratic tone, then Claypool's *Guyver: Dark Hero* score and cues tap into the darker side of this superhero. For that, it should be applauded. It really is amazing the score, and to an extent the finished film, ever saw the light of day.

Following the preview screening, *Guyver: Dark Hero* would release a month later in Japan on April 20, 1994. It would find its way to U.K. rental stores (albeit in a trimmed down version 100-minute cut) on August 5, 1994, and in Europe (specifically Germany) a month later on September 27, 1994. It wouldn't be released in the United States until October 19, 1994.

Reviews were kinder to this sequel/reboot, with it being more faithful to Yoshiki Takaya's source material, darker in tone, and had praise lavished at its exceptional fight sequences. *Guyver: Dark Hero* quickly became more highly regarded than its more comedic predecessor.

After *Dark Hero* was starting to make its way to video stores for rental, Kathy Christopherson and David Hayter had a brief encounter with a potential viewer. "A funny thing happened after the movie came out. David and I popped into a video store and strolled over to where *Guyver: Dark Hero* was sitting on the shelf," recalls Christopherson.

"A customer just happened to be looking at the video box, so we stood nearby, waiting to see if they noticed anything unusual. Finally, David asked him about the movie. The guy looked right at us and said, '*Oh, it's about these young people trying to act like they're in their 20s*'. It never occurred to him that he was talking to the two leads. We cracked up as we were in our 20s," remembers Christopherson.

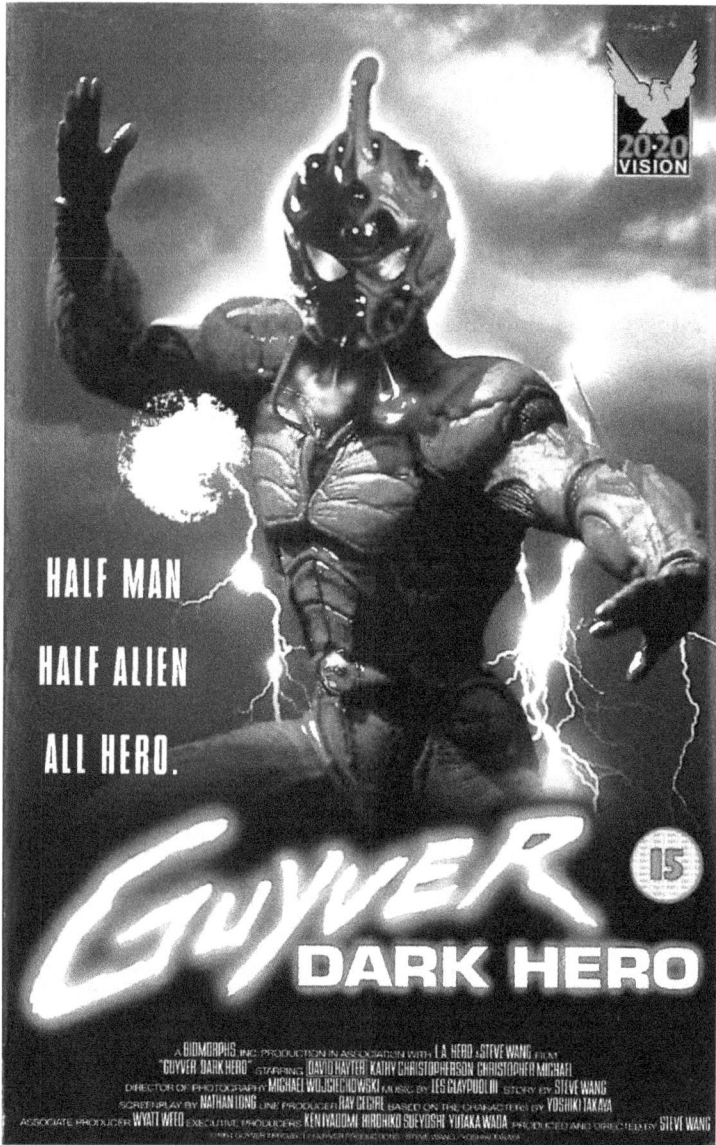

The U.K. VHS big box cover for the rental version of *Guyver: Dark Hero*.
20•20 Vision. Photo courtesy of Peter Hayward-Bailey

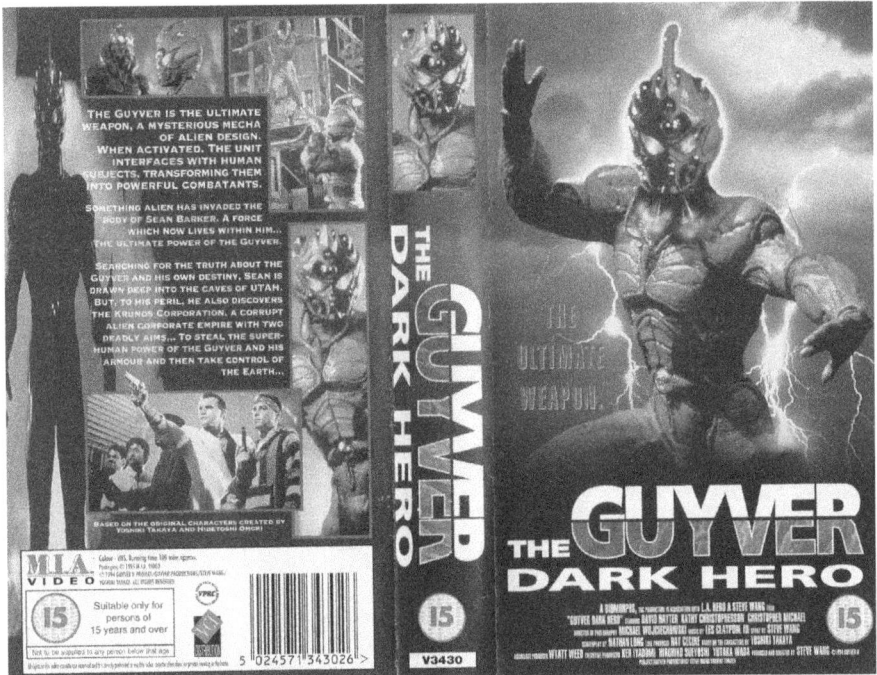

The second U.K. VHS cover for the retail version of *Guyver: Dark Hero*. For this release, the cover font would be changed, giving it a more sterile look compared to the previous release's more stylised font. M.I.A. Video/ VCI Distribution. Photo from Author's Own Collection

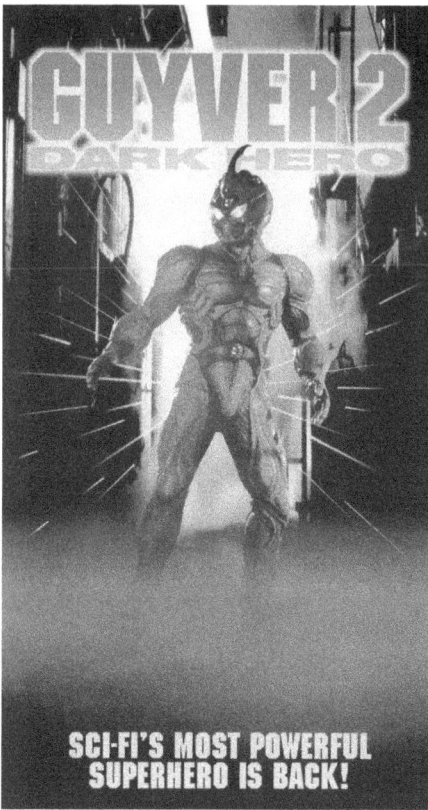

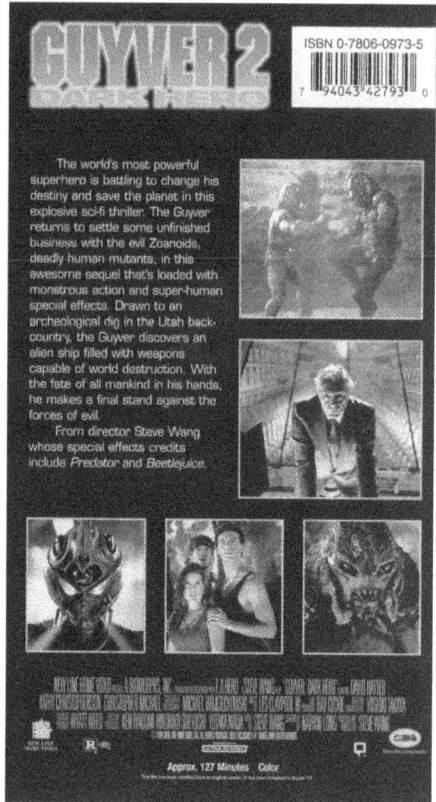

The front and back of the U.S. cardboard cover for *Guyver: Dark Hero* or *Guyver 2: Dark Hero* as it was called in the States due to the non-title change of the first film. New Line Home Video/ Turner Entertainment. Photo courtesy of Wyatt Weed (from his personal collection)

The Japanese VHS cover for *Guyver: Dark Hero*. Bandai/Emotion

An alternative cover for the Japanese VHS of Guyver: Dark Hero. Note the different background to the prior image. The alternative cover also lists this as the 'Japanese Dub Version'. The other VHS release would have subtitled for Japanese audiences. Bandi/Emotion

The Japanese Laserdisc release of *Guyver: Dark Hero*. The film came on two 12' discs and played on three sides (Sides A, B, C). On the third side of the disc, once the film finished, Takuya Wada's 20-minute *Making of Guyver: Dark Hero* would play (in English with Japanese subtitles). Bandai/Emotion

The Swiss VHS cover for *Guyver: Dark Hero* which was also sold in Germany. The DVD release from Phoenix Distribution several years later would contain the 20-minute "Making of" that was on the Japanese Laserdisc. Both the VHS and DVD would be significantly cut for violence due to Germany's censorship laws. MPC

The first U.K. DVD for *Guyver: Dark Hero* would, like its VHS counterpart, contain a trimmed-down version of the film (100-minutes) and was released as a budget disc. M.I.A./VCI.

The second (and currently final) U.K. release of *Guyver: Dark Hero*. This would be released in 2007, several years after the M.I.A version and was the first time Steve Wang's full two-hour version would be released on a physical format in the U.K. and included everything prior fans in the U.S. would have seen from its original release. It was marketed as the 'Special Extended Version', despite it being Wang's original vision. Again, it would be a budget release. Pegasus Entertainment/Showcase Entertainment. Photo from Author's Own Collection.

Chapter Twelve

A Bio-Boosted Legacy

Few films, particularly those that are direct-to-video, have such enduring legacies as both *Guyver* films, which is in large part due to the talent behind and in-front of the camera. With both films being video store staples in the 1990s, it was only a matter of time before their low-budget special effects magic would go on to inspire a whole new generation of filmmakers.

Whether it was because of the comparisons to other Tokusatsu entertainment from the 1990s, such as *Power Rangers*, *Masked Rider*, *VR Troopers* or *Big Bad Beetleborgs* - all of which had their action footage taken from other Japanese Tokusatsu productions and retrofitted for Western audiences by Saban Entertainment – the practical effects, stunt work or the visual aesthetic of the Guyver suit would ingrain themselves into the minds of many aspiring filmmakers.

Despite their more mature age ratings (especially within Europe), many pre-teens would discover the violent pleasures of both *Guyver* films due to many parents' rental mistakes – as was the trend of the 1990s and the accessibility of video stores.

The *Guyver* films – particularly *Guyver: Dark Hero* – would go on to inspire two low-budget filmmakers, countries apart from each other.

First, there is Canadian filmmaker Steven Kostanski, who has garnered a sizable reputation for himself among the horror community for his elaborate practical effects feature films, usually on miniscule budgets. Kostanski gained notoriety during his time with filmmaking company Astron-6 and their violent schlock, which took inspiration from the Grindhouse era of low-budget and low-brow drive-in cheapies.

Astron-6's most well-known features among schlock aficionados are the Troma Team distributed *Father's Day (2011)*, a delightfully lewd descent into shock and gross excess, harking back to the Video Nasty era of film. *The Editor* (2014) would show a more refined side to Astron-6 as they delved into Italian Giallo, paying homage to the likes of Dario Argento, Mario Bava and Sergio Martino and their oeuvre of psychedelic serial killer thrillers.

Although all these features were co-directed by Kostanski, Adam Brooks, Jeremy Gillespie, Matt Kennedy, and Conor Sweeney, in the same year as *Father's Day* Kostanski would direct his first solo feature *Manborg* (2011). This loving homage of straight-to-video post-apocalyptic action flicks, which lined the rental shelves of the 1980s, was met with acclaim from various film festivals such as Austin, Texas' Fantastic Fest.

Produced by Astron-6 on a micro-budget of $1,000 (CAD) and shot against a green screen in Kostanski's parent's garage; it quickly gained a cult reputation and cemented Kostanski as a micro-budget pioneer, creating features like those he grew up watching. The influence of the VHS era was clear with his follow-ups *The Void* (2016), *Leprechaun Returns* (2018) and *Psycho Goreman* (2020), the latter proudly wearing the Guyver inspired aesthetics on its blood-soaked sleeve (most notably using the aforementioned 'Guyver Kick' during a fight sequence).

"When I was a kid growing up with my parents in the 90s, we had a cabin that we'd go to on weekends in the summer that my parents bought. We'd pretty much go up there every weekend, that's just kind of the thing to do when you're young in Canada. So, we'd go there and just swim and do nature stuff," recalls Kostanski.

"I wasn't really interested in doing the nature stuff, so we had a TV set up there and VCR and every weekend we would go rent movies. We had a few video stores in our area, so we'd be pretty spoiled as far as options. But there was this one place, I believe called Video Cluster, where we'd rented from and my mom would go and just like grab movies, like 10, seven-day rentals and bring them to the cabin because she knew that I would probably want to just sit and watch movies. We'd also do the typical, family movie night hang as well, an activity that the whole family can do."

"I have so many memories of watching just so many random movies that my mom would pick out and we'd just all sit and watch collectively. So, one weekend in this stack of movies was a copy of *Guyver: Dark Hero*. My mom didn't understand that it was a sequel, but she saw it had like a cool alien suit on the cover and she was probably like '*Steve will like this. He's big into Power Rangers and stuff*. And I guess she didn't clock the rating on it. Because I believe it was R rated," chuckles Kostanski.

Turns out it was a defining moment for the young Kostanski, as both he and his family sat and watched it together during their movie night, despite none of them being into the film itself, as Kostanski recalls.

"My family wasn't into it and were like '*What the hell is this thing?* whereas I was just so enthralled by it. It was one of those cases where it gave you just enough information to understand what was going on. Like I kind of felt like it had a *Star Wars* vibe if you're coming into the middle of an adventure. And so, I didn't really know who the characters were and what their relationships were at the beginning, and that's because it's tying up loose ends from the first movie."

"I remember when the movie first starts with that great fight scene in the warehouse with those really diverse criminals and their flamboyant wardrobe, and they're talking about this scam where they put cocaine in plastic dolls and then melting it down. It's like the wildest thing committed to film."

"As a kid I was like, '*Oh, maybe this is gonna be a little too intense for me*', but to be honest watching R-rated movies as a kid was special and magical because you're always scared that it was going to get too intense for you. Like something was going to happen. That it was too much. Like the guy melting at the end of *Robocop*, that sort of thing just gets burned in your brain and becomes this trauma that you have to deal with for the rest of your life."

Despite the traumatic R-Rated violence, *Dark Hero* still managed to hook Kostanski, particularly when the action started to take place.

"When the Guyver shows up, I was just like, totally hooked. I loved how much detail they gave him like glowing eyes and having those insect-like nodules moving around on the sides of his head, and then the air blasting out. I was just like, '*Okay, this is all the things I like*'. Then there's a bunch of like kicky-punchy martial arts stuff and I'm like, '*Yes, now it's just like Power Rangers. This is awesome*'. But then the scene ends with him slitting the guy's throat, and I remember being horrified like, '*Oh my God! The Red Ranger would never do that in the Power Rangers*'. I loved it and I was terrified of it at the same time," recalls Kostanski.

Guyver: Dark Hero continued to absorb into Kostanski's imagination and despite the love-hate relationship he had with it during his formative years, he learnt to really appreciate the stylistic choices and aesthetics applied throughout the film. None more so was this the case than during the final climatic fight, as the director explains.

"There was this tug-o-war between loving it and fearing it, and it just made me respect it so much. Even as a kid, watching that end fight, to me, it's one of the best end fights in a movie ever. Even now, if I can get to a point where I am making something that's like that scene in my career, I think I will have considered myself a success."

There are a few parallels between Kostanski and Wang for those versed in each of the director's works and careers. Both started out as effects artists on other people's projects and in-between each film, they would direct their own shorts or features. Kostanski sees Wang as both an inspiration and role model of sorts to creature effects, particularly for the millennial generation.

"Steve is absolutely an inspiration to me and he's just on another level that, I don't know if we'll ever really see it again. His style and aesthetic look; I just I love it so much. It's so specific and you can tell he's putting his own spin on everything that he does. That's what I want more of in creature effects, especially now where everything feels very homogenized to me, where a lot of creature design feels very over-designed," says Kostanski.

"I feel like in Steve Wang's heyday, like the late 1980s, 1990s and 2000s, he was just making stuff look so cool and iconic. I also feel like there's less of a push to make things iconic nowadays than there was back then, where everything did have its own look and its own vibe. There's so much personality and character to these creatures that are, ultimately, kind of inanimate and unrealistic."

"But it's more just about the overall kind of tone they set and I just love that style so much. It's the kind of thing that I want to make, by getting away from this obsession with realism and being more just about looking cool and, again, looking exciting, fun, and memorable. You know, it doesn't have to be the most articulate thing," says Kostanski.

Kostanski would even go on to pay homage to both of the *Guyver* films in his effects heavy creature feature *PG: Psycho Gore-man* (2020). Whether it's in a few design choices on characters or a nice call back to the films which inspired him and left an indelible impression that both *Guyver* films had on him as a child.

For instance, the previously mentioned Guyver Kick found its way into one action sequence due to another Guyver fan being on the crew.

"That was Alex Chung our stunt coordinator who played Dark Scream. He really wanted to put the Guyver Kick in somewhere. It was a really hellish two days of trying to shoot that whole sequence and it originally had way more chorography in it. We got to a point where we're just running around with cameras trying to get shots. Thankfully, Alex is super smart and was able to plan the choreography to what I want to get within a reasonable amount of time. We still managed to get a bunch of fun stuff in there and the Guyver Kick was part of that."

Steven Kostanski wasn't the only young cinephile in the 1990s who was instantly hooked in and then inspired by Wang and Co's work on the *Guyver* films. In the far-flung county of Lancashire, a pre-teenage wannabe filmmaker, MJ Dixon, would view a 12-part anime series that led to his obsession of low-budget filmmaking found within *The Guyver* and *Guyver: Dark Hero*.

In more recent years, Dixon (along with his producing partner and wife Anna Dixon) has gained a steady fan base among the micro-budget horror crowd, not just within the U.K. but several other regions as well (especially in the U.S.).

Even with the minuscule budgets that Dixon and his wife have secured, it has not hindered the ambition of Mycho Films. The duo has created a slasher film universe filled with characters who often crossover or appear in each other's films. It's a low-budget slasher cottage industry filled with collectables, comic crossovers, video games, and other merchandise. Budget, it seems, does not outweigh Dixon's ambitious nature or creative endeavors.

While films such as *Halloween (1978)* and *Friday the 13th (1980),* along with their slew of sequels and reboots, helped inspire Dixon's mythical slasher villains, he'd also find inspiration from the *Guyver* films, all of which set him off on his filmmaking path. It all started with personal discovery through a lack of finances, which led to a wealth of otherworldly creativity.

"I didn't have a lot of money as a kid, so I was constantly trading in games and stuff at this little second-hand shop that did VHS and video games," recalls Dixon.

"I'd be constantly trading stuff in to watch *The Guyver* anime series. In my head I'd go '*If I trade this in, I have enough to swap for, like, a cheaper game and an episode of* Guyver *and bring that episode of* Guyver *back and I can trade that against another game, then I can get two episodes of* Guyver'. It went on like that and eventually, I kind of filled the gap of my knowledge with all 12 episodes, although completely out of order. It was just whatever I could get hold off in second-hand shops and things like that."

With Dixon's love of all things Guyver only being further cemented, even if the anime titles were out of order, his young pre-pubescent mind was about to be changed after learning of the live-action features.

"After working through those episodes, I remember someone asked if I'd seen the film. I was like, '*What? What film?*' I managed to convince someone I went to school with to tape it off their satellite movie channel. I think it might have been on the Sci-Fi (now Syfy) Channel, and so for years, I had this videotape that had two films - *Bill and Ted's Bogus Journey* (1991), followed by *Guyver: Dark Hero* straight after. I just used to bunk off school, saying to my parents '*err...I don't feel too good today*' and I'd stay at home and when everyone was out of the house, I would just sit and watch this tape."

With the discovery of the second film – although this was unknown to him at the time – Dixon's love affair with *Dark Hero* now far exceeded his passion for the anime series. The film had a hold over him, a powerful hold from the looks of things. Very few films could make one want to ditch school to indulge in the action-packed, low-budget insanity on display in *Dark Hero*.

There were to be further revelations for Dixon, though, as unbeknownst to his younger self the Guyver back catalogue would have one further surprise for him. As previously touched upon, territories outside of the U.S. (for supposed marketing reasons to capitalize on the live-action *Teenage Mutant Ninja Turtles*) the first *Guyver* film went by the title of *Mutronics: The Movie* in an attempt to appeal to a broader audience. This was mainly because *The Guyver* had not yet transitioned from its Eastern origin and would be a little-known title until a few years later, particularly with the (the now defunct) Manga Video VHS release of the 1989 OVA series in 1994 - the same year as *Dark Hero's* VHS release.

With *Dark Hero* not given a numeral on its cover in the U.K. (albeit in certain regions such as the U.S. where the numeral of two was added for clarity), most people who rented *Dark Hero* didn't make the connection between the two films and often viewed it as a standalone title. Dixon was no different and was elated to know there was another live-action version of this character which had passed him by.

"I was talking with someone about *Dark Hero*, and they said to me '*Have you not seen the first one?*' and I was like, '*What first one?*' They told me about *Mutronics: The Movie* aka *The Guyver* and it became like, this legendary thing to me. Every time I went to my local Blockbuster, which was about an hour and a half walk away from my house, it was out every single time as they only had one copy."

"Back then I was, like, someone's always got this film out, you know, and every time I'd go back, they'd say something like '*Oh, it was due back three days ago*'. I was always like '*How do I keep missing this*'? I think it was my 13th or 14th birthday. I went to HMV, and it was just there, sat on the shelf. I think it was a deleted title at the time as well," recalls Dixon.

"Looking back on it now, I'm 100% sure that my grandfather had gone and ordered it in, so it'd be on the shelf on that day. To me it just seemed like a bit of a miracle, that on my birthday I went in and this film that I talked to him about every week when he'd taken us out, was suddenly on the shelf. Finally, I had my copy of *The Guyver / Mutronics: The Movie*."

Like many creatives during their formative years, Dixon had found something his young mind could latch onto and help inspire him with his pursuits. If Wang and Co. could make these impressive sets, fight sequences and creatures with some skill and minimal money, then a lad from the U.K.'s North could do the same. These elements alone were not the only parts that piqued Dixon's interest, but also how both films felt so uniquely different from most major studio productions.

"It was the low-budget of *Dark Hero* that felt very organic, as it's all very much shot on location, apart from the soundstage ship sequences. The first *Guyver* definitely feels like a more polished production, you can tell it has a bit more money behind it, at least compared to the second film. Whilst the second one genuinely feels like independent filmmakers are making the movie," says Dixon.

It was this rough and ready, seat-of-your-pants style of filmmaking that continued to impress Dixon with each recurrent viewing.

"I watched the Director's Cut / Extended Version recently, having not revisited it in about two or three years, and started to look at a lot of the background details. What I really like about it, is that it taught me a lot about what you can do in terms of when you have absolutely nothing. One really great example of how low budgets breed creativity is the cliff jumping scene. Is it a short sequence? Nope, it's almost like an anime itself with its shots. It's a cleverly planned sequence with some basic animation, and a few other people in the Guyver suits, etc. I think that's the moment when I realized, '*Wow! I could do so much with so little*', just by thinking of where the camera is placed and how it moves."

"I mean Steve is genuinely like the master of doing stuff like this when you look over these films, especially with *Drive* (1997) which just solidifies the whole kind of theory that he really knows what he's doing, in terms of where and how he's moving the camera, and how it's all done with purpose. That's one of the other things I've absolutely carried with me for my entire career, just using the camera with purpose. It's like the no budget rules, to some degree, of smashing through your budget shortcomings by making each shot count," says Dixon.

When Dixon got around to making his first short film starring his infamous slasher Thorn, it was during the early days of social media connecting on a more global level. Keen to get as many people to view his short as possible, Dixon would eventually stumble upon Steve Wang's own social media profile (during the early Myspace days). Dixon took the plunge and thought it was the perfect opportunity to engage with his favourite filmmaker,

"I made a short film version of *Thorn* in 2009 and I remember sending that to Steve via Myspace. He wrote me back an incredibly lovely letter saying how much he enjoyed the film, then gave me some advice on filmmaking. It was just absolutely like one of the best moments of my life," recalls Dixon.

"Looking back at *Dark Hero*, I know I want to pass the ideal they had while making it, along to our stuff. Each of our films is held together with sheer willpower, we can't make these films with the resources we don't have. I take a lot of that spirit with me whenever we go on to our own sets."

"I think no budget can work in a film's favour. There's kind of a thing where suddenly there isn't all the contracts and infighting over who gets what and such. Suddenly, you're just all in it together. It's like, '*Look guys, can we stay an extra couple hours to get this shot, and it can be done*', you know."

The features from Mycho are much like Wang's and Kostanski's features, made with passion and devotion to the craft of low-to-micro-budget filmmaking. When a viewer forgives or embraces the imperfections and can sense the love these features are made with, they take on a whole new meaning outside of conventional film criticism.

And what of the cast and crew in the years since the release of *Guyver: Dark Hero*? Wang and Co. would reteam for one final film: the cult martial arts darling *Drive*, a fast-paced action comedy with some of the best action ever committed to a DTV action film. Often seen as a progenitor to the more widely discussed *Rush Hour* (1998), *Drive* remains a fitting finale for Wang and Co's style of filmmaking, particularly with the Director's Cut version.

Drive feels like an accumulation of all the work Wang and Co. put into *Dark Hero*. The crew would set new standards for inventive low-budget martial arts action by creating another low-budget action epic. One that continues to garner new fans, even now.

Although Wang wouldn't direct another feature film after *Drive* (at least at the time of writing), his brother Michael, Nathan Long, Kathy Christopherson and himself would work together on the Westernised and retrofitted version of *Kamen Rider Ryuki* – retitled *Kamen Rider: Dragon Knight*.

Since *Drive*, a lot of the cast and crew have gone on to prolific careers within the film industry. David Hayter, while most known to gamers as the iconic Solid Snake from Hideo Kojima's legendary *Metal Gear Solid* series, would go on to co-write the first two X-Men films (*X-Men* (2000) and *X-Men 2* (2003) aka *X2*) and direct the low-budget creature feature *Wolves* (2014).

Kathy Christopherson continues to act, appearing in several high-profile TV series such as *Criminal Minds: Beyond Borders* (2017), *Lucifer* (2019), *Dexter* (2009), and *CSI: Crime Scene Investigation* (2001), as well as reteaming with a good portion of the *Dark Hero* crew on the aforementioned *Kamen Rider: Dragon Knight*.

For Christopherson, playing Cori in *Dark Hero* remains a highlight of her career, as it's a point in her life she holds deep feelings for. "I feel nostalgic about having had the opportunity to play Cori. It's still one of the most fun shoots I've been on, partly because of it just being crazy sci-fi fun, and partly because Steve Wang is so fun," reminisces the actor.

"A few years ago, I got talking to local police who were on a call. As I thanked them, one of the officers quickly said, '*I just have to ask you, are you Cori from Guyver?*' It turned out the officer and his son have been obsessed with *Guyver* for years and they're huge fans. We've remained friends ever since. I invited him to one of my birthday parties so he could meet Steve Wang."

Even now, the *Dark Hero* legacy lives on in her day-to-day life and this was especially the case during a more recent event for Christopherson.

"I had another birthday party in which *Guyver: Dark Hero* was playing on a loop on this big screen. It was one of those novelties we decided to throw in for the festivity. I was surprised just how many of my friends had already seen it. Plus, Steve, David Hayter and Marisa were there, and it was great fun."

"I love that *Guyver* has its dedicated fan base, and the movie makes so many people happy; what more could I ask for? I honestly consider Steve a lifelong friend and after working on *Kamen Rider* together, I'd be tickled pink to work on anything he's doing. I appreciate his unmatchable perfectionism, which is balanced with his ridiculous Bruce Lee impressions," says Christopherson.

Christopher Michael who played C.I.A. Agent Atkins has carved an illustrious career in TV post-*Dark Hero*. Even if you don't know his name, chances are you've still seen the actor in a multitude of roles, most notably playing cop or security guard characters in *GLOW* (2017-2019), *Community* (2009-2015), *Brooklyn Nine-Nine* (2013-2021), and *ER* (1994-2009). Outside of TV, Michael has had roles in films such as Mario Van Peebles' *Baadasssss!* (2003), the schlocky creature feature, *New Alcatraz* (aka *Boa*, 2001), and *F.R.E.D.I.* (2018). On top of the supporting roles, Michael has also written and directed his own film called *Limp Fangs* (1996), a vampire comedy that was a labour of love for Michael.

Ted Smith and Wyatt Weed would both direct genre films in the early 2000s, with high-concept monster-hunting schlock *Guardian of the Realm* (2004) directed by Smith (also co-written and edited by Weed) and atmospheric vampire feature *Shadowland* (2008) directed by Weed. *Guardian of the Realm* would also have several *Guyver* film alumni present in various crew roles.

Since these features, Smith would continue to be a creature performer in a number of horror films, Rob Zombie's *House of 1000 Corpses* (2003) for instance, and in more recent years has become affectionately known as the 'Bob Ross of Foam' with his Evil Ted channel, which focuses on building elaborate and fantastical designs for cosplayers.

Weed has gone on to create a slew of short films based on existing properties and has effectively played one of the best on-screen interpretations of Bruce Wayne for his short film *The Dark Knight Returns: An Epic Fan Film* (2016). Outside of directing and producing, Weed has become a champion for starting out filmmakers in St. Louis and runs filmmaking courses to help the next generation of filmmakers.

Co-Writer for *Dark Hero* – Nathan Long – would (after *Kamen Rider: Dragon Knight*) become an author for tabletop miniatures company Warhammer and in more recent years has branched out into writing within the video game industry, most notably with Brian Fargo's RPG company InXile and on projects such as *Wasteland 3* and *Torment: Tides of Numeria*.

Asao Goto would continue to work on several features following *Dark Hero* and would apply his diverse skill set to a handful of genre films, such as *Children of the Corn III: Urban Harvest* (1995) as part of Screaming Mad George's S.M.G. Effects Inc. effects shop, and on the late Stuart Gordon's wonderfully insane *Space Truckers* (1996), again as part of S.M.G. Effects Inc. Following his stint in the U.S., Goto has returned to Japan and continues to create high-detailed models and miniatures for exhibitions, along with teaching young film fans how to create miniature effects.

The Alpha Stunts team continues to go from strength to strength and has expanded in size significantly since its early days. In recent years they are primarily responsible for stunt work on a broad range of Tokusatsu shows such as *Super Sentai/Power Rangers*, *Kamen Rider*, and *Ultraman* in Japan, with Koichi Sakamoto continuing to work as a director on several of these shows.

Sakamoto has also directed a slew of budget action features, all using the unique action choreography he is known for. These include the impressive and physically exhausting *Broken Path* aka *Broken Fist* (2008), *Extreme Heist* aka *Wicked Game* (2002), horror-actioner *Devon's Ghost: Legend of the Bloody Boy* (2005*)*, *Black Fox: Age of the Ninja* (2019) and *009-1: The End of the Beginning* (2013), all of which have garnered devoted fans the world over.

Akihiro 'Yuji' Noguchi continues to work with Alpha Stunts, but also found success post-*Dark Hero* on several DTV Isaac Florentine features as stunt coordinator, including post-apocalyptic western *Cold Harvest* (1999), *Special Forces*, and *Ninja* (2009). Noguchi would also branch out into video games by being the action director on titles like *Binary Domain* or stunt work motion-capture on *Devil May Cry 3: Dante's Awakening* and *Yakuza 2* (2006).

Tatsuro Koike as gone onto be a prolific stuntman, along with taking on second unit director responsibilities. Post-*Dark Hero*, Koike has provided his extensive skill set on a couple of Isaac Florentine features as well as Noguchi, having worked on the Dolph Lundgren starrer *Bridge of Dragons* (1999) and *High Voltage* (1998). In recent years, Koike has found himself working on several gaming titles from Ryu Ga Gotoku Studio (the team responsible for the *Yakuza* series), including *Yakuza 6: The Song of Life* (2016), *Fist of the North Star: Lost Paradise* (2018), and Yakuza spin-offs *Judgement* (2018) and *Lost Judgement* (2021) as a stunt coordinator.

Steve Wang continues to create amazing effects for film with his company Onyx Forge, whether that's creating suit designs or giant character stands for gaming expos. Additionally, his other company

Elite Creature Collectables (ECC) creates limited edition statues with eye-watering sculpts based on various film properties, including *Guyver: Dark Hero* and several other creature features that Wang created designs for films such as *Blade II (2002), Underworld: Evolution (2006)*, and *Gremlins 2: The New Batch*.

Hopefully, *Drive* will not be Wang's last directorial feature. Maybe one day, if the stars align, Wang will bellow into the megaphone once again. Until that moment, the special effects wizard and director continues to create exceptional pieces of creature work, all bearing his distinct style and aesthetics.

In a world full of big-budget comic book epics, self-congratulatory Oscar bait and an almost cookie-cutter/manufactured mass-market appeal for countless cinema releases, the average viewer may forget or even be unaware of the low-budget or micro-budget features which are often released.

These titles, seen by many as bargain bin fodder, are the ones which frequently contain the most heart and passion, where they may be lacking in budget. In fact, a lot of these micro-budget titles – while having a niche following themselves – will always continue to inspire the next generation of independent filmmakers.

What budget filmmakers like Steven Kostanski and MJ Dixon do, will hopefully inspire more young filmmakers much like Steve Wang and Co. did during the 1990s. With the distant memories of the halcyon video rental days – with only a few still existing in this age of streaming – getting their smaller films discovered, despite the accessibility on digital platforms, has become harder for indie filmmakers.

Thankfully word of mouth via social media sites, small-scale and independent film festivals and fans who champion the indie filmmaking scene are singlehandedly keeping the flag flying for these unique, niche, and passionate pieces of filmmaking.

Although the general public might be oblivious to just how expansive the micro-budget scene has become, having evolved from the SOV (shot-on-video) era through to the quickly produced, cheap and cheerful DVDs always present in the local supermarket electronics section, it's a world of cinema that's ripe for discovery.

And again, thanks to the internet fandom, social media, and film memories of a better time, both *The Guyver / Mutronics: The Movie* and *Guyver: Dark Hero* are being discovered by new fans on a near daily basis. For those fans who grew up with the films, there remains a certain ownership over their schlocky and entertaining nature.

Both films, or more specifically *Dark Hero*, became watershed moments for a young generation of effects hungry pre-adolescents. Given the fact *Dark Hero* was released during the height of *Power Rangers* mania in the Western world, it's easy to see why the likes of MJ Dixon and Steven Kostanski were able to dupe their parents into renting this violent delight, particularly with the *Power Rangers* mania at its most extreme during this period.

Several decades on, both *The Guyver* and *Guyver: Dark Hero* continue to inspire fans in countless ways, whether they are creating their own collectables, unique pieces of artwork, or other filmmakers adding nods to the films in their work. It seems the legacy of Wang and Co's work continues to inspire generations. Additionally, during the making of both films, relationships and friendships (both professional and personal) would blossom forth, and (as Hayter mentioned earlier) more than a few Guyver babies arrived as well.

The accumulation of all these things is undeniably the best legacy a set of schlocky, low-budget action films could hope to achieve.

Afterword

By Steve Wang (Co-Director of *The Guyver* and Director of *Guyver: Dark Hero*)

When I was in the 3rd grade, I watched *Ultraman* for the first time in the cinemas. It changed my world, literally. I didn't know how I knew it, but I knew someday this life-changing event would become my life. My fascination with Tokusatsu was just beginning and I started to discover shows like *Diamond Eye*, *Kikaider*, *Himitsu Sentai Gorenger* and *Kamen Rider*. The 1970s was a great time to be a kid.

In the mid-1980s, I found my way into the makeup/creature effects business. I loved monsters and I taught myself how to make them. I was very lucky that my employers, the likes of the legendary Stan Winston and Rick Baker saw potential in me and gave me many opportunities to work on what are now iconic creature films.

Eventually this led me to travel to Japan to meet the creators and artists that were responsible for those Tokusatsu shows. I'll never forget meeting Shotaro Ishinomori, the creator of *Kamen Rider*, *Kikaider* and a bunch of other famous Japanese superheroes. He told me that I look like I could be a *Kamen Rider*. I was floored! At the time I was 21 and in pretty good shape. I struck up life-long friendships in Japan and which eventually led me to getting involved with co-directing the first *Guyver* film with my good friend, Screaming Mad George.

As covered earlier in the book, by late 1992, I got a phone call from Screaming Mad George telling me that Hero Communications, the company which financed the first *Guyver* film had offered him to direct the sequel. George declined as it was only half of the original $3 million budget. I asked him if it was ok that I talked to them about directing the sequel. He gave me his blessing.

I brought in Ray Cecire, a relatively new Line Producer, with me to the meeting. We pitched Hero Communications the idea of us making a *Guyver 2* and told them we could work with the $1.5 million budget.

They said the budget was actually $850,000, much smaller than even I was comfortable with. They added that I would have full autonomy, but all they asked was to have one Zoanoid and one cute girl in it. I accepted. As Ray and I left the office, we looked at each other and said, 'Ok. *I guess we gotta go make a movie now*?!' This was a huge step for both Ray and I, and the trial by fire way of figuring out how to make a movie would eventually cement our life-long friendship.

Out of our inexperience, we proceeded to break every rule in Hollywood as we went. A lot of trial and error, but we made the film. With the budget so low and my script so ambitious, I ended up paying myself $175 per week to co-write, direct, produce, edit, create creatures etc. for a period of 15 months. That's how long it took from writing the initial script with my long-time collaborator Nathan Long, to the final delivery of the film. If it were not for the teaching job I had in Japan helping to pay my bills, I would have never been able to make this movie.

I always made sure my cast and crew got paid first before I would take any salary. I remember at one point I only had $90 in the bank. It was really tough when you have a new-born son and a mortgage to pay.

My wife at the time was very supportive even though she had to take care of our new child, mostly on her own while I was shooting the film. Some days I would drive for an hour and a half home from location to see her sprawled out on the floor, asleep from exhaustion, while the baby was still up. I would take care of our son till the morning so she could sleep. When she awoke, I handed our son back to her, got back in my car and drove back to location to continue shooting the film. This happened a lot.

The old adage that hard times build character is beyond true and the hard experience of making a film on a super low budget makes one fearless. I don't remember ever panicking because the financier was late with our regularly scheduled payment during production. This happened quite often, but the payment would eventually show up and we would have to apologize to our crew…again.

Most of them held on and worked with us. I like to think that they were able to see how ambitious we were and also see that our enthusiasm during such hard times was unwavering.

After we wrapped production, I finally got to relax a little. I scrubbed all the paint off the floors of our rented 15000 sq. ft warehouse where the massive sets used to stand. That was fun, and probably was the start of my back problems, but I wouldn't have traded the experience for anything. I loved every minute of making *Guyver: Dark Hero*, no matter how hard some days would get. It was a labour of love for me, and I was incredibly fortunate to have a project that fuelled my intense passion for Tokusatsu filmmaking. I think I normalized the idea of me not sleeping when I make movies and little did I know, this was just a warm-up for the incredible hardship I was going to endure on my next film, *Drive*. But that's another story.

It's been over 30 years since I first stepped into the Guyver's universe, and I am still floored by the outpouring of love the fans have for our little movies. I am forever grateful and inspired by them. And for our future generation of filmmakers, I share my experiences in the hope that you get a taste of the scope of the personal sacrifices and persistence your journey into independent filmmaking may demand of you. And I hope you will stop at nothing to make your vision a reality. It's hard, very hard, but so worth it!

Steve Wang,
January 2023

Steve Wang striking a pose and calling the shots as director on *Kamen Rider: Dragon Knight*. Photo courtesy of Steve Wang.

About the Author

Dom O'Brien is a UK based writer and has written for several publications such as Attack from Planet B, Game Rant and 88 Films Ltd. He was brought up on a diet of 1980s and 1990s action and creature features (which kickstarted his love affair with films and filmmaking in general), and he primarily writes about low-budget genre fare and the history of oft-forgotten films.

This is his first book.

Acknowledgements

This book wouldn't have been possible without the help and openness from several people. I would like to take this opportunity to thank Steve Wang, David Hayter, Wyatt Weed, and Ted Smith for allowing me to quiz them at a moment's notice for additional information, for their help elaborating on specific details from either of the film productions. I'd also like to thank them for their support and encouragement on this project and happily discussing memories from over 30 years ago to a random and highly excitable Brit, usually at silly o'clock in the morning.

Thank you to all those I have interviewed for the book including: Brian Yuzna; Screaming Mad George (Joji Tani); Nathan Long; Gabe Bartalos; Kathy Christopherson (and her wonderful anecdotes); Christopher Michael; Eddie Yang; Mat Morse; Les Claypool (beer is on me, mate); Sandy Collora; Johnnie Saiko Espiritu (enjoyed our thought provoking discussions on life, the universe and everything); Spice Williams-Crosby; Jennifer McManus; Levie Isaacks (truly an honour, sir); Asao Goto; Akihiro 'Yuji' Noguchi (a thank you to Miho Noguchi too); MJ Dixon; Steven Kostanski; Stan Giesea (for some truly wonderful behind-the-scenes insight, video and support).

A thank you to my mum, my family, and my extended family, for their support and understanding over this project, and an additional thank you to close friends, Ricky and Alexsia Dee, Charlie Cox, and Edd Hassall.

Thank you to Jonathan Melville; Em McGowen; Lee B Golden; Andrew Marshall-Roberts; David Hood and Stephen Biro at Unearthed Films; Fabien Mauro; Matthew Essary; Ken Wynne; Tuomas Lius; Lucas Peverill; Mike Scott; Jérémie Damoiseau, and also to Dakota Drobnicki for originally putting me in contact with Wyatt Weed.

Thank you to Tara Ansley, Jimmy Shaw, and the rest of the team at Fangoria for their help during part of the editing process for the book.

A thank you to my beta readers Jade Lindley; Paul Saunders and Dion Dassanayake, for their guidance and critiques on the manuscript.

Thank you to Ben Ohmart, Stone Wallace and the team at Bear-Manor Media for taking a chance on my first book and the support they provided, and my dad for working with me on creating the unique chapter images.

Although I didn't get to interview everyone, I would also like to acknowledge the special effects crew and stunt teams who brought the creatures and action to life on both *Guyver* films.

Firstly, for *The Guyver*: Shozo Ano; Joanne Bloomfield; Andy Clement; Pat Conrad; Michael Deak; Masaaki and Yoichi Fukuoka; Misa Uo Gardner; Mika Hagiwara; Glen Hanz; Nori Honda; Koji Hoshi; Michiko Ishikawa; Mike Jolly; Yasuko Kudo; Takao Kumaoka; Jake McKinnon; Joey Orosco; Timothy Ralston; Sally Ray; Jordu Schell; Aaron Sims; James Slavin; Shaun Smith; Heidi Snyder; Ken Tarallo; Wayne Toth; Chieko Watanabe; T.C. Williams; Jeanna Crawford; Lynette Eklund; Tom Gleason; Ted Rae; Kenny Ferrugiaro; Dennis Madalone; Hauro Matsuoka; Kimberly L. Ryusaki; Luis J. Silva; Doug Simpson; Brian Simpson; Tony Snegoff; Tim Trella and Bob Yerkes.

For *Guyver: Dark Hero*: Rob Freitas; Brian Wade; Miwa Hata; Yumi Nakano; Ted Ng; Kyomi Suzuki; Ken Tarallo; Toshimitsu Usui; Kimika Yamazaki; Gary Yee; Mykel Denis; Rick Hilgner; Bret Mixon; John Teska; Joe Esparza; Steve Harris; Jeff Himmel; Art Martyn; Gabriel Navarro; Derek Olsen; Willie Palomarez Jr; Paul Pistore; Paula Thompson; Ted Van Dorn; Raul Varela; Coburn Hawk; Shane Williams; Shyam Yadav; Gary Young; Mike Wang; Koichi Sakamoto; Tatsuro Koike; and Takuya Wada for his original Laserdisc documentary which, for many years, was the only way of seeing any behind-the-scenes information on *Dark Hero*'s production.

A huge thank you to Si Heard for the great cover art. You managed to turn my abstract sketch into something truly exceptional, which very much taps into the 1990s aesthetic I was going for.

Thanks to Robert Beardsley, Dylan Demasi, Mike Leeder, Ronan Kelly, Christoph Kellerbach, David Malcom, and Kris Wall for their Ko-Fi support during the latter half of the book's development.

Finally, I would also like to remember a number of cast and crew who were associated with *The Guyver* and *Guyver: Dark Hero* in some capacity, but are sadly no longer with us: David Gale, Moto Hata, Thomas C. Rainone, Eric H. Lasher, Merritt Yohnka, Cleve Hall, and Matt Rose. I hope this work honours your legacies and the friendships with those involved on both *Guyver* films.

Index

Numbers in **bold** indicate photographs

Milton Keynes UK
Ingram Content Group UK Ltd.
UKHW011012150324
439468UK00009B/672

9 798887 713014